TIMEKEEPERS

HOW THE WORLD
BECAME OBSESSED WITH TIME

SIMON GARFIELD

CANONGATE

To Ben, Jake, Charlie, Jack and Justine
And to the memory of Rena Gamsa

Alice: How long is forever?
White Rabbit: Sometimes, just one second.

Contents

TIMEKEEPERS

Simon Garfield is the author of seventeen acclaimed books of non-fiction including *A Notable Woman* (as editor), *To the Letter*, *On the Map*, *Just My Type* and *Mauve*. His study of AIDS in Britain, *The End of Innocence*, won the Somerset Maugham prize.

www.simongarfield.com

'Scholarly but jokey, with a magpie's appetite for glittering trivia, Garfield is as eager to amuse as to inform, and achieves both' *Telegraph*

'An eclectic collection of explorations of our relationships with time . . . Very readable' *The Times*

'Delightful' *Sunday Telegraph*

'Delightful . . . Gloriously funny . . . Garfield has an astonishing capacity for meticulous research and a wonderful ability to select the best stories to entertain us' *Daily Express*

'Engaging . . . Engrossing' *Mail on Sunday*

'In this book, brilliant cultural historian Simon Garfield assembles a host of intriguing characters who have tried to bend time to their own rules, and questions how we came to be ruled by something so arbitrary' *Elle*

Also by Simon Garfield

Expensive Habits
The End of Innocence
The Wrestling
The Nation's Favourite
Mauve
The Last Journey of William Huskisson
Our Hidden Lives (ed.)
We Are at War (ed.)
Private Battles (ed.)
The Error World
Mini
Exposure
Just My Type
On the Map
To the Letter
My Dear Bessie (ed.)
A Notable Woman (ed.)

Introduction:

Very, Very Early or Very, Very Late

We are in Egypt. Not Ancient Egypt, which would be a reasonable place to begin a book about time, but in modern Egypt, an Egypt out of *Condé Nast Traveller*, with the fine beaches and the tourists at the pyramids and the sun beating down on the Mediterranean. We are sitting at a restaurant above a beach near Alexandria, and at one end of the beach we can see a local fisherman catching something tasty for dinner: a nice red mullet perhaps.

We are on holiday after a punishing year. After our meal we stroll towards the fisherman. He speaks a little English. He shows us his catch – not much yet, but he's hopeful. Because we know a little about fishing and opportunity, we suggest he might move to that rock over there, just a little further out, a higher cast than his present position on his old folding stool, and a greater chance of hooking his daily haul of fish faster.

'Why would I want to do that?' he asks.

We say that with greater speed he could catch more fish, so that he could not only have enough for his dinner, but sell the surplus at the market, and with the proceeds he could buy a better rod and a new icebox for his catch.

'Why would I want to do that?'

So that you can catch even more fish at greater speed, and then sell those fish, and swiftly earn enough to buy a boat, which means deeper seas and still more fish in record time with those big nets they use on trawlers. In fact, you could soon become a successful trawler yourself, and people would start calling you Captain.

'Why would I want that?' he asks smugly, annoyingly.

We are of the modern world, attuned to ambition and the merits of alacrity, and so we advance our case with growing impatience. If you had a boat, your haul would soon be of such size that you would be a kingpin at the market, be able to set your own prices, buy more boats, hire a work-force and then, fulfilling the ultimate dream, retire early, and spend your time sitting in the sun fishing.

'A bit like I do today?'

*

Now let us briefly consider the case of William Strachey. Strachey was born in 1819, and from his schooldays had set his heart on becoming a civil servant. By the mid-1840s he was working in the Colonial Office in Calcutta, where he became convinced that the people of India, and the people of Calcutta in particular, had found a way to maintain the most accurate clocks (the best clocks in India at this time were probably made in Britain, but no matter). When he returned to England after five years away he determined to carry on living his life by Calcuttan time: a valiant move, for this was usually five-and-a-half hours ahead of London time.

William Strachey was the uncle of Lytton Strachey, the eminent Victorian critic and biographer. Lytton's own biographer, Michael Holroyd, has noted how William was among the most eccentric of all the Stracheys, which was really saying something, given the amount of general weirdness ritually favoured by the Strachey clan.*

---

* Another of Lytton Strachey's uncles, Uncle Bartle, wrote the definitive book –

William Strachey lived until his mid-80s, and thus spent more than 50 years in England on Calcuttan time. This meant having breakfast at teatime and a candlelit lunch in the evening, and making decisive calculations regarding train timetables and other routines of daily life, such as shopping and banking hours. But in 1884 it got more complicated still, as Calcuttan time jumped 24 minutes ahead of much of the rest of India, making Strachey's day 5 hours and 54 minutes ahead of London time. Sometimes it was just impossible to tell if he was very, very early or very, very late.

Many of Strachey's friends (not that he had many friends) grew used to this eccentricity, although he severely tried the patience of his family when he bought a mechanised bed at the Paris International Exposition of 1867. The bed came with a clock designed to wake the occupant at an appointed hour by tipping him or her out, and Strachey rigged it up in such a way that it tipped him into his bath. Despite his planning, he was apparently so enraged when he was first woken in this way that he saw no other option but to smash the clock to ensure he wouldn't be tipped up again. According to Holroyd, William Strachey spent his remaining years in galoshes, and shortly before he died he bequeathed his nephew a considerable assortment of coloured underpants.

*

Between the serenity of the fisherman and the madness of Strachey lies the compromised life of us all. Do we want the fishing life or the clock life? We want both. We envy those

---

definitive up to that point at any rate – on the orchids of Burma. Yet another, Uncle Trevor, was married to a woman named Aunt Clementina, who, whenever she visited Lytton's home in Lancaster Gate, spent her time making chapattis on the living-room carpet. One of Trevor's and Clementina's children died while embracing a bear.

with a carefree existence but we don't have time to examine it for long. We want more hours in the day but fear we'd probably only waste them. We work all hours so that we may eventually work less. We have invented quality time to distinguish it from that other time. We place a clock by our bed but what we really want is to smash it up.

Time, once passive, is now aggressive. It dominates our lives in ways that the earliest clockmakers would have surely found unbearable. We believe that time is running away from us. Technology is making everything faster, and because we know that things will become faster in the future, it follows that nothing is fast enough now. The time zones that so possessed William Strachey are rendered almost obsolete by the perpetual daylight of the Internet. But the strangest thing of all is this: if they were able, the earliest clockmakers would tell us that the pendulum swings at the same rate as it always has, and the calendars have been fixed for hundreds of years. We have brought this cauldron of rush upon ourselves. Time seems faster because we have made it so.

This is a book about our obsession with time and our desire to measure it, control it, sell it, film it, perform it, immortalise it and make it meaningful. It considers how, over the last 250 years, time has become such a dominant and insistent force in our lives, and asks why, after tens of thousands of years of looking up at the sky for vague and moody guidance, we now take atomically precise cues from our phones and computers not once or twice a day but continually and compulsively. The book has but two simple intentions: to tell some illuminating stories, and to ask whether we have all gone completely nuts.

I recently bought the smartphone app Wunderlist. It's designed to 'sort out and synchronise your to-dos for home, work and everything in between' and 'take a quick peek inside a to-do' and 'swipe down from any app to get a glance of your due to-dos with our Today widget'. Buying the app was a tough choice, for there are also apps named Tick Task Pro, Eisenhower Planner Pro, gTasks, iDo Notepad Pro, Tiny Timer, 2Day 2Do, Little Alarms, 2BeDone Pro, Calendar 366 Plus, Howler Timer, Tasktopus, Effectivator and many, many hundreds of others. In January 2016, these Business and Productivity apps – the vast majority concerned with time-saving, time management and increased speed and efficiency in all aspects of our lives – accounted for a greater share of smartphone apps than Education, Entertainment, Travel, Books, Health & Fitness, Sports, Music, Photos and News, all of which were also vaguely concerned with improving efficiency and getting more done faster. Yes, that name was 'Tasktopus'. How did we arrive at this terrible and exciting place?

*

Timekeepers examines some important moments in an attempt to find out. For most of the time we will be in the company of contemporary and modern witnesses, among them some remarkable artists, athletes, inventors, composers, film-makers, writers, orators, social scientists and, of course, watchmakers. The essays in this book will consider the practical rather than ethereal applications of time – time as a lead character in our lives, and sometimes the only one against which we judge our worth – and examine a few instances when our measurement and notion of temporal things enhanced, restricted or restruc-tured our lives in significant ways. The book will not scold us for our fast living, although several people will suggest how to apply the brakes. Nor will it be a book about theoretical physics, so we will not figure out whether time is real or imaginary, or what came before the Big Bang; instead, the book examines what came after the big bang of the industrial revolution. Equally, we're not going to mess around with science fiction or the mind-bending mechanics of time travel: all that going back to kill your own grandfather and suddenly-waking-up-in-the-Field-of-the-Cloth-of-Gold rigmarole. I'm leaving that to the physicists and *Doctor Who* fanatics, and taking the rational Groucho Marx line on all of this: time flies like an arrow but fruit flies like a banana.*

Timekeepers tracks time's arrow in the modern age. The pace picks up with the railways and the factory, but our tour is primarily a cultural one, and occasionally a philosophical one, gathering momentum with Beethoven's symphonies and the fanatical traditions of Swiss watchmaking. There will be the occasional sampling of wisdom from Irish and Jewish comedians. The timeline will be cyclical rather than linear, because time has a habit of folding back upon itself (the early days of cinema appear here before the early days of photography, for example). But, chronological or not, it comes with one inevitability – that sooner or later we will track down the person responsible for the adverts that claim 'You never actually own a Patek Philippe, you merely look after it for the next generation', and try not to kill him. A little later the book will also evaluate the wisdom of time-saving gurus, examine why the CD lasts the length it does, and explain why you should think very seriously before travelling on 30 June.

But we begin at a football match, an event where timing is everything.

---

* The joke is *attributed* to Groucho Marx, although one can spend a very pleasurable weekend searching in vain for even one occurrence of him actually saying it. The expression probably originates in an article on the uses of computers in science written for *Scientific American* in September 1966 by the Harvard professor Anthony G. Oettinger.

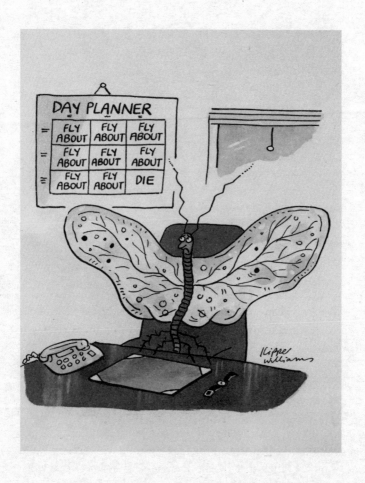

Chapter One

The Accident of Time

i) Leaving the Ground

You know that thing they say about comedy being tragedy plus time? The thinking is that any terrible misfortune can be made hilarious given a suitable period to recover and reassess the situation. The film director Mel Brooks (who found that the passage of time permitted him to make fun of Hitler in *The Producers*) had his own version: 'Tragedy is when I cut my finger. Comedy is when you fall into an open sewer and die.'

*

We had been to a football match. After three minutes of extra time, my son Jake and I untied our bikes from the railings and cycled towards Hyde Park. Chelsea's opening game of the season had been an easy thing, 2–0 over Leicester, goals from Costa and Hazard, and we'd enjoyed being back at the ground after the summer layoff. The cycle home was good too: late August sun, the park packed with tourists.

The day was dominated by a fixture list that had appeared two months before, and the kick-off time was dictated about a month after that by the television companies. But when the day of the match finally came it was all about old rituals: when to meet up, when to have lunch, how long the pizzas take, how long until the bill arrives, the walk to the ground, the length of the turnstile queue, the songs on the PA before the game – always Blur's 'Parklife' these days, coordinated with the big-screen video of past glories. And then the game itself: how slow it seems when you're winning and waiting for the final whistle, and how quickly it goes when you're behind.

We left a minute early to avoid the crowds, also a temporal negotiation: how does one measure the possibility of missing a last-minute goal with the value one attaches to saving ten minutes of crowd congestion? Many in the crowd chose the early departure, which almost defeated the object, and we weaved our bikes through the throngs on the Fulham Road. My youngest son Jake was 24, full of energy, slightly ahead of me along Exhibition Road and past the Albert Hall. The nice thing about Hyde Park is the modern division of the pavement, half for cyclists, half for pedestrians, and you glide past the Serpentine Gallery, a show by an artist I'd never heard of, and then suddenly I had blood pouring from my face, a pulsing gash just above my eye, my sunglasses smashed, my bike in the road, a heavy numb pain around my right elbow, a lot of concerned people, the sort of frowns on their faces that suggested to me that my head wound must be serious. Someone was calling an ambulance and another was giving me paper towels to clutch to my head, and the towels were turning crimson.

It was just as people had said: time did indeed seem to slow down. I can see the fall not exactly in slow motion but extended, each tiny event surrounding the accident elongated and logged as if it might be my last, my flight from bike to ground an elegant swoop through the air rather than an ungainly, panicky confusion, people saying 'ambulance' all the time. The ambulance arrived in six long minutes or so, probably finding it hard to work itself past all the supporters, and I can remember being worried about my bike, and who would tell my wife. One of the ambulance men cut open the sleeve of my jacket and flinched a little as he saw the state of my elbow. No bones exposed, but swelling like a dinner plate, and he said, 'You'll have that X-rayed, but I can tell you now that it's broken!!', and we sped on to the hospital on the Fulham Road we had passed not fifteen minutes earlier. I asked him if they were going to put the sirens on, and he asked me what had happened.

I had been undone by time. I wasn't going fast, because the pavement was crowded. Jake was ahead of me, and there were a lot of people on our left up ahead, and one of them, a visitor from Portugal we find out later, drifted out slightly from her friends, and walked directly into my path. I knew I was going to hit her before I did, but there was no time to brake or even put my hand out, and my bike seemed to disappear underneath me as I fell forward. The Portuguese woman, perhaps mid-20s, was shocked and concerned, and Jake took her mobile number, but we have no idea where that is now. Even at the time, sitting on the grass near the Serpentine Gallery, I think I knew it could have been much worse, and my sunglasses could have shattered into my eyes, and I would have lost my sight.

Neuroscientists may be a little worn out with the amount of stories they hear of time slowing down at the scene of an accident, and they will tell you why it seems that way. Accidents are alarming and fearful things. For those tumbling over a bike or a precipice, our brain finds plenty of space for new memories to imprint themselves upon our cortex. We remember them as significant events with lots of vivid action, and when we reframe that narrative in our own heads, or tell it to others, there appears to be so much going on that it simply must have taken longer than the split second it actually did. Compared to familiar occurrences that have hardened in our cortex until we no longer have to think about them (the drive to the shops with our mind on other matters, the routines so familiar we say we can do them in our sleep), a sudden new event will require more of our brain's attention. The unfamiliar shape of a woman as she crosses a painted white line, the loose chips of gravel, the shrieks of brakes and passers-by – these are unusual things to process when one is trying to limit the damage to vulnerable flesh.

But what actually happens in this flashbulb moment? How does a flashbulb moment seem to collide with a long exposure, something that we know to be impossible? Two small portions of our brain known as the amygdalae – groups of hyper-responsive nerve bundles in the temporal lobe concerned primarily with memory and decision-making – commandeer the rest of the brain's functions to react in a crisis. It is something that seems to stretch a one-second fall to five seconds or more, set off by fear and sudden shocks that hit our limbic system so hard that we may never forget them. But our perceived duration distortion is just that; clock time has not in fact offered to pause or elongate for us. Instead, the amygdalae have laid down memories with far more vivid detail, and the time distortion we perceive has just happened in retrospect. The neuroscientist David Eagleman, who has conducted many experiments into time perception and as a boy experienced a similar elongation of time when he fell off a roof, explains it in terms of 'a trick of the memory writing a *story* of a reality'. Our neural mechanisms are constantly attempting to calibrate the world around us into an accessible narrative in as little time as possible. Authors attempt to do the same, for what is fiction if not time repositioned, and what is history if not time in retrospect, events re-evaluated in our own time?

Not that I could have explained this in the ambulance on the way to the hospital; the ambulance had its own routines and schedules. As did A & E, where I sat for what seemed like an eternity waiting to be seen. With my amygdalae returned to equilibrium, there was now a different sort of elongated time – the elongation of boredom, two hours or so looking at other patients and wondering how I would cancel most of my packed week ahead. Jake had planned to take the last train that evening to St Ives, but the train would leave without him. After a while my wife Justine arrived, and I took her through what happened, still with bloody paper stuck above my eye, and after a further while the process began properly, and I was on a gurney in a screened cubicle, a nurse seeing whether I could make a fist. It was almost midnight when they started putting my elbow in plaster to keep it from moving before they could operate on it, and past one by the time a kind doctor at the end of his shift said he had to get back to his wife and their three-week-old baby, but he would sew me up rather than let a junior do it because it was such a deep wound.

And then at around 3 a.m. I was alone in the bowels of the Chelsea and Westminster. My wife and son had driven home with the bikes in the back of the car, and I didn't yet have a bed in a ward so I lay in a darkened room in a speckled gown tied at the back, with my arm in plaster on my chest and nine stitches just above my eyebrow, and painkillers inside me. I wondered how long I would be there, and how long until they operated, and I could hear dripping somewhere and a person calling outside my room, and I began to feel cold.

I thought I could feel every granule of time. It was August 2014, but the date seemed irrelevant and arbitrary. My over-wound mind had been prised open by a fall, and everything had been upended. In a dead space in a clinical setting I felt myself drifting towards a consciousness where time took on not only a new urgency, but also a new laxity. I was back in a cradle where time was no longer my own, and it made me question to what extent it ever had been. Was everything chance or was everything fixed? Had we lost control of something we had created? If we'd left the ground just a half-minute earlier, or pedalled just that bit harder, one wheel rotation more, or if the traffic lights by the Royal Albert Hall had slowed us down, and if the woman from Portugal had lingered over her cake that afternoon, or, even better, hadn't come to London at all, then this would have never happened, and Jake would have caught his train, and I would have watched the highlights on *Match of the Day*, and the doctor would have arrived home earlier to help his wife. Everything that passed for time in this setting had been self-imposed and self-ordained, a modern arrangement calibrated gradually over generations. It made me wonder how such an alliance had come about. Time regulated transport, entertainment, sport, medical diagnostics, everything – and the people and processes that set these connections in motion are the subject of this book.

ii) The Shortness of Life and How to Live It

Someone feeling sorry for themselves in a hospital ward today would do well to think of Seneca 2,000 years ago. *On the Shortness of Life* advised his readers to live life wisely, which is to say not frivolously. He looked around and didn't like the way people were spending their time, the way 'one man is possessed by an avarice that is insatiable, another by a toilsome devotion to tasks that are useless; one man is besotted with wine, another is paralyzed by sloth.' Most existence, he reasoned, was not life, not living, 'but merely time'. In his mid-60s, Seneca took his own life by slitting his wrists in the bath.

The most famous line in Seneca's essay comes right at the start, a reminder of a famous saying by the Greek physician Hippocrates: 'Life is short, art is long.' The exact meaning of this is still open to interpretation (he was probably not referring to the queues at the hot Richter show, but the length of time it takes to become an expert at something), and Seneca's employment of the phrase confirms that the nature of time was a topic that thinkers in Ancient Greece and Rome found highly engaging. Around 350 BC, Aristotle saw time as a form of order rather than measure, an arrangement in which all things are related to each other. He saw the present not as fixed, but as a moving entity, a component of continuous change, ever dependent on the past and the future (and, idiosyncratically, the soul). Around AD 160 Marcus Aurelius believed in fluidity: 'Time is a river of passing events and as strong as its current' he found. 'No sooner is a thing brought to sight than it is swept aside and another takes its place. This too will be swept away.' Saint Augustine of Hippo, who lived a long life between 354 and 430, caught the fleeting essence of time that has confounded quantum physicists ever since: 'What then is time? If no one asks me, I know what it is. If I wish to explain it to him who asks, I do not know.'

My elbow was made in the summer of 1959, and it had been shattered on its 55th anniversary. The X-rays showed it now resembled a puzzle, with the bones of my joint chipped and scattered like fleeing prisoners. During my forthcoming operation, which I was assured would be fairly routine, the bits would have to be rounded up and held in place by pieces of wire.

The watch I was wearing at the time of the accident was also made in the 1950s, and lost between four and ten minutes a day, depending on how often I wound it, and other things. I liked the fact that it was old (you can trust an old watch because it's been doing the same thing for years). To be punctual at appointments I had to calculate exactly how late my watch may be. I had been meaning to take it in for recalibration, but I never seemed to have the time. Most of all I enjoyed the analogue factor, the cogs and springs and flywheels that didn't need a battery. But what I really liked was the suggestion that time shouldn't control how I conducted my life. Time could be the most destructive force, and if one could protect oneself from its ravages, one could somehow attain a sense of control, and a sense of directing one's own destiny, at least on an hourly basis. The best thing of all, of course, the ultimate temporal freedom, would be to give my watch away, or to throw it from the window of a speeding train.

Four minutes of time, fast or slow – that was a useful thing to consider when lying supine and semi-conscious in a dark room, drifting in a boat along the reeds, searching for the place, in a phrase Clive James once employed in a song, where you trade your shells for feathers. I admired the optimism of Aristotle who believed that time should be measured by the heart, and I liked the words of the 19th century poet Philip Bailey: 'We live in deeds, not years; in thoughts, not breaths; in feelings, not in figures on a dial. We should count time by heart throbs.' I wanted a time holiday; I approved of J.B. Priestley's dictum that a good holiday is one spent among people whose notions of time are vaguer than one's own.

They operated on me the next morning, and not long after lunchtime my mouth was dry and there was a surgeon standing over me and a nurse was measuring the throbs of my heart. The procedure had gone well, and I could expect to get about 90 per cent of my flexibility and pronation back within eight weeks if I worked hard at the physiotherapy.

In between the physio I watched a lot more television than normal, and got far angrier than usual, and read a lot on my Kindle, normal books being unmanageable with just one good hand, as was watch-winding. I read *Zen and the Art of Motorcycle Maintenance*, that inflated spiritual road trip by Robert M. Pirsig that became a phenomenal bestseller by tapping into some sort of Western cultural zeitgeist, or what the Swedes call a *kulturbärer*, an ultra-timely book that challenged our assumptions about cultural values. In this case, *Zen* challenged our assumptions that what we wanted was more and faster – more materialism, a faster and more connected life, a greater reliance on things beyond our control or understanding.

Beneath the surface, *Zen and the Art of Motorcycle Maintenance* is all about time. It begins with the words 'I can see by my watch, without taking my hand from the left grip of the cycle, that it is eight-thirty in the morning', and for the next 400 pages the grip barely loosens – the exploration of what one values and treasures in life, and what one sees and feels at the core of the journey. The bike ride through a scorching landscape lends it an immediate consciousness. The riders – the writer, his son Chris and some friends – are heading through the Central Plains to Montana and beyond, and they are not dawdling. 'We want to make good time, but for us now this is measured with emphasis on "good" rather than "time" and when you make that shift in emphasis the whole approach changes.'

I thought about the man who had turned me on to books and words, a school English teacher named John Couper. Mr Couper let me bring the lyrics of Dylan's 'Desolation Row' into our A-level seminar and analyse it like it was a Shelley poem, even though it was obviously much better. One day, Couper had stood up at the podium in our Great Hall during morning assembly and delivered a speech about time. I think he began with some famous time quotes: 'Time spent laughing is time spent with the Gods' (anonymous); 'Beware the barrenness of a busy life' (Socrates). He then read from a list, and I remember it like this: 'Time. You can spend it, make it, lose it, save it, squander it, slow it down, speed it up, beat it, keep it, master it, spare it, kill it.' There were other dainty uses too, but his big final message was that we were privileged to be young and have time on our side, for time waits for no man (it was an all-boys school then) and that whatever else we did with our time, we shouldn't waste it. That stuck with me, but it was a hard rule to live by.

Sometimes I think I can measure out my childhood with images of timekeeping. Perhaps we all can. One day when I was three or four my father brought home a gold carriage clock in a case lined with crimson crushed velvet, and when my tiny finger pressed the button at the top a bell chimed the hours. The school clock in the Great Hall, the kitchen clock, and in my bedroom I had an alarm clock called Big Ben made by Westclox.*

Then one day we turned on the television to watch the Irish comedian Dave Allen. This was as risky as it got in my house: Allen was a 'dangerous' comedian, often outraging religious groups, drinking and smoking on air, stretching out stories well beyond bedtime. He looked a little louche, and had lost the tip of his left forefinger in what he claimed was a spooky comic accident, but we found out later that it happened when a cog chewed it in a mill when he was six.

One night he got off his tall chair, put down his cut-glass

---

* Which reminded me of that joke where Big Ben talks to the Leaning Tower of Pisa and says, 'I've got the time if you've got the inclination.'

tumbler, and started one of his stories about the peculiar way
we order our lives. 'I mean,' he said, 'how we *live* by time . . .
how we live by the *watch*, the *clock*. We're brought *up* to the
clock, we're brought up to *respect* the clock, *admire* the clock.
Punctuality. We live our life to the clock.' Allen waved his
right arm around in astonishment at the craziness of it all.
'You clock *in* to the clock. You clock *out* to the clock. You
come home to the clock. You eat to the clock, you drink to
the clock, you go to bed to the clock . . . You do that for
forty years of your life, you retire, what do they fucking give
you? A clock!'

His swearing triggered lots of phone calls from viewers
(there were people who were just *poised* by their phones when
Allen was on, like contestants on a quiz show). But no one
quickly forgot the joke, nor the perfect comic timing, every
pause like the air in a drum solo.

Recovering, I wasted a lot of time on my iPhone. One
night as I lay in bed I had an urgent need to watch films
starring Bill Nighy. I dimmed the screen on my phone and
feasted on YouTube, and was watching addictive flows of
Richard Curtis movies and David Hare's play *Skylight*, and
when I was done I did something unforgivable: I paid to
download *About Time*. It was a preposterous thing about how
the men in the fictional Nighy family can travel back in time,
correct the mistakes of the past – a wrong word here, a
bungled meeting there – and end up happy in love. As the
film critic Anthony Lane pointed out, the really smart thing
to do would be to look at the day's papers and travel back
to bet on winning horses, *Back to the Future*-style, but, as has
been clear for over a century of such fictional wanderings,
time travel is seldom practised by the most astute. Obviously
I wished I could have travelled back and not clicked Purchase.

But it wasn't just his work that drew me to Nighy. I once
had dinner with him and his then-wife Diana Quick, and

found him to be exactly the same as he was in most of his movies and plays: the immaculate suit and heavy glasses, of course, and the impeccable debonair English manners and chivalry that makes you believe everything he says is either knowing or hilarious. What I really liked about him was that he seemed to have his life mapped out perfectly. When asked how he spent his spare time he said he watched a lot of football on television, particularly Champions League games. He was just fascinated by the Champions League. In fact, he said, he measured out his remaining time on earth by how many Champions League seasons he had left. If FC Barcelona could entertain an elegant but exhausted soul for the next 25 years with their swift passing style and a strict dressing-room edict that they were to hold the ball for no longer than seven seconds, then that would amount to a fantastic mortal span for him.

As I recovered from my accident, and my elbow healed, and I was able to hold a book again, I discerned an exploration of time in almost everything I encountered: every story, every book. And every film too: every plot was time-sensitive or time-dependent, and everything that wasn't set in an imaginary time was history. In the newspapers and on television, little seemed to be worth covering unless it was linked to an anniversary.

And the word dominated. Every three months, the *Oxford English Dictionary* adds about 2,500 new and revised words and phrases to the online version of its third edition (in print, the second edition runs to 20 volumes, containing 615,000 entries). Many of the new words are slang, and many of the others derive from popular culture or digital tech. In contrast to the new words, the *OED* also maintains a list of the old words we use most often, and they are words we might expect: the, be, to, of and, of course, and. But what are the most commonly used nouns? Month is at number 40. Life is number 9. Day is 5, and Year is 3. Person is at number 2, while the most commonly used noun in the English language is time.*

The *OED* observes that our lexicon relies on time not merely as a single word, but as a philosophy: more actions and phrases depend on time than any other. On time, last time, fine time, fast time, recovery time, reading time, all-time. The list goes on for ages. It leaves us in no doubt of time's unassailable presence in our lives. And reading just the beginning of that list might lead one to imagine we have come too far, and are travelling too fast, to reinvent time or stop it altogether. But as we shall see in the next chapter, we once had a notion that such things were both possible and desirable.

*Oxford University Press conducted its research online, consulting books, newspapers, magazines, blogs and Hansard.

Counter-revolutionary: the 10-hour clock finds a new admirer.

Chapter Two

How the French Messed Up the Calendar

Puffball, walnut, trout, crayfish, safflower, otter, basket of gold, truffle, sugar maple, wine press, plough, orange, teasel, cornflower, tench. At the end of January 2015, Ruth Ewan positioned the last of her 360 objects in a large bright room overlooking London's Finchley Road and tried to turn back time. Ewan, who was born in Aberdeen in 1980, was an artist much interested in time and its radical ambitions, and this new project, entitled *Back to the Fields*, represented an act of historical reversal so audacious and unsettling that a casual visitor might have suspected both sorcery and lunacy.

It does look like witchcraft. The objects, placed primarily on the parquet floor, also included winter squash, skirret, marshmallow, black salsify, a bread basket and a watering can. Some of the fresh produce ruined easily in the indoor conditions, and so there were occasional gaps in the display. Grapes, for instance, rotted fast, and it was up to the artist, or one of the assistants at Camden Arts Centre, to visit a nearby supermarket to replace them. The objects resembled a giant church harvest festival, but had a distinctly non-religious intent. And they were not chosen or arranged at random. The winter barley, for example, was deliberately separated from the six-row barley by salmon and tuberose, and the button mushroom was 60 items away from the shallot.

The items were divided up into groups of 30, representing the days of the month. Each month was divided into 3 weeks of 10 days, while the number of days in a year remained the familiar 365 or 366. The 5- or 6-day shortfall in the new calculation was made up by festival days: Virtue, Talent, Labour, Conviction, Humour and, on leap years, Revolution. But the whole concept was a revolution, and certainly more than just elaborate and provocative art: it was a vivid representation of the idea that time could begin anew, modernity running wild in the fields of nature.

Ruth Ewan was recreating the French Republican calendar. This was both a political and academic rejection of the *ancien régime,* and the practical conclusion to the logical theory that the traditional Christian Gregorian calendar should be stormed alongside the Bastille and the Tuileries.

Astonishingly, this new calendar caught on for a while (or perhaps not so astonishingly: the guillotine still glistened in the autumn sun). It came into being officially on 24 October (*Poire* of *Brumaire*) 1793, although it was backdated to 22 September (*Raisin* of *Vendémiaire*) 1792, which became the start of the Republic Year 1. This radical notion lasted more than 12 years until 1 January 1806, when Napoleon Bonaparte presumably reasoned *ça suffit.*

Outside this agricultural and seasonal room in north-west London was a second Ruth Ewan re-creation, hung high on the wall: a clock with only 10 hours. This was based on another Revolutionary and doomed French experiment in the re-formatting of time – the decimalisation of the dial, a complete refiguring of the day.

Four years earlier, Ewan had tried to confound a whole

town with her wrong clocks. The Folkestone Triennial of 2011, a show utterly reliant on time passing regularly and predictably, featured 10 of her 10-hour clocks positioned strategically throughout the town, including one above Debenhams, one above the town hall, one in an antiquarian bookshop and one in a local taxi.

For a few minutes, the 10-hour clock seemed to make sense, or at least as much sense as the 12-hour one. The day was reduced to 10 hours, while each hour was divided into 100 minutes, and each minute split into 100 seconds. (One revolutionary hour was thus 2 regular hours and 24 standard minutes, while 1 revolutionary minute was 1 standard minute and 26.4 standard seconds.) The midnight hour 10 was at the top, the noon hour 5 at the bottom, and, if you were used to the regular 12-hour face, 8 minutes to 4 on the Revolutionary one was in fact anyone's guess. The French – or at least those French citizens to whom precise time was important in the 1790s and could afford a new timepiece – struggled to come to terms with the new state-imposed clock for 17 months and then shook it off like a bad dream. It remains an anachronism of history, although one to which obsessives will occasionally return, like those who want to put Australia at the top of the globe.*

Ewan told me that she wanted to make the clocks because she wanted to see how they would look; she knew of only one working example in a museum in Switzerland and a handful in France. But when she approached clockmakers with her idea 'I just got laughed at'. After phoning round six or seven clockmakers she found a keen firm called the Cumbria Clock Company (its website announced a specialism

* The French had another shot at time transformation in 1897, albeit on a modified scale. The *Commission de décimalisation du temps* suggested maintaining the 24-hour day, but changing to 100-minute hours with 100-second minutes. The proposal lay on the table for three years but was brought into effect for nought minutes.

in 'turret clock horology', and claimed the staff were as happy oiling cogs in the smallest church as they were fixing bigger problems, which recently included work at Salisbury Cathedral and Big Ben). The company also offered services such as 'night silencing'. The company had never made a 10-hour clock mechanism before, let alone 10 of them.

Ewan's disruptive show at Folkestone had a brilliant name: *We Could Have Been Anything That We Wanted To Be.* The title came from a song in the film *Bugsy Malone*, and Ewan particularly liked the second line: 'And it's not too late to change.' The clocks were 'an old item, but they also seemed to talk of a possible future,' Ewan says, putting her finger on the nature of time itself. 'I wanted to allude to the fact that we had rejected this clock once, but it may come up again.'

Once the clocks are mounted in a public space, they are ridiculously hard to read. 'A lot of people look at it and go, "all right, I get it", but they realize they haven't fully understood it: they read it as being a 20-hour clock and not a true 10-hour clock. In the course of a day, the hour hand rotates only once, not twice.'

When we spoke, Ruth Ewan's energetic obsession with time showed no sign of slacking. She had just started her stint as an artist in residence at Cambridge, where, alongside plant scientists, she was analysing Carl Linnaeus's great flower clock of 1751. Linnaeus, a Swedish botanist, had proposed an intricately arranged display of plants, designed as a circular dial, that would open and close at naturally appointed times of the day to enable accurate (or at least approximate) timekeeping. Influenced by light, temperature, rain and humidity, Linnaeus's list of responsive plants in Uppsala (60° north) did not, however, all flower in the same season, so the clock – as many attempts at practical demonstration in the nineteenth century showed – remained largely theoretical. But it was time reborn and reimagined, and the names of its components struck a similarly mellifluous air as those seen in France 40 years later. Jack-Go-To-Bed-At-Noon (open at 3 a.m.); Rough Hawkbit (open by 4 a.m.); Wild Succory (4–5 a.m.); Spotted Cat's Ear (6 a.m.); Marsh Sow Thistle (by 7 a.m.) and Pot Marigold (3 p.m.).

An artist involved in reinventing time faces dilemmas that do not befall the modern printmaker or ceramicist. The trickiest thing about Ewan's *Back to the Fields* calendar show was obtaining the obscure plants and objects that had fallen out of favour in the last 200 years. 'I thought initially that you could get everything you want online,' Ewan acknowledges, 'but I know now that you can't.' The last object to join the show was a winnowing fan, a type of basket. 'Not that long ago they were probably everywhere, but the only place we could find one was in an Oxford professor of basketry's own collection. You'll see one in a painting by Millet. It was literally used to sort the wheat from the chaff.'

One visitor to Ewan's show at Camden Arts Centre knew more than most about the dislocations of time. Matthew Shaw, a curator at the British Library, had written his Ph.D. on post-revolutionary France and turned it into a book. He had also turned it into a 45-minute talk that began with that famous bit of optimism from Wordsworth: 'Bliss was it in that dawn to be alive / But to be young was very heaven!' Shaw explained that the calendar was an attempt to lift an entire nation out of the earth's existing timeline, to start history afresh and give each citizen a shared and finite collective memory; it was a good way to impose order on a disordered country.

Shaw examined the calendar's secular elements (it abolished religious festivals and the saints' days), and stressed its inbuilt work ethic – the way time was newly arranged to make pre-industrial France more productive in the field and battlefield. The month was split into three 10-day *décades*, granting only one day off in ten rather than one in seven. With the Sabbath gone, the population found that the new day of rest carried many active obligations. 'The observant of you will notice there's a pattern here,' Shaw said as he guided his visitors round. 'Every fifth and tenth day there's something slightly out of sequence, either an animal or an implement. On the tenth day you're all supposed to gather in your village, sing patriotic songs, read out the laws, have a big meal together – and learn about the pickaxe.'

This, perhaps, was one explanation for the calendar's eventual failure. But there were other, more astronomical, reasons, such as a misalignment of the equinox. It was also a calendar that was more than a calendar: it was political, radically agrarian, and imposed its own weighty sense of history. Besides, Shaw observes, 'it was quite hard to rule an empire with it.' To complicate matters further, the 12 months had new names too, each selected by the flamboyant poet and playwright Fabre d'Églantine (who was guillotined not long afterwards for financial misdemeanours and his associations with Robespierre; he died on the day of the lettuce). *Brumaire* (Fog) lasted from 22 October (the day of apple) to 20 November (the day of roller), while *Nivôse* (Snow) lasted from 21 December (the day of peat) to 19 January (the day of sieve). All very simple when you get the hang of it, which few French citizens did, or seemed to want to.

Shaw was reaching the end of his tour, and his audience was beginning to pull away, shaking heads. He paused at 15 February, represented by hazel. 'It's very appropriate, as today we've just heard the news that Michele Ferrero has passed away at the age of 89, who made his fortune from Nutella.' Shaw's penultimate stop in the room was at the 10th of *Thermidor*. This was Republican high summer, and the day (28 July 1794) when Robespierre was executed. The Terror was eating its own. The day was represented by a watering can.*

Insane and wonderful as it was, the utopian French Republican calendar seems to have existed outside time. From today's perspective it appears as absurd as the prospect of a global commune or free money, but it is only routine and time itself that has brought us to this judgment. Earth has many calendars in which it has set its frame, and all blend logic, natural science and arbitrariness to their cause. The calendric system of time that apportions our lives into a semblance of progressive shape – and perhaps, we hope, consistent meaning – is not something that may be conclusively proven or even relied upon. One day we may wake up, as did the citizens of Auvergne and Aquitaine, and find that Tuesday is not where it used to be, and that October has gone completely.

The Republican calendar was also unusual in one other respect. It was history overnight, and unrecognisable from what had preceded it; it destroyed what calendrical historians like to call the 'deep fixity' of all earlier conceptions.** Previously, or so we would like to assume, calendars in Europe and the civilised ancient world had progressed gradually with emerging astral awareness and mathematical computation. Religious calendars also built upon each other, drawing on common baselines of solstice, equinox and eclipse.

But we'd be wrong to believe that the French Revolutionary calendar was the first to impose a political perspective upon

---

* Rather than face the guillotine, the principal architect of the calendar, Gilbert Romme, fell on his own sword almost a year later on 17 June 1795 (or, as he would have preferred, 29 *Prairial*).

** See Sanja Perovic, 'The French Republican Calendar', *Journal for Eighteenth-Century Studies*, vol. 35, no. 1.

the days. All calendars impose order and control to a greater or lesser degree, and all are political in their own way (particularly the religious ones). The ancient Mayan calendar, for example, was a beautiful and truly baffling thing, intricately maintaining two years in parallel, one of 365 days and one of 260. The 260-day system, or Sacred Round, contained 20 different names of days, including Manik, Ix, Ben and Eiznab, and these ran on the perimeter of an inner circle of 13 numbers, so that the year ended on 13 Ahau. The 365-day calendar contained 18 months of 20 days each, but as this made up only 360 and rendered it out of step with lunar and solar cycles, the remaining five days were judged fateful, with Mayans wont to stay indoors and pray to the Gods lest terrible things occur. These were terrible *religious* prophecies, an indication of the power of the priesthood. The Aztec calendar of the fifteenth and early sixteenth centuries ran on similar cycles, and institutional control: disparate provinces of a vast empire were purposely unified by religious festivals and other dates. (The Aztec calendar culminated in the New Fire ceremonies performed at the end of the full cycle every 52 years.)

We will be more familiar with the Julian calendars (effective from 45 BC, and consisting of 12 months and 365.25 days, based on a solar year), and the Gregorian reform of 1582, which retained the Julian months and lengths but slightly shortened the duration of the year (by 0.002 per cent) to accommodate more accurate astronomical rotations and reposition the date of Easter to the date it was first celebrated.* The Gregorian

---

* We are vaguely familiar too with the Julian months: Januarius, Februarius, Martius, Aprilis, Maius, Iunius, Julius, Augustus, September, October, November, December. In the first centuries of the modern era, newly appointed Roman emperors made their own egotistical modifications. The most extreme was Commodus, who delighted in changing all the months to variations of his own adopted names: Amazonius, Invictus, Felix, Pius, Lucius, Aelius, Aurelius, Commodus, Augustus,

calendar took a while to be widely accepted, with the grudging adoption by non-Catholic countries causing anomalies throughout Europe. When Edmond Halley observed a total solar eclipse in London on 22 April 1715, much of the rest of Europe saw it on 3 May. Great Britain and its American colonies finally switched over in 1752, but not without a bit of half-hearted rioting from people shouting 'Give us back our eleven days!' Japan only changed in 1872, Bolshevik Russia came in at the end of the First World War, and Greece in 1923. Turkey clung on to its Islamic calendar until 1926.

The apparent arbitrariness of how we have chosen to govern our lives was expertly parodied by B.J. Novak in the *New Yorker* in November 2013. 'The Man Who Invented the Calendar' wrote plainly of the great logic of his invention: 'A thousand days a year, divided into twenty-five months, forty days a month. Why didn't anyone think of this before?' Things go well for the calendar initially, but the first crisis hits after four weeks. 'People really hate January and want it to be over,' the inventor noted. 'I tried to explain that it's just a label, and that ending it wouldn't make any difference, but no one got it.' On 9 October, the inventor writes: 'Can't believe I haven't written in so long! Summer was amazing. Harvest was amazing . . . This year has been amazing and it's still only October. There's still November, December, Latrember, Faunus, Rogibus, Neptember, Stonk . . .' He soon decides to end the year earlier than planned, and he receives huge acclaim from friends. But there is disquiet around Christmas: 'December 25th – Why do I feel so lonely today?' and 'December 26th – Why am I so fat?'

Herculeus, Romanus and Exsuperatorius. And then he was assassinated, and subsequent emperors changed the months back.

By the time of the Second French Revolution in 1830, no one dared suggest new calendars or clock dials.* Instead, another obsession seemed to engulf early nineteenth-century France, or at least its psychoanalytical casebooks: the act of looking back became a certifiable disease. Medical studies of the 1820s and 1830s were fascinated with what appeared to be an outbreak of *nostalgia*.

One of the earliest cases concerned an elderly occupant of a lodging in rue de la Harpe, in the Latin Quarter. This man took great pride in his apartment and was devastated when he heard the news that it was to be demolished to make way for street improvements. So devastated that he took to his bed and, despite his landlord's assurances that his new home would be better and brighter, refused to budge. 'It will no longer be my lodging,' he complained, 'the one I loved so much, that I embellished with my own hands.'** He was found dead in his bed just before the demolition, having apparently 'suffocated of despair'.

Another example, also from Paris, featured a two-year-old boy named Eugéne who couldn't bear to be separated from his wet nurse. Returned to his parents, Eugéne became limp and pale, with eyes fixed on the door from where his nurse exited. When returned to his nurse, all joy broke loose. Such cases rendered French citizens useless to the state. The cultural historian Michael Roth has classified nostalgia as 'an affliction that doctors regarded as potentially fatal, contagious, and

* Although, as with the revolution of 1789, time momentarily, and perhaps mythically, did stand still. The German philosopher Walter Benjamin claims (in *On the Concept of History*, 1940) that 'during the evening of the first skirmishes . . . it turned out that the clock-towers were shot at independently and simultaneously in several places in Paris'. Two plausible reasons: to show contempt for an old unconstitutional establishment, and to mark the exact time of its overthrow. Then again, bullets may just have been flying everywhere.
** Quoted in 'Dying of the Past' by Michael S. Roth, *History and Memory*, vol. 3, no. 1 (Indiana University Press).

somehow deeply connected to French life in the middle of the nineteenth century.' The common cause was an over-fondness for one's earliest memories, and in a century of intended modernity, nostalgia cast the patient as an outcast, destined for the madhouse or the jail. The affliction was first classified in 1688 by the Swiss physician Johannes Hofer, who aligned the Greek words *nostos* (or homecoming) with *algos* (pain). Earlier in the century the affliction *mal de corazón* had seen a group of soldiers sent home during the Thirty Years War, and it did seem to be a disease that particularly afflicted the army. Swiss soldiers could apparently be left in puddles of tears if they heard cowbells, reminding them of their native pastures, not least the milking song 'Khue-Reyen'. This was such a weakener that anyone who played it – or consciously hummed it – was liable for the firing squad. Today we might just be homesick or *unhappy*. But nostalgia was the first disease associated with time, its victims longing for days gone by.*

But nostalgia is not a disease of the past. Nowadays we are nostalgic for all sorts of things, even if the analyst's couch has been vacated for more critical concerns. We like retro and vintage and distressed and heritage, and we adore history (history as a subject worthy of academia and literature barely existed before the French Revolution). The Internet thrives on the desire of the middle-aged (mostly men, it must be said) to buy back a lost youth, be it auctionable toys or salvageable cars (time has not withered these things, only increased their resale value). Nostalgia is increasingly viewed not as a punishable disease but as a consumerist one, and its connotations are no longer entirely negative. As we shall see in a later chapter, a desire to turn back the clock pervades an increasingly popular way of living: the slow life (incorporating

---

* Today's diseases associated with time? There are many: ADHD, cancer, smartphone addiction.

slow food, mindfulness, a back-to-the-lathe 'maker' mentality) has long since transformed itself from a dilettante's diversion into a monetisable movement.

The French tradition of redirecting the traditional flow of time continues today, with similarly ineffective results. But the objections are now more extreme, and more self-parodic, and are based not just upon reformatting the calendar but cancelling it altogether. On New Year's Eve 2005, a protest group calling itself Fonacon gathered in a small coastal town near Nantes to try to halt 2006. There were a few hundred people in all, and their reasoning was simple: 2005 had not been a great year, and 2006 had all the potential to be worse, and so they would symbolically try to stop time by singing some songs and smashing up a few grandfather clocks. Astonishingly, it didn't work. They tried again the year after, and a few more innocent clocks lost their lives, but globally things just kept ticking.

Next year they tried again, but still no joy. It was playful anarchy, and proof, if it was needed, that the French will protest about anything, but it brought to mind a more serious incident from more than a century before. On 15 February 1894, a French anarchist called Martial Bourdin met an unfortunate fate in the grounds of the Royal Observatory at Greenwich, the traditional home of empirical timekeeping. Bourdin was carrying a bomb, and when it exploded accidentally it blew off one of his hands and ripped a hole in his stomach.

When two Observatory staff ran from their office at the sound of the explosion, they found Bourdin still alive. But he survived only half an hour, and when his body was examined by the police they found he was carrying a large amount of cash; it was fleeing money, they suggested, quite enough to get him swiftly back to France once his mission had been accomplished. But what precisely was his mission? Speculation gripped London for weeks, and a decade later it inspired Joseph Conrad's novel *The Secret Agent*. Bourdin's motive remains unclear. He may have been carrying a bomb for an accomplice. He may have simply been trying to cause panic and chaos, the way terrorists aim to do today. But the most romantic theory, and the most French, is that he may have been trying to stop time.

The people at Fonacon do not hold up Bourdin as a hero, not in these straitened times. But they do possibly share an ambition. On New Year's Eve 2008, Fonacon tried to stop time once more, and they had a new slogan: 'It was better right now!' As a man named Marie-Gabriel explained, 'We're saying no to the tyranny of time, no to the merciless onslaught of the calendar, and yes to staying put in 2008!' The protest in Paris saw the largest turnout yet, with about a thousand people gathering to boo the arrival of the new year on the Champs-Élyseés. The clocks struck midnight, and the protestors struck the clocks, and then, *merde*, it was 2009.

The idea that time may be stopped in its tracks we happily recognise as a fanciful one, or the stuff of movies. If, in revolutionary France, such a thing once seemed plausible, it is a desire we should credit to optimism and enthusiasm, and to the fact that another revolution, a revolution in travel, was yet to occur. A train was coming down the track, and it was a solid and earnest thing: in terms of time, the train would change everything.

Mallard: small boy not included.

Chapter Three

The Invention of the Timetable

i) The Fastest Thing You Ever Did See

Do you plan on being alive for the next two-and-a-half years? If the answer is yes, you may begin building *Mallard*. This magnificent British steam locomotive, streamlined and garter blue, is available for construction each week from your newsagent, and if you keep the faith for 130 weeks, and buy all the bits required and assemble them, you will end up with a 500-millimetre-long engine and tender (almost 20 inches), weighing about 2 kilos.

Mallard was originally built in Doncaster in 1938, but in 2013 the publishers Hachette offered the amateur modeller the chance to build a highly detailed replica as a part-work, a precision-tooled miniature of the 'O'-gauge variety, designed to run on 32mm track ('track not included'). The model is made from brass, white metal, etched metal and an intricate metallic casting process called 'lost wax', and requires not only considerable patience and skill to assemble, but also tools including round-nose pliers and top-cutter pliers, and a recommendation to wear protective gloves and a face mask. When you have finished making your model, you may then paint it (paint not included).

Issue no. 1, priced at only 50p, consists of the first metal parts and a magazine that tells you a bit about *Mallard*'s history and great railroad enterprises such as the Trans-Siberian Railway. The magazine is hole-punched for easy storage, and, after a few weeks, the magazines should be put in a binder (first binder and dividers included free with your second magazine; subsequent binders not included).

The first choice you must make is whether to superglue or solder (solder not included and not recommended). Instructions for the first week's parts, which will make the driver's cab, come in twelve sections and include using the top-cutter pliers to remove all parts from the fret, smoothing the edges with wet and dry sandpaper, punching three dots in each tab to form raised rivets, and placing the left-front cab window bead in position with the pliers. If you actually like doing this you will be delighted with the free Modeller's Magnifying Glass to inspect the smaller parts (if you reply within 10 days), and a black-and-white A3 print of the original *Mallard* in thunderous action down a slope.

Issue 2, priced at only £3.99, contains the next part of your model (nose section and boiler skirts) and a feature on the West Highland Line. If you subscribe, you will also get a magnificent set of *Mallard* drink coasters in a tin. Not much happens with issue 3, apart from the arrival of the main boiler and a price hike to £7.99 (the standard price for each issue from now on), but with issue 4 you get a free Modeller's Toolkit, including a stainless steel ruler and two mini-clamps. With issue 5 there are details of how to motorise your *Mallard* when you have completed it (motor not included).*

The bit-part *Mallard* is a costly enterprise. If you wish to make the whole thing, and surely there can be little point stopping at issue 10 or 50 or 80, then you need to buy all 130 issues, and all 130 issues will cost a total of £1,027.21. The original locomotive from Doncaster, 70 feet long and 165 tons,

---

* A neat loop: Hachette's founder, Louis Hachette, founded his publishing and part-work empire on train station bookstalls in the 1820s, in the same manner as W.H. Smith.

taking hundreds of thousands of passengers on an express journey from London to Scotland and back for 25 years – about one and a half million miles of track travel in all – cost £8,500. It would be cheaper to buy the kit direct from DJH Model Loco in Consett, County Durham, where, for just £664, you get it all in one delivery in one big box. DJH Model Loco even offers a service in which someone will speed everything up and build the damn model for you in a couple of weeks, although that would surely be missing the point. For *Mallard* has always been about time. Time is why she was built.

Perhaps you can imagine *Mallard* coming down the track on Sunday, 3 July 1938. The engine, tender and cars are blue, although whether you'll be able to see this as it speeds past you is questionable. There is also a rickety brown carriage early in the chain, known as a dynamometer car, and within this are men with stopwatches and machines that resemble primitive lie detectors and heart monitors. The train is travelling so fast that it appears to be 'hunting', the phrase engineers use to describe a locomotive hurtling at such a velocity that it is swaying from side to side, as if it was searching for the fastest route to its destination, happy to jump to another track if need be. Its destination is London, but it will overheat long before then.

You are watching the train from Stoke Bank, not far from Grantham. The threat of war hovers. Twelve-year-old Margaret Roberts is at school up the road. The hurtling train, and its memory, will swiftly become one of those iconic pre-war images, like the last of the country-house shooting parties before Britain went dark. What it is about to do will never be bettered, and the anniversaries – 25th, 50th, 60th and so on – just can't come soon enough. People who love trains love this train as much as they love anything.

Similar locomotives in this group, known as A4 Pacifics, were designed to look and perform like *Mallard*, and their engineer Nigel Gresley gave them all similar names: *Wild Swan*, *Herring Gull*, *Guillemot*, *Bittern* and *Seagull*.* But to Gresley – 62, in failing health, his designs internationally recognised and copied, his trains, including the *Flying Scotsman*, lauded for both safety and comfort, an engineer comparable in achievement to the Stephensons and Brunel – none of them appeared to be *chosen* like *Mallard*, with her dynamic lines and increased cylinder pressure, and her new brake valves, double chimney and blast-pipe maximising steam production.

At Stoke Bank it has its chance. The ride through Grantham has been slow due to track maintenance, but it has reached Stoke Summit at 75 mph and accelerates now over a long downhill stretch. The speeds at the end of each mile from the summit were recorded as: 87½, 96½, 104, 107, 111½, 116 and 119 mph. The subsequent half-mile readings then gave 120¾, 122½, 123, 124¼.** And so Joe Duddington, aged 61, an Englishman based in Doncaster, employed by the London and North Eastern Railway since its formation in 1921, and *Mallard*'s driver that day, pushed her on a little as she thundered past the Lincolnshire village of Little Bytham.

---

* When a statue, bound for King's Cross, was cast in 2015 to mark the 75th anniversary of Gresley's death, there was some controversy in the railway and duck press over whether a mallard should appear at his feet. The duck appeared in the early designs, but in the end, it was decided against.

** At that very moment, the world record set by a steam train was still 124.5 mph, recorded two years earlier on a run between Hamburg and Berlin. The passengers on board, jubilant in their achievement, included Reinhard Heydrich and Heinrich Himmler. Hitler would hear of the news directly from Joseph Goebbels, who had drawn up the passenger list. The achievement was a victory not just for German engineering, but for Nazi supremacy.

'She just jumped to life like a live thing!' he would recall a few years later. 'Folks in the [dynamometer] car held their breath.' The train achieved a top speed of 125.88 miles per hour, a steam record that stands to this day.

Time passed. Seventy-five years later, a great gathering of 90 old-timers assembled at the National Railway Museum in York to talk of crewing *Mallard* and manning the sheds, and to tour another great gathering in the main hall, all six of the surviving A4 streamliners (of 35 built), huge and gleaming, a product of England: *Mallard, Dominion of Canada, Bittern, Union of South Africa, Sir Nigel Gresley* and *Dwight D. Eisenhower*. They were all wonderful engines, but *Mallard* had the celebrity status – the fastest, the only one purchasable in 130 parts, its creator's favourite – and it did seem to glow more than others, the way Marilyn Monroe or Cary Grant used to. And, as with movie stars, adults who should know better sighed in the train's presence, as if they weren't worthy, as if the train was of a different and higher species. Iron and man-made as it was, it was also a deity, shining huge above us. I queued up to step on its boiler plate, and I would have put on overalls and cap and begun shovelling coal if they had let me.

Trains, and steam trains in particular, serve as the holding pen for deep male longing. For a person over 70, the notion of 'times past' usually invokes foggy stations and whistles and the presence of grime. A great hall with men dragging tired wives around, lots of plastic bags with lots of souvenirs – it could only be childhood revisited at a railway museum; the French would have locked you away for such nostalgia.

I specifically went to hear one of the old-timers, a man named Alf Smith. Smith was 92, funny and direct, the fireman (coal-shoveller and oiler) on the boiler plate of *Mallard* for almost four years, and 'I never had a bad day, never had a bad day'. He spoke of his driver and his train with deep respect, telling a story of how, when the pair were lodging overnight and came down for their cooked breakfast, his driver would scrape three-quarters of his meal from his plate and give it to him. 'Not once, not twice, but every day that we was there, that's what he done. I said to him, "Joe, what are you doing?" He said, "I can get home on a bloody egg, you've got the work to do – eat it!" *Mallard* was part of our story. Well, it *was* our story. That was my engine.' His engine was being mobbed downstairs as he spoke. In the shop, the train was basking in the glory of an anniversary, which meant posters and magnets on sale, and small tins of garter-blue paint suitable for modelling.

Speed records on trains tend to be maintained for a long time: you push the absolute limit for a few miles, and then safety concerns or a basic lack of ambition seals the record shut for decades. The London to Aberdeen run, for example, took 8 hours 40 minutes in 1895 and didn't get any faster for 80 years. In the mid-1930s it took about 2 hours 20 minutes from London to Liverpool, and we have shaved barely 15 minutes from this. But in the twenty-first century the train is once more beholden to records and speed. The birthplace of the railways has come relatively late to this party; HS2, the first phase of which is due to open in 2026, will cut the journey between London and Birmingham from 1 hour 24 minutes to just 49 minutes.

Elsewhere in the world, progress has been faster. In Spain in 2010, the 205 mph AVE S-112, a train shaped like and nicknamed 'The Duck', cut the time it takes to get from

Madrid to Valencia by more than two hours, to 1 hour 50 minutes. In the same year, travellers between St Petersburg and Helsinki managed the cross-border trip in 3 hours 30 minutes, two hours faster than before the Sm6 Allegro arrived from its works in Italy. In China, the CRH380, new in 2011, travelled at 186 mph to cut the journey from Beijing to Shanghai to less than half the journey time in 2010: from 10 hours to 4 hours 45 minutes. And, with a certain inevitability, Japan has gone a little faster than everyone: in April 2015, on a test track near Mount Fuji, its Maglev ('magnetic levitation') train, hovering 10cm above the track, carried 49 passengers at a speed of 374 mph, smoothly outgunning the French TGV. It is expected to begin service in 2027 between Tokyo and Nagoya, a journey of 165 miles that it should manage in 40 minutes, half the time of the current Shinkansen bullet train.

But for the most extraordinary advance of all we need to go back to the birth of the *idea* of the train, and a sooty dawn in pre-Victorian north-west England.

ii) Was Ever Tyranny More Monstrous?

On the day it opened in 1830, the Liverpool and Manchester Railway revolutionised the way we thought about our lives. The fact that it linked the thriving cotton mills to a major shipping port about 30 miles away is almost incidental. The steam engine both shrunk and expanded the world; it enhanced trade; it hastened the spread of ideas; it fired global industry. And more than any other invention – save the clock itself and possibly the space rocket – the railways changed our appreciation of time.

The train wasn't like the computer: its early champions knew fairly well what they were unleashing on the world. Proposing the idea of the Liverpool and Manchester line to prospective backers and nervous crowds in the late 1820s (people thought their lungs would collapse, that cows would fail to milk, that the countryside would be set alight), the line's secretary and treasurer Henry Booth spoke of how the passenger journey time between the cities, previously only possible by horse-drawn coach over turnpike roads, would be cut in half.* 'The man of business in Manchester will breakfast at home,' Booth predicted, 'proceed to Liverpool by the railway, transact his business, and return to Manchester before dinner.' (In 1830, dinner was at lunchtime.) Booth, a man who should be more remembered than he is, foretold the impact of the railway far more eloquently than the Stephensons or Brunel. The railway, he correctly suggested, would change 'our value of time'. 'Our amended estimate of the occupation of an hour, or a day' would affect 'the duration of life itself'. Or, as Victor Hugo would later claim, 'All the armies in the world are not so powerful as an idea whose time has come.'**

The Liverpool and Manchester railway was the biggest mechanised engineering project the world had seen. It was, of course, at that time also the fastest railway in the world, covering the 31 miles in around 2 hours and 25 minutes.*** Within a few years of its opening, there were accidents all over the country, but also a huge sense of industrial adventure and release: the destiny of the world's economies was now

---

* Seasonably unreliable canals, the other slow method of transport at the birth of the railways, were principally for freight.

** Paraphrased translation from 'Histoire d'un crime', 1877.

*** The actual journey on the opening day, 15 September 1830, attended by the Duke of Wellington and other dignitaries, took a little longer, owing to the fatal accident involving William Huskisson, MP for Liverpool and a great local supporter of the new railway. A frail man who failed to gauge the time it would take for *Rocket* to travel up the track to where he was standing, he was struck by it as passengers milled around on the track and as the engines took on water midway in the journey. Oh, the symbolism of progress! At the time it was an easy mistake to make.

hurtling on iron wheels, and the minute hand had found its vital and indispensible purpose.

British steam engines were being shipped throughout the world. In February 1832 a new publication called the *American Rail-Road Journal* carried news of a rail alongside the Erie and Hudson canal, and plans for imminent openings in New Jersey, Massachusetts, Pennsylvania and Virginia. Passenger railways opened in France in 1832, Ireland in 1834, Germany and Belgium in 1835, and Cuba in 1837. In 1846 the whole of Britain was being dug up or drilled through or laid upon: there were 272 railway acts that year.

With the openings came another innovation – the passenger timetable. In January 1831, the Liverpool and Manchester Railway dared list only its departure times, although its journey time was shortening. The company now hoped that the trip between the cities 'is usually accomplished by the First Class carriages [in] under two hours'. The first-class coaches did indeed seem to travel faster – more coal, perhaps a more efficient engine – and there were two distinct schedules: first class, costing 5 shillings each way, ran at 7 a.m., 10 a.m., 1 p.m. and 4.30 p.m., with late departures for Manchester tradesmen at 5.30 on Tuesdays and Saturdays; second class, costing 3 shillings and sixpence, left at 8 a.m. and 2.30 p.m.

But what happened if you wished to travel further afield, perhaps from Lancashire to Birmingham or London? This was already possible by the late 1830s, although the competing rail companies – the Grand Junction Railway running north-west from the Midlands, the London and Birmingham Railway, the Leeds and Selby Railway, the York and North Midland Railway – failed to coordinate their schedules to oblige a passenger keen to use more than one line in a day.

The first popular railway timetable combining several lines appeared in 1839, but carried an inbuilt flaw: clocks throughout

Great Britain were not synchronised. Before the railway network few saw the need. If the clocks in Oxford ran 5 minutes and 2 seconds behind London time, or those in Bristol 10 minutes behind, and those in Exeter 14 minutes behind (this was indeed the case with all three westward cities in the 1830s, each enjoying a later sunrise and sunset than London) it was simply a matter of adjusting your time-piece when you arrived.* The clock at the town hall or main church tended to be the master timekeeper for the local community, the time still set according to the midday sun; a relatively static populace cared little for the time elsewhere in the country so long as their own local timepieces ran at the same time. If road or waterway journeys were undertaken, the time differences would either be adjusted en route (some coaching companies provided adjustment lists), or be judged to be commensurate with the unreliability of a traveller's pocket watch or carriage clock. But with railways, a new time consciousness affected all who travelled: the concept of 'punc-tuality' was born anew.

Passengers who prided themselves on the accuracy of their watches (and as the century went on, there were many more of these) were joined by an entirely new watch-owning class – railwaymen. Neither would be satisfied with what they saw as unnecessary wrinkles in precision. If railway station clocks were left unsynchronised, composite and comparable time-tables between destination and arrival points would not only cause confusion and frustration, but would be increasingly impossible and dangerous to maintain. As railways filled the countryside, a driver's watch at variance with another's would almost certainly end in collision. And then, a year later, a

* The disparity was evident northwards of London too: Leeds was 6 minutes and 10 seconds behind London; Carnforth was 11 minutes and 5 seconds behind; Barrow was 12 minutes and 54 seconds.

solution was found, at least in Britain. For the first time, timekeeping achieved nationwide standardisation: the railways began to imprint their own clock upon the world.

In November 1840 the Great Western Railway was the first to adopt the idea that time along its route should be the same no matter where a passenger alighted or departed. This task was made possible with the advent of the electric telegraph the year before, with time signals from Greenwich being sent directly along trackside wires. 'Railway time' thus aligned itself with 'London time', and by 1847 it was running on the North Western Railway (where its greatest champion was Henry Booth), the London and South Western, the Lancaster and Carlisle, South Eastern, Caledonian, the Midland and the East Lancashire lines.

There were other maverick champions too. In 1842, Abraham Follett Osler, a glassmaker and meteorologist from Birmingham, believed so strongly in the establishment of standardised time beyond the railways that he took matters into his own hands. Having raised funds for the erection of a new clock outside the Birmingham Philosophical Institution, he proceeded one evening to change its time from local to London time (moving it forward 7 minutes and 15 seconds). People noticed, but they also admired the clock's accuracy; within the course of a year, local churches and shopkeepers changed their time to match it.

By mid-century, about 90 per cent of Britain's railways were running on London time, although the regulation met a little local opposition. Many city officials objected to *any* interference from London, and showed their disapproval by maintaining clocks with two minute hands – the later one usually denoting their local, older time. In an article titled 'Railway-time Aggression', a correspondent in *Chambers' Edinburgh Journal* in 1851 offered comical disgust: 'Time, our best and dearest possession, is in danger. [Inhabitants were] now obliged, in many of our British towns and villages, to bend before the will of a vapour, and to hasten on his pace in obedience to the laws of a railway company! Was ever tyranny more monstrous or more unbearable than this?' The writer backs his disdain with many examples, including a dinner party and a wedding both ruined as a result of time discrepancies, before rallying the readership:

> Is it possible that this monster evil, with its insidious promises of good and its sure harvest of evil, will be tolerated by freeborn Englishmen? Surely not! Let us rather rally round Old Time with the determination to agitate, and, if needs be, to resist this arbitrary aggression. Let our rallying cry be 'The Sun or the Railway!' Englishmen! Beware of delay in opposing this dangerous innovation! No time is to be lost – 'Awake, arise, or be forever fallen!'

Railway time could kill you just by being there. In 1868, one Dr Alfred Haviland, an epidemiologist and author of the guide *Scarborough as a Health Resort*, published *Hurried To Death: or, A Few Words of Advice on the Danger of Hurry and Excitement Especially Addressed to Railway Passengers*, in which, in fairly breathless prose, he warned of the risks of over-studying a train timetable and running to catch a departure, and being overly concerned with the era's new schedules. His evidence, which managed to be both conclusive and dubious, centred on research suggesting that those who ventured regularly on the Brighton to London line aged faster than those who didn't.

The new pressure of time was the cause of some amusement. In 1862, the *Railway Traveller's Handy Book*, an indispensible guide to what to wear and how to comport oneself on the rails, and how to behave when going through a tunnel, contained a passage about the inexperienced traveller running to catch a train with time to spare:

About five minutes before a train starts, a bell is rung as a signal to passengers to prepare for starting. Persons unaccustomed to travel by railway connect the ringing of the bell with the instant departure of the train, and it is most amusing to watch the novices running helter-skelter along the platform, tumbling over everything and everybody in their eagerness to catch the train which they believe is about to go without them.

Those who travelled often, on the other hand, would use the bell as a signal to stand 'by the carriage door coolly surveying the panic-stricken multitude'.*

The final unifying stroke came in 1880, with the passage in parliament of the Statutes (Definition of Time) Act. It was now a public order offence to knowingly display the wrong time on municipal buildings. But beyond Great Britain, time ran on different tracks. France, a nation that had embraced the railways later than many of its European neighbours, found a way to adapt its traditionally perverse attitude to time to its new transport. While most stations adopted Paris time for their schedules and external clocks, clocks within station buildings consistently and deliberately ran five minutes early to ease the pressure on passengers who might arrive late (this lasted from about 1840 to 1880; regular passengers, of course, grew wise to the ruse and adjusted their own scheduling accordingly, a nice display of laissez-faire).

In Germany the railways seemed to shrink time, as if a magical invention. When the theologian David Friedrich Strauss travelled from Heidelberg to Mannheim in the late

---

* For some, the helter-skelter of railways represented merely one more unwelcome intrusion of the fast modern world. 'What with railways, steamships, printing-presses it has surely become a most *monstrous* "tissue" this life of ours,' Thomas Carlyle wrote from London to Ralph Waldo Emerson in America in 1835. He was horrified at 'the roaring Loom of Time', a reference to Goethe's *Faust*. The printing press, it should be acknowledged, was by then 300 years old, and one wonders where the two authors would have been without it.

1840s he marvelled at a journey that took 'half an hour instead of five hours'. In 1850 the Ludwigs railroad company shrunk time even more, advertising a trip from Nuremberg to Fürth, travelling 'one and a half hours in ten minutes'. In his *History of the Hour*, the German theologian Gerhard Dohrn-van Rossum notices persistent contemporary references to the railways causing 'the destruction of space and time' and 'the emancipation from nature'. As with Henry Booth in Liverpool, travellers cutting through mountains and spanning valleys estimated that the eradication of these obstacles practically doubled their lifespans. The imagination accelerated all possibilities.

The character of the nation, the *volksgeist*, determined that the trains not only consistently ran according to schedule but were shown to do so by station clocks synchronised from Berlin. But the acceptance of the transformation from 'external' local time to 'internal' railway time took more than fifty years. Germany was unified by railway time only in the 1890s, but it was political and military expediency, rather than a concern for the passenger, that forced the move. In 1891, Field Marshal Helmuth von Moltke, who had employed the railways effectively in his military campaigns in France, spoke in the Reichstag of the need for one clock throughout the country. The railways facilitated the greatest single improvement the military had encountered in his lifetime – enabling him to amass 430,000 men in four weeks – but there was a problem to be overcome.

> Gentlemen, in Germany we have five different time zones. In north Germany, including Saxony, we use Berlin time; in Bavaria, Munich time; in Würtemburg, Stuttgart time; in Baden, Karlsruhe time; and in the Rhenish Palatinate, Ludwigshafen time. All the inconveniences and disadvantages which we dread encountering on the French and Russian frontiers, we experience

today in our own country. This is, I may say, a ruin which has been left standing, a relic of the time of German disruption – a ruin which, now that we have become an Empire, should be completely erased.'

And thus did Germany adopt the precision of Greenwich.*

But it was on the vast continent of North America that the issue of a standard time faced its greatest challenge. Even in the early 1870s, an American rail traveller would have to have faith indeed, for the station clocks offered 49 different times from east to west. It was noon in Chicago, but 12.31 in Pittsburgh. The issue assumed particular urgency after 1853, when irregular timekeeping caused several railway fatalities (it didn't help that trains usually travelled in both directions on a single track).

A set of timekeeping instructions issued in August 1853 by W. Raymond Lee, the superintendent on the Boston and Providence Railroad, laid bare the complexities, and the propensity for human error. In part, it read like a Marx Brothers script: 'Standard Time is two minutes later than Bond & Sons' clock, No 17 Congress Street, Boston' the first of these began. 'The Ticket Clerk, Boston Station, and the Ticket Clerk, Providence Station, are charged with the duty of regulating Station Time. The former will daily compare it with Standard Time, and the latter will daily compare it with Conductor's Time; and the agreement of any two Conductors upon a variation in Station Time shall justify him in changing it.'**

And so the call went out to an unlikely group of specialists.

*Or as the proclamation in the Reichstag stated, 'The legal time in Germany is the solar mean time of the fifteenth degree latitude east of Greenwich.'

** Parallel tracks: in the twenty-first century, the lines of ultra-fast fibre-optic cables used for high-frequency trading between, for example, stock exchanges and traders in New York and Chicago, followed the telegraph laid down by the railways some 150 years before.

American astronomers had long argued that their observatory time was the most accurate available, and they were now required to set station clocks wherever possible (taking over from town clocks and jewellers' windows as the custodians of reliability). Around 20 astronomical institutions administered time to the railways in the 1880s, with the US Naval Observatory taking the lead.

Apart from the astronomers, one figure stands out. A railway engineer named William F. Allen was permanent secretary of the General Time Convention, and had long seen the advantages of a universal time system. At a meeting in the spring of 1883 he had laid out two maps before the assembled officials that seemed to establish his case beyond doubt. One was a forest of colours showing almost fifty lines, as if scribbled by an angry child, and the other was a smooth display of four broad colour bars, running north to south, each fifteen degrees of longitude apart. Allen claimed that the new map carried all 'the enlightenment we hope for in the future'.* Allen was proposing a remarkable thing: that his continent's timekeeping be based not on its national meridian, but on a meridian beyond its borders, and upon signals received by electric telegraph from the Royal Observatory at Greenwich.**

In the summer of 1883, Allen sent maps and details of his proposals to 570 railway company managers, and gained approval from the vast majority; he then supplied them with 'translation tables', to convert local time to standard. And so the familiar era of public timekeeping began at noon on Sunday, 18 November 1883, and the 49 previous time zones

---

* He was building on the maverick ideas of Professor C.F. Dowd, the principal of Temple Grove Seminary for Young Ladies in Saratoga, New York, who first suggested separating the continent into four or more 'time belts'.

** Before this standardization, the first message transmitted telegraphically some forty miles along the Baltimore to Washington line was 'What hath God wrought!'

were reduced to four. Observing the transition from the Western Union Building in New York City, Allen noted, 'the bells of St Paul's strike on the old time. Four minutes later, obedient to the electrical signal from The Naval Observatory . . . local time was abandoned, probably forever.'

As in Europe, the railways' strictures gradually spread to the locale in which they operated, and adhesion to the time-table on the tracks spread to all aspects of daily life. But, as in Europe, not every city delighted in the imposition of uniformity. Pittsburgh banned standard time until 1887, while Augusta and Savannah resisted until 1888. In Ohio, members of the Bellaire school board voted to adopt standard time and were promptly arrested on the orders of the city council. Detroit protested louder than most: although strictly part of the Central time zone, the city maintained local time (28 minutes behind Standard Time) until 1900. Henry Ford, who trained as a watch repairer before he revolutionised the car business, made and sold a watch that told both standard and local time simultaneously, and both remained in use until 1918.*

Towards the end of 1883, the *Indianapolis Centennial* noted that in the ultimate quarrel between man and nature, man had finally and irrevocably pulled ahead: 'The sun is no longer to boss the job . . . The sun will be requested to rise and set by railroad time.' At the heart of the newspaper's distaste for this new system lay the diminishing role of the church and its bells calling congregants to prayer (and in effect the whole

---

* No such delineations in Russia, though: throughout the construction of the Trans-Siberian Railway between 1891 and 1916, and despite the great distances involved, the route ran entirely on Moscow's civil time. The route now spans seven time zones across an eight-day journey.

God-given scheme of things). 'The planets must, in the future, make their circuits by such timetables as railroad magnates arrange . . . People will have to marry by railroad time.'* A reporter in Cincinnati observed that 'the longer a man is a commuter the more he grows to be a living timetable'.

The word 'commuter' was brand new (one who 'commuted' or shortened their journey). But the notion of the railway timetable, novel at the launch of the Liverpool and Manchester line in 1830, was by now ingrained in the soul.** The first international railway timetable conference took place in Cologne in February 1872. Representatives from Austria, France, Belgium and Switzerland joined delegates from a newly unified Germany. The debate was both a simple and a complicated one: how to coordinate trains running across international borders to facilitate smooth travelling for passengers and freight and an efficient service by the operators? And then how to advertise this service in a way that would encourage and simplify this procedure? One of the most important agreements was how the timetable would be represented visually: it was decided to use roman numerals based on the 12-hour format. The conferences increased in number and productivity each year: the founding members were soon joined by Hungary, the Netherlands, Spain, Poland and Portugal, and the standardisation of time from London

---

* Quoted in Jack Beatty, *Age of Betrayal: The Triumph of Money in America 1865–1900* (New York, 2008) and in Ian R. Bartky, *Selling the True Time: Nineteenth-Century Timekeeping in America* (Stanford, 2000). The latter is especially comprehensive, and has been a useful source for the American details in this chapter.
** Those within even touching distance of railway fanaticism, and admirers of Michael Portillo (more now than there used to be), will be aware of Bradshaw's, the guide that began in England as a pocket-sized timetable in 1839 and soon expanded into a UK railway atlas, a traveller's guide and a European handbook. It was both infinitely useful and highly accurate, and its popularity obliged railway companies to run punctual trains; the printed timetable dictating the service rather than the other way around.

ensured that passengers increasingly made the right connections. The meetings were held twice a year, for summer and winter timetables, until the First World War brought cooperation and, in many cases, cross-border travel to an end. (War undid much that was noble about the railways; their potential facilitated modern warfare. The Duke of Wellington would surely have recognised their worth, as of course did Mussolini.*)

It won't be so long before the train shifts its symbolic status as a model of speed and alarm to a model of sedateness; we shall soon see the car overtake it as the epitome of speed and stress. But first let us travel back to other tracks and tempos, and to charming old Austria, where a man with crazy hair is about to conduct a nervous orchestra.

---

* Many eyewitness accounts suggest punctual Fascist trains were a myth, but there can be no doubting the hitherto unavailable possibilities of synchronised troop movements.

A revolution in sound: three minutes of bliss from the Beatles.

Chapter Four

The Beet Goes On

i) The Way to Play the Ninth

At 6.45 p.m. on Friday, 7 May 1824, a large crowd gathered at a theatre in the centre of Vienna for the first performance of the greatest piece of music ever written. Beethoven's Ninth Symphony, composed in almost total deafness, was a work so radical in form and free in spirit that even those who interpret it almost two centuries later never fail to find within it something revelatory. When the world falls apart or unites, this is the music it reaches for.

No one could predict this at the time, of course. Since its construction in 1709, the Theater am Kärntnertor had witnessed premieres by Haydn, Mozart and Salieri, and its audience was versed in high opera. The last great work by Beethoven performed at the theatre had been the newly revised version of *Fidelio*, which was received rapturously, but that was exactly 10 years before. The composer, now aged 53, the state of his finances always precarious, had accepted many commissions from royal courts and publishers in London, Berlin and St Petersburg, had frequently missed his deadlines, and was thought to be overwhelmed not only with work but also with legal battles over the custody of his nephew Karl. Besides, he had developed a reputation for obstinacy and cantankerousness. So there was no reason to expect that Beethoven's latest work was going to be much more than another worthy milestone, not least since it became known that the piece was long and complex, involving a larger orchestra than usual, with solo singers and a chorus in the finale, and had undergone less than four days' rehearsal. And there was one more thing. Despite the announcement that the concert was to be conducted by the theatre's regular maestro Michael Umlauf, assisted by first violin Ignaz Schuppanzigh, it was agreed that Beethoven would also appear onstage for the entire performance, placing his own conductor's stand next to Umlauf, ostensibly to guide the orchestra in the dynamics of the symphony's tempo (or as it said in the official announcement of the concert the day before, 'Mr Ludwig van Beethoven will himself participate in the general direction'). This would, of course, create a complicated dilemma for the orchestra to negotiate. Where to look? Whose tempo to follow? One eyewitness, the pianist Sigismond Thalberg, claimed that Umlauf instructed his players to honour Beethoven by occasionally looking at him, but then to totally ignore his beating of time.

The evening began well. Before the premiere there were two other recent compositions: the overture *Die Weihe des Hauses*, which had been commissioned for the opening of another Viennese concert hall two years earlier, and three movements from his great D Major Mass *Missa Solemnis*. As his new symphony began, Beethoven was a dramatic figure on stage, his hair and arms wild and everywhere – or, in the words of one of the orchestra's violinists Joseph Böhm, 'he threw himself back and forth like a madman'. Böhm further remembered, 'he stretched to his full height, at the next he crouched down to the floor. He flailed about with his hands and feet as though he wanted to play all the instruments and sing all the chorus parts.' Helène Grebner, a young member of the chorus, recalled that Beethoven's timekeeping may have been a little tardy: although he 'appeared to follow the score with his eyes, at the end of each movement he turned several pages together'. On one occasion, possibly at the end of the second movement, the contralto Caroline Unger had to tug on Beethoven's shirt to alert him to the applause behind him; these days the audience holds its approval until the end of the entire piece, but in those days praise arrived at regular intervals. Beethoven, still facing the orchestra, had apparently not heard the clapping, or was too busy readying his score for the *adagio*. Could this really have happened? Or was this last story a myth subtly amplified by time?* The performance throws up bigger questions too. How could one so profoundly deaf compose a piece of music that would send almost all who heard it into raptures? Beethoven's secretary Anton Schindler wrote how 'never in my life did I hear such frenetic yet cordial applause . . . The reception was more than imperial – for the people burst out in a storm four times.'** A reviewer in the *Wiener Allgemeine Musikalische Zeitung* suggested that Beethoven's 'inexhaustible genius had shown us a new world'. Everyone – friends, critics, the whipped-up cream of Viennese connoisseurship – had delightedly thrown their hats in the air. But had they heard what the composer intended? And have we?

We know the score. The first movement in sonata form that never settles down, the orchestra in an elemental battle with itself, the hovering tension of the first gentle bars soon

* The principal source seems to have been Joseph Böhm again. 'Beethoven was so excited that he saw nothing that was going on about him, he paid no heed whatever to the bursts of applause, which his deafness prevented him from hearing in any case. He had always to be told when it was time to acknowledge the applause, which he did in the most ungracious manner imaginable.' Translated in H.C. Robbins Landon, *Beethoven: A Documentary Study* (London, 1970). See also: R.H. Schauffler, *Beethoven: The Man Who Freed Music* (New York, 1929); George R. Marek, *Beethoven: Biography of a Genius* (London, 1970); Barry Cooper, *Beethoven* (Oxford, 2000); Thomas Forrest Kelly, *First Nights* (Yale, 2000).

** Schindler wrote this in one of Beethoven's 400 Conversation Books, the verbal scrapbooks used by his visitors to communicate with the composer once his deafness took hold.

colliding with the full swaggering crescendo that announces a work of unshakeable emotional force. The second movement, the scherzo, a juggernaut of engaging and urgent rhythm before the controlled and heart-stoppingly beautiful melody of the slow third. And then the last visionary movement, the stirring optimism of Schiller's *Ode to Joy*, thunderous as to Heaven, a rhapsodic symphony in itself, described by the German critic Paul Bekker as rising 'from the sphere of personal experience to the universal. Not life itself portrayed, but its eternal meaning.'

But how well do we *really* know the score?

The notes are one thing, the tempo quite another. The symphony has long become part of the landscape. It has an official title: 'Symphony No. 9 in D Minor', and the catalogue number Opus 125; it has a vernacular title: the 'Choral', and an insiders' shorthand title 'B9'. But what it doesn't have, through all its thousands of performances, is even the loosest of agreements on its timing. Just how aggressively should the second movement be played? And how sluggishly the third? By what electrifying licence can Toscanini drive home the fourth movement more than five minutes faster than the relatively glacial interpretation by Klemperer? How can one conductor from the nineteenth century get the audience home a comfortable 15 minutes earlier than one in the twenty-first century? How can Felix Weingartner conduct the Ninth with the Vienna Philharmonic in February 1935 at a lick of 62.30, Herbert von Karajan lead the Berlin Philharmonic in the autumn of 1962 in 66.48, and Bernard Haitink and the London Symphony manage 68.09 in April 2006? What about Simon Rattle's take of 69.46 back in Vienna in 2003? And then there are the live recordings complete with pauses and coughing between movements – most famously Leonard Bernstein conducting a multinational orchestra in Berlin on Christmas Day 1989 to mark the fall of the Wall, the performance at

which the word 'joy' was replaced by the word 'freedom' at
the choral finale, clocking in at a remarkable 81 minutes 46
seconds. Has our patience for the symphony expanded against
all the faster odds in our modern world? Does our modern
appreciation of genius demand that we savour every note?

The glory of music rests as much with its interpretation
as its composition, and it is the interpretation that supplies
the life force. Art cannot be reduced to absolutes; emotion
cannot be measured in a timescale. But at the beginning of
the nineteenth century, the method of interpreting contemporary music changed, and Beethoven's impatience and
radicalism had much to do with it. The composer found a
new way of marking time.

Although each movement of the Ninth Symphony carries
the usual form of general introductory guidance for tempo
and mood, even the casual listener will acknowledge the
inadequacy of these instructions for such a varied and uncon-
ventional piece. The first movement plumps for '*Allegro ma
non troppo, un poco maestoso*' (lively and joyous, but not too
much so, and then a tad stately); the second '*Molto vivace*'
(very fast and forceful); the third '*Adagio molto e cantabile*'
(slow and lyrical); and the fourth, with its groundbreaking
choral finale, '*Presto – Allegro ma non troppo – Vivace – Adagio
cantabile*' (trippingly fast, lively but steady, slow and sweet).

Where did these tempos come from? From the human
heartbeat and the human stride. Any definition of tempo
required a baseline from which to operate – the *tempo giusto*
from where one may either run fast or slow. An accepted
average for both a leisurely stroll and a relaxed heart rate
stood at around 80 beats per minute (bpm), and this was
considered a 'normal' place to start. (In 1953 the fabled music
historian Curt Sachs suggested that there was an upper and
lower limit which prevented a concert performance descending
or accelerating into incomprehension. 'The maximum of

slowness, which still allows for a steady step or beat, is possibly 32 (bpm) . . . and the maximum of speed, beyond which the conductor would fidget rather than beat, is probably 132.' Sachs also made his own table, approximate at best but certainly original, linking precise bpm with vague terminology. Unfortunately, it slightly contradicted his estimation above. Thus he calculated that *adagio* would be 31 bpm, *andantino* 38, *allegretto* 53 ½ and *allegro* 117.*

It was the Italians who introduced the descriptions of tempo we're still familiar with (all those *vivaces* and *moderatos*), and by 1600 the *moods* of classical music were well established. Emotions were no longer merely intuited but inscribed: 'gaily' (*allegro*) and 'at leisure' (*adagio*). When he played in Bologna in 1611, Adriano Banchieri's organ scores already carried very particular instructions for *presto*, *più presto* and *prestissimo*. Fifty years later the musical vocabulary stretched to the most staccato *nervoso* and the most beautiful *fuso* ('melting'). The fabled link to the heartbeat found further resonance in the Italian term for a quarter-rest: *sospiro*, a breath or a sigh.

But there was a problem: emotions are pliable things, and they didn't always translate from composer to conductor. Nor did they translate between nations. In the 1750s, C.P.E. Bach, son of Johann Sebastian, found that 'in certain countries [outside Germany] there is a marked tendency to play *adagios* too fast and *adagios* too slow.' Some twenty years later, a young Mozart found that when he performed in Naples his

---

*There are echoes. From the beginning of the twentieth century, music has splintered into so many genres that often it is only attitude and tempo that defines them. Jazz found myriad ways of defining the undefinable: bebop always meant fast; cool jazz was predominantly airier. From ballad to speed metal, the definitions extend to pop and dance music too. The modern club dance scene may be entirely delineated by its bpm, with house set somewhere between 120–130 and trance at 130–150. You'll find breakbeat somewhere between them. And speedcore only gets serious at 180.

interpretation of *presto* was so unparalleled that the Italians assumed that his virtuosity was somehow connected to his magic ring (which he then removed to rule out foul play).

By the 1820s we know that Beethoven regarded these instructions as perfunctory and outmoded. In a letter to the musician and critic Ignaz von Mosel in 1817, he suggested that the Italian terms for tempo had been 'inherited from times of musical barbarism'.

> For example, what can be more absurd than *Allegro*, which once and for all means cheerful, and how far removed we are often from the true meaning of this description, so that the piece of music itself expresses the very opposite of the heading! As far as these four main connotations are concerned [*allegro, andante, adagio, presto*], which, however, are far from being as right or as true as the main four winds, we would do well to dispense with them.

Mosel agreed with him, and Beethoven feared they would both be 'decried as violators of tradition' (although he regarded this as preferable to being accused of 'feudalism'). Despite these protestations, Beethoven reluctantly persevered with the old style; right to the last quartets his work was proceeded by the Italian settings he despised.* To temper his dissatisfaction he occasionally included slight modifiers in the body of the score: *ritard*, he writes early on in the first movement of the Ninth Symphony, short for *ritardando*, a signal to slow down gracefully when the rhythms start running off in all directions. But throughout his score for the Ninth, Beethoven also provided a new and far more significant instruction to the conductor and players – a measure of exact timing supplied by a newly invented musical gadget.

---

* There is some suggestion in his correspondence that he still regarded the use of *allegro, andante* and the rest as a useful indicator of *character*, if not of tempo.

The metronome was as revolutionary to Beethoven as the microscope was to seventeenth-century bacteriologists. It afforded both ultimate steadiness and minute variableness, and it transmitted to the entire orchestra the composer's precise intentions. What, at the beginning of a musical sequence, could be clearer and more exacting than a notation of regimented beats to the bar and beats to the minute? And what would bring an ageing composer closer to God than the belief that he was transforming the essence of time itself?

In his letter to Mosel, Beethoven credited the invention of the metronome in 1816 to the German pianist and inventor Johann Mälzel, although Mälzel had copied, improved and patented a device developed in Amsterdam several years earlier by a man named Dietrich Winkel. (Winkel had been inspired by the reliable movement of a clock's pendulum, which had been used as an aid to musical composition since the days of Galileo in the early seventeenth century. But the early musical pendulums were cumbersome, inexact machines closer in appearance to an upright weighing scale than the small pyramids we are used to today. The key innovation of Winkel's device was the fact that the pendulum pivoted around a lower central point with movable weights; the old machines swung pendulously from the top. When Mälzel took out patents for Winkel's machine across Europe, his sole innovation appears to have been a newly notched measuring plate.)*

Mälzel had a talent for copying and claiming as his own:

---

* Another note from Beethoven, however, suggests that the composer was well aware of the old-style metronome a few years before the Winkel/Mälzel improvements. He was certainly aware of the obvious connection between the old pendulum metronome and the clock, and may have acknowledged the link in his Eighth Symphony. Although listeners argue about his intentions, the brief second movement has the staccato tick-tock rhythms of a clock, and is believed by some to be the composer's tribute to the metronome. It is also possible that this passage was inspired by the second movement of Haydn's Symphony No. 101 ('The Clock').

Beethoven had once accused him of taking undue credit for writing 'Battle of Vitoria', his short piece celebrating the Duke of Wellington's victory over Napoleon in 1813. The two had initially worked on the composition together; Beethoven had intended to use Mälzel's panharmonicon (a mechanised organ-style box able to reproduce the sound of a marching band), but later expanded the scale of his piece, rendering the new instrument redundant.*

Mälzel was the Caractacus Pott of his day. The son of an organ maker, his obsession with mechanical wonders reached both its zenith and nadir in his promotion of the automaton chess-playing 'Turk' (a fraud, of course: a small and masterful player sat beneath the Turk in a cabinet controlling every move; intriguingly, the Turk was taken on a European tour lasting several years in the first part of the nineteenth century, and was occasionally demonstrated during the interval of Beethoven's concerts). Mälzel also developed four ear trumpets for Beethoven, two of which hooked around his head to free both hands, which may explain Beethoven's later desire to patch up their differences and support his metronome. At the end of his letter to Mosel, the composer envisaged a situation in which 'every village schoolmaster' would soon be in need of one. And in this way a familiar musical teaching and performance tool entered common use: 'It goes without saying that certain persons must take a prominent part in this exercise, so as to arouse enthusiasm. As far as I am concerned, you can count on me with certainty, and it is with pleasure that I await the part which you will assign to me in this undertaking.'

His support did not diminish with the passing years. On 18 January 1826, some 14 months before his death, he wrote

---

* The word metronome (*metronom* in German) derived from the Greek *metron* and Latin *metrum*, 'to measure'. Metre (length) and metre (poetic) ditto.

to his publisher B. Schott and Sons in Mainz, promising 'everything adapted for metronome'. And later that year he wrote to his publishers again: 'The metronome marks will follow soon: do not fail to wait for them. In our century things of this kind are certainly needed. Also, I learn from letters written by friends in Berlin that the first performance of the [Ninth] symphony received enthusiastic applause, which I ascribe mainly to the use of a metronome. It is almost impossible now to preserve the *tempi ordinari*; instead, the performers must now obey the ideas of unfettered genius . . .'

And that, one may have reasonably believed, would have been the end of it. The unfettered genius would get his way, and henceforth his music would have but one tempo, and almost two centuries later we would sit in a concert hall and hear essentially the same piece of music that an audience heard when the music was new. Fortunately for us, things didn't work out that way. Beethoven's metronome marks have been confounding musicians since their ink was wet, and many have responded in the only way they feel able – by almost completely ignoring them.

In a landmark talk to the New York Musicological Society in December 1942, the violinist Rudolf Kolisch addressed the issue of Beethoven's tempo with wry understatement. 'These marks have not been generally accepted as altogether valid expressions of his intentions or been uniformly adopted in performance. On the contrary, their existence has failed to enter the consciousness of musicians, and in most editions they are lacking. The traditions and conventions of perform-ance deviate widely from the tempi denoted by the marks.' In other words, musicians and conductors placed their own interpretations above those of the original composer. They preferred, Kolisch suggested, the traditionally vague Italian markings over the more precise, newfangled ones. 'This strange situation,' the speaker reasoned, 'deserves investigation'.

A common reason offered for the decision to ignore Beethoven's sense of timing is that the marks do not accurately convey his musical desires; Schumann is commonly cited as someone else who wrote metronomic marks he couldn't have possibly meant. Other non-adopters claim that Beethoven's metronome was different to the one that came factory-built in the twentieth century; it was probably slower, so that the marks it threw up are now too fast, and almost impossible to play; critics find it useful to refer to them as 'impression-istic' and mere 'abstractions'. And then there is a more philosophical suggestion: the feeling that using a metronome was somehow rigidly mathematical and therefore 'inartistic'. Beethoven seemed to be working against himself; according to Kolisch's talk, such a free-spirited organic composition 'cannot . . . be forced into so mechanical a frame'.

When a revised version of Rudolf Kolisch's talk was published in the *Musical Quarterly* fifty years later, it included Beethoven's earliest written reference to Mälzel's metronome. He called it 'a welcome means of assuring that the perform-ance of my compositions everywhere will be in the tempi that I conceived, which to my regret have so often been misunderstood.'* We shouldn't forget that Beethoven had a maniacally high opinion of himself; he once derailed one critic of his work with the suggestion, 'Even my shit is better than anything you could create.' (And of course his opinions changed over time. Before he championed the metronome, the value he attached to the tempo of his compositions appeared much looser: on one occasion he suggested that his markings should apply only to the first few bars; on another he wrote, 'Either they are good musicians and ought to know

---

* A century later, and a century apart in musical composition, Arnold Schoenberg would agree with Beethoven's creative wish for control over timing. Writing in 1926, he asked, 'Doesn't the author have at least the right to indicate, in the copies of the work *he himself* publishes, how he imagines his ideas should be realized?'

how to play my music, or they are bad musicians and in that case my indications would be of no avail.')

Perhaps only the most challenging and gifted of composers deserve to be reinterpreted anew at each performance; perhaps only a masterpiece can withstand this new scrutiny on a regular basis. Or perhaps even the most exacting of a composer's musical timings should provide only the loosest guidelines: to provide, as the aesthetics professor Thomas Y. Levin has suggested, a frame within which music may simply *live*. Because everything else, 'its breathing, its phrasing, the endlessly complex and subtle structuring of time within this constitutive constraint remains, as always, the responsibility of the performer'.*

But does the responsibility of the performer vary with the generations? Our innate measurement of time today may be quite different from two centuries before. The Swiss-born American conductor Leon Botstein confronted these issues in 1993 when he was in a great hurry to catch a train. 'I was driving a car on a back-country road and found myself behind a black semi-covered carriage pulled by two horses,' he wrote in the *Musical Quarterly* a few months later. 'What struck me was that the horses seemed to be going really quite fast. This was not a Central Park tourist drive. Yet as I tailgated the contraption I became painfully aware how intolerably slow it moved.'

Botstein grew agitated, and began to wonder how long it would take him to reach his destination if this was the top speed of all forms of travel – which once, of course, it was. 'By the time I could pass it, my anger turned to free association. Was it at all significant that Beethoven probably never experienced motion any faster than the velocity of this carriage – that his expectations with respect to time, duration, and

* *Musical Quarterly*, Spring 1993.

the relative possibilities of how events and spaces might be related to one another in time might be radically different from our own?'

Beethoven's metronome marks, which appeared to Botstein much too fast, are countered by many works that appear too slow. Schumann's markings for *Manfred* appear sluggish; Mendelssohn's marks in parts of *St Paul* painfully so; Dvořák's final movement of the Sixth Symphony also has markings that appear to the musician to be quite out of keeping with the energy of the music. It begs yet another unanswerable question: should the musical time allotted to a work at a particular period in history necessarily feel correct in a modern, faster life many decades later? Will innovation always date? The world spins and the impact of an artistic revolution turns from shock to analysis. Cubism is a movement not a controversy; the Rolling Stones are not a scary parental proposition.

And there is, of course, more to an interpretation of a masterpiece than mere timings on a manuscript or CD insert. There is intent. When Wilhelm Furtwängler famously chased down the final movement of the Ninth Symphony at the Bayreuth Festival in 1951, he was following more than a metronome. He was following the Second World War. Contemporary accounts suggest that sometimes he appeared not even to be paying heed to the notes, let alone the tempo, with his direction carrying enough indignation to burn through the score. Passion is an overused word these days, but Furtwängler's audience and his orchestra may have been reminded of the passion of Beethoven himself, flailing at the premiere, furious at the noise in his head.

There is yet another realm of exploration: the notion that there was, in Vienna in 1824, very little acceptance of what the concepts of speed and quickening time might yet entail. Viennese society was not yet a modern one, and conducted itself much as it did two or three centuries before. Clocks were not always accurate timepieces, time ran liberally fast and slow, and there was little need for greater accuracy and synchronisation. The railways and the telegraph had not yet transformed the city. Throw a precise and unforgiving metronome into this mix and you had an explosion big enough to deafen the world.

Perhaps it is inevitable with Beethoven that the story always returns to deafness. Stanley Dodds, a second violin with the Berlin Philharmonic, has wondered whether it isn't freedom itself that underlies the key mysteries of Beethoven's Ninth: 'I ask myself sometimes if when you become completely deaf and music exists only in its imaginary form in your head, it of course loses a certain physical quality. The mind is completely free, and this would explain and helps maybe to understand where this enormous creativity, this freedom in his compositional creativity, came from.' Dodds was interviewed for a digital tablet app that forensically contrasts performances of the Ninth by Ferenc Fricsay from 1958, Herbert von Karajan from 1962, Leonard Bernstein from 1979 and John Eliot Gardiner from 1992.* He also finds Beethoven's metronome values to be 'rather ridiculous' and much too quick. The recordings that attempt to honour those values 'sound a little bit like music notation programmes which just play it off as a machine would play it off', and humans require something else.

Music itself, when executed in its physical form, has a little bit of weight. That weight could be defined as the weight of a bow, which needs to moved up and down and turned at every bow

---

* The app, published by Touchpress and Deutsche Grammophon in 2013, is a rather magnificent thing, enabling the listener to follow and contrast each performance either from the 1824 score or any of the orchestras' instruments. The accompanying notes and interviews are also fascinating.

change, or even just the few grams of the lips which need to vibrate to cause the brass instrument to sound, or the timpani skin which needs to oscillate. A double bass sound, for example, seems to take longer to travel.

The sum of all these slight practical delays might mean that Beethoven's notations are not actually physically realisable. 'But because Beethoven was imagining it in his mind, in your mind you are completely free. I know from my own experience that I can *think* about music in a way that is much faster than actually when I am *playing* the music.'

Beethoven died three years after his Ninth Symphony first brought the house down in Vienna.* The city came to a standstill for his funeral; the clocks stopped in his honour. His final months were spent revising earlier works specifically to add marks for the metronome, for he could think of nothing more important to fortify the future performances of his work. We know things didn't work out that way. But there is one further peculiar twist to the story, and it didn't happen for another 150 years.

ii) Just How Long Should a CD Be?

On 27 August 1979, the chief executives and leading engineers of Philips and Sony sat around a table in Eindhoven with the simple intent to alter the way we listen to music. Decades before the term was invented, they planned disruptive technology on a grand scale. The grooved vinyl LP had hardly changed in 30 years, and was blighted by dirt, dust, scratches and warping, and a truly tedious limitation: how could you lose yourself in even the shortest symphony if halfway through

---

* The concert hall has been demolished, and in its place stands the Hotel Sacher, home of the famous torte.

you had to lift the needle, remove the fluff, flip the disc and start anew? (The LP was, of course, also beautiful, tactile, warm of sound and transformative, but progress is progress.)

And so the compact disc was born, or at least conceived. The idea was to combine the neat modern ease of the compact cassette with the aural durability and random access of the videodisc, and in so doing persuade music lovers to become gadget lovers.* The CD was to be a smaller object, a digital recording read optically by a laser, and what it lacked in aural warmth it made up for in dynamism, accuracy, random access and a wipe-clean surface. (It was also a cool new thing, and although few who handed over their money for Dire Straits' *Brothers in Arms* could have anticipated it, the CD was also the public on-ramp to the nascent digital universe.)

There was one problem to overcome before this could happen: the format. Stung by the video wars between Betamax and VHS, during which two competing technologies slugged it out for the consumer to the detriment of all, Philips and Sony now agreed to work together on an unprecedented scale.** Both had developed a similar technology and announced it to the world in March 1979, but they differed on the specs;

* The cassette had been launched by Philips in 1962, and had been a huge hit for a new generation of pop fans and car drivers, but was let down by its poor fidelity and its overwhelming desire to unspool; the record industry loved the cassette for a while (until it was used to record music from the radio, when it started to love it less). The video disc, also known as the laserdisc, had also been partially developed by Philips, but had proved popular only with the Bang & Olufsen crowd and boffin cineastes – early adopters without any later adopters.
** Much of the video format war focused on a videocassette's duration. If Sony's Betamax lasted an hour, but JVC's VHS lasted two or four, then anyone interested in sport or movies had an easy decision. There was another incompatible competitor in the shape of Video 2000 (Philips and Grundig both lost their shirt on that one), and, for a short while at least, a system from Panasonic called VX. This offered an early and primitive programmable timing device: the box itself was called the Great Time Machine.

consumers would again face an incompatible choice of players. They needed a united front, particularly if they were to convince music lovers to buy the same music they already owned.

But precisely how compact should the disc be? And how much digital information should it contain?

The meetings between chief executives and engineers took place over several days in Eindhoven and Tokyo, and resulted in the industry standard manual known as the Red Book. Summarising the agreement years later in *IEEE Communications*, the journal of the Institute of Electrical and Electronics Engineers, a long-standing member of the Philips audio team named Hans B. Peek took great pride in contributing to a product that nudged the culture. Peek suggested that the LP was simply out of time: in an age of miniaturisation it just stood there, the records stout in the stacks and the player bulky on the sideboard. Peek wrote of the tiny 'pits and lands' of the CD grooves and how the pitfalls of the digital registration of audio signals were mastered. Unlike the LP, a CD would be read from the inside to the outside edge. Skipping, clicking, dropouts – all the errors of optical reading that could be caused by such a simple thing as fingerprints on the disc – had to be overcome, and an agreement had to be reached on information density. Prior to Sony's involvement, the diameter of the disc was agreed at 11.5cm, the same as the diagonal length of a cassette. The initial playing time was set at one hour, a nice round figure and a considerable improvement on the LP.

In February 1979, prototypes of a CD player and discs were played to audio experts at PolyGram, the newly formed record company founded by Philips and Siemens (a synergy that provided access to the entire catalogue of Deutsche Grammophon). The PolyGram people loved it: crucially, when several samples of music were played, they could detect no difference between the playback of a CD and the playback of the original master tapes. Journalists got to hear a CD for the first time a month later; again, the sound astonished: on one of the earliest recordings, a complete collection of Chopin waltzes, one could hear the pianist's assistant turn the pages. The media also liked what they didn't hear – there was no sound at all as they paused music in the middle of a track: the precision pause button, the suspension and elongation of musical time, was itself revolutionary. The CD also offered something else: a whole new consciousness of musical time. It's a thrill, really – seeing the first seconds of the track appear on a digital read-out in green or red, with the ability not only to pause, but also to repeat and scan back. The operator was in charge of time in a novel way, everyone a DJ with precise control, Abbey Road in everyone's road.

Philips then went to Japan to talk manufacturing part-nerships. Representatives spoke to JVC, Pioneer, Hitachi and Matsushita, but only Sony signed a deal. Norio Ohga, Sony's vice-chairman, arrived in Eindhoven in August 1979 to begin hammering out the details of what would become the industry standard, and it wasn't until further meetings had concluded in Tokyo in June 1980 that an agreement was reached and final patent applications were filed. By then, the original formats proposed by Philips had changed. According to J.P. Sinjou, who led a team of 35 at the Philips CD lab, the 11.5cm disc was changed to 12cm on the personal wish of Norio Ohga. The extra width would allow Ohga, who was a trained baritone and passionate classical music lover, to extend the duration of the disc by a crucial amount. 'Using a 12cm disc,' Hans B. Peek wrote, 'a particular performance of Beethoven's Ninth Symphony, a favourite of N. Ohga with a length of 74 minutes, could be recorded.' Other issues were met with even neater solutions: 'J. Sinjou put a Dutch coin, a dime, on the table. All agreed that this was a fine size for the hole [in the middle of the disc]. Compared with other lengthy discussions, this was a piece of cake.'*

Could it be that its initial length was really inspired by a lengthy recording – Furtwängler's interpretation at Bayreuth in 1951 – of Beethoven's Ninth? Wouldn't that be wonderful? The story is quoted only as an 'anecdote' by an engineer, and doubts have crept in. Another version suggests the Beethoven fan was not Mr Ohga, but his wife. It may be that the Beethoven story was concocted in retrospect, an inspired marketing wheeze. And there was one further twist: Furtwängler's 74-minute performance could technically be accommodated on a single CD, but it couldn't be played; the earliest CD players could only handle 72 minutes. It was a fate the conductor was to share with Jimi Hendrix's *Electric Ladyland*: today both masterpieces fit on a single disc, but initially they were split between two.

But who buys CDs these days? Who but the purist has time to visit a record shop and buy a physical product when a song may be downloaded in three seconds? In an age of SoundCloud and Spotify, who has time to even *listen* to an entire uncompressed album as it was conceived by the artist? The format no longer restricts the art form; but once, as we shall see from the records kept by the cashier at Abbey Road, the format used to be very strict indeed.

iii) Revolver

A little hush now please: the Beatles are about to record their first LP. It is early in the morning on Monday, 11 February

---

* Between August 1982 (when the first CDs and players reached the market) and the beginning of 2008, global CD sales were estimated at 200 billion. The product spawned the CD-Rom and became a key method of computer storage. The record-able CD followed, and then the DVD and Blu-ray on the same platform.

1963, and Studio 2 at Abbey Road is booked for three sessions: 10 a.m.–1 p.m., 2.30–5.30 p.m. and 6.30–9.30 p.m. The timings comply with standard Musicians' Union rules. A session may last no more than three hours, from which no more than 20 minutes of recorded material may be used. Each artiste will be paid the same amount per session – 7 pounds and 10 shillings – and you have to sign your chit at the end of the day to get your Musicians Union Fees from Mr Mitchell, the Abbey Road cashier. When they first register for payment, the band are an unfamiliar presence: John Lennon gives his details as J.W. Lewnow of 251 Mew Love Ave; the role of bass guitarist is credited to George Harrison.

The fact that the Beatles are there at all that day is unusual. When the studio was booked, the group had released only one single; when Parlophone's label chief George Martin broke the news that the band were going to make a long-player, it was a remarkable announcement. Pop music was restricted to singles. The biggest-selling LPs in Britain over the previous two years were not by Cliff Richard or Adam Faith, or even Elvis Presley: they were by the George Mitchell Minstrels with songs from *The Black And White Minstrel Show*.

The morning session began with the Beatles recording an original song called 'There's a Place', inspired by 'Somewhere' from *West Side Story*.* There were seven full takes, and three false starts, with the last take, lasting 1.50, being credited on the studio recording sheet as 'best'. Then it was straight into a song listed as '17'. There were nine takes in all, including false starts, and after playback it was decided that the first take had been the best, and within a few days the title had changed to 'I Saw Her Standing There' and it was decided that the song should open the album, just as it opened many

---

* As with the rest of the tracks on the album, the song was originally credited to 'McCartney–Lennon'.

of their live shows. But George Martin sensed there was something missing – a certain dynamism that the Beatles displayed when he had recently seen them play live at Liverpool's Cavern Club. So at the very beginning of take one he spliced in the four words that Paul McCartney had used at the start of take nine: 'One-two-three-FOUR!' And then it was time for lunch.

So much happened in 1948 – the establishment of the state of Israel, the Berlin airlift, the birth of the NHS and the Marshall Plan – that the launch of a 12-inch record that spun at 33⅓ revolutions per minute seems like a minor thing in comparison. But the impact of the LP was astounding. The possibilities of 22 minutes per side, rather than 4 or 6 on the older 10-inch or 12-inch 78 rpm records, changed the way composers and musicians thought about music and wrote it. It changed the way a generation obtained much of their pleasure and enlightenment, and it's not for nothing that Philip Larkin dates the start of sexual intercourse around the time of the Beatles' first LP.

It would be simplistic to claim that the standard lengths of musical performances have been determined largely by the technical constraints of recording them. But before the wax recording cylinder and the gramophone there was certainly far less need for structure. Songlines on the African plains rang continuously through the centuries; in medieval courts, entertainment lasted for as long as it pleased the throne, or until the money ran out. In more recent times, performance merely tested human patience: how much could we concentrate, and how long would we behave ourselves? A concert would often end when the candles ran down. It was the same with ancient theatre: how long would an audience sit in an unheated space without demanding the Roman equivalent of a choc ice?

But the recording of music – which effectively began in the 1870s – did change our capacity to hear it. The two-minute and then four-minute limit of the early Edison and Columbia wax cylinders concentrated the mind like a guillotine. Likewise the 10-inch shellac 78 rpm record lasted about three minutes; the 12-inch record (before the micro-grooved long-player) ran about four-and-a-half. The 7-inch 45 rpm vinyl single, introduced in 1949, varied little from this, perhaps three minutes, before the grooves wound so tightly that the sound would deteriorate and the needle would skip.*

Mark Katz, a leading historian of recorded sound, has noted that listening to music at home before the LP was a distinct nuisance.** He quotes the blues singer Son House from the 1920s, who bemoaned 'gettin' up, settin' it back, turnin' it around, crankin' the crank, primin' it up and lettin' the horn down'. Bad enough for blues and jazz, fairly catastrophic for classical, for which a recording of a symphony was split into 20 sides on 10 discs (which is how the 'album' got its name – a collection of 78s in a folder).

One got used to it, of course, and in the early days recorded sound must have seemed like a miracle. But creatively it was more than a nuisance; it was a hindrance. An opera or a concerto was no longer split up into the acts or movements intended by the composer, but into false movements created by the limitations of a four-minute wax cylinder or disc.

---

* If you're Ray Charles with 'What'd I Say' (1959, 6 minutes 30 seconds) or Bob Dylan with 'Like a Rolling Stone' (1965, 6:13) or Don McLean with 'American Pie' (1971, 8:42) you just carry on over and put part two on the B-side. The most notable exception to the trend was the Beatles' 'Hey Jude', remarkable because in 1968 the sophistication of mastering techniques and pressing plants enabled a song lasting 7:11 to appear on one side. The B-side, neatly, was 'Revolution'.

** Mark Katz, *Capturing Sound: How Technology Has Changed Music* (University of California Press, 2004)

Music would suddenly stop, and the only way it would continue was when someone got up from the armchair. What was the effect of this? Shorter recordings, or more recordings of shorter pieces. Mark Katz has noted that while concerts in the early half of the twentieth century contained the usual array of symphonies and operas, 'any survey of record catalogues . . . will reveal the dominance of character pieces, arias, marches and brief popular song and dance numbers . . . It was not long before the time limitation affected not only what musicians recorded but also what they performed in public.' Audiences increasingly wanted the short pieces they knew from their records.* The length of the three-minute pop song was cemented, if not created, by the ability to record little more, but it is more surprising that this practice existed both before and beyond pop.

When Igor Stravinsky composed his Serenade for Piano in 1925, there was a specific reason why the piece only lasted 12 minutes and appeared in four almost equal segments. 'In America I had arranged with a gramophone firm [Brunswick] to make records of some of my music,' Stravinsky explained. 'This suggested the idea that I should compose something whose length should be determined by the capacity of the record.' Hence four movements of under three minutes, each of which fit snugly on one side of a 10-inch, 78 rpm disc.**

---

* The relationship between familiarity and popularity is captured nowhere better than at the live pop concert. Whereas once a debut performance of a new piece was judged an occasion for excitement and privilege – the first performance of Beethoven's Ninth, say – it is now judged an occasion to go to the bar. The story is told of how Neil Young, during one of his more recalcitrant phases (i.e. anytime in the last four decades), announced to an audience that the first half of his concert would be new material, and the second half would be songs they already knew. He played the new material, and then in the second half, with the new material no longer new, he played it again.

** Many composers and musicians distrusted the LP for this and other reasons. They log mistakes for posterity; they remove surprise excitement. Béla Bartók noted how even a composer's own recordings immediately restrict the 'perpetual variability' of

Composers were also willing to cut their own work to fit the limitations of a record. In 1916, Edward Elgar reduced the score of his Violin Concerto to fit four 78s; an uncut performance would easily last more than twice that length.

The performance offered by musicians may also change from a concert recital to a recorded version. The visual texture of a live performance may have to be somehow recreated in the listener's mind by the introduction of vibrato and other resonances. The conductor Nikolaus Harnoncourt believes that 'if you don't see the musicians . . . you have to add something which makes the process of music making somehow visible in the imagination of the listener.' The timing may also change, not least the gaps between movements or other dramatic pauses. A silent musician in a concert hall may provide drama to proceedings by wiping a bow or brow, or damping percussion; on CD this would be dead air. In becoming tighter, a performance may become less broad, and the rhetorical effect reduced.

When the Beatles returned to Studio 2 after lunch they recorded 'A Taste of Honey', 'Do You Want to Know a Secret' and

---

their music, while Aaron Copland wrote that 'the unpredictable element, so essential in keeping music truly alive . . . dies with the second playing of a record'.

Most famously, John Cage loathed the LP beyond compare. It was a dead thing, he believed, and once told an interviewer that they could 'destroy one's need for real music . . . [Records] make people think that they're engaging in a musical activity when they're actually not.' In 1950, just two years after the LP was launched, Cage wrote to Pierre Boulez (himself no slouch in his promotion of the unorthodox) only half-joking that he was about to establish 'a society called Capitalists Inc (so that we will not be accused of being Communists); everyone who wants to join has to show he has destroyed not less than 100 discs of music or one sound recording device; also everyone who joins automatically becomes President.' (For more on Cage and his relationship with sound recording see *Records Ruin the Landscape* by David Grubbs, Duke University Press, 2014).

'Misery'. Then there was another break for supper, and in a marathon evening session between 6.30 and 10.45 p.m., for which they would have been paid overtime, they recorded 'Hold Me Tight', 'Anna (Go To Him)', 'Boys', 'Chains', 'Baby It's You' and 'Twist and Shout', most of them in one or two takes.

'It's amazing really how creative we could be in those circumstances,' George Martin said in 2011, reminiscing with Paul McCartney about their time in the studio. McCartney replied, 'I say to people now, "10.30 a.m. to 1.30 p.m., two songs". And you would just remind us about halfway through the three-hour period, "Well, it's just about enough on that one, chaps, let's wrap it up." And so you learnt to be brilliant, he said modestly, in one-and-a-half hours.'

'But I was under pressure because I got so little time with you,' Martin remembered. 'You were running all over the world, and I would say to Brian [Epstein], "I need more time in the studio." And he said, "Well, I can give you Friday afternoon, or Saturday evening," and he would dole out time to me like giving scraps to a mouse.'*

Nothing was wasted. Every song recorded on 11 February 1963 was used on the album, which was called *Please Please Me*. To the 10 new tracks were added 4 songs already recorded as A- and B-sides for two singles ('Love Me Do'/'P.S. I Love You' and 'Please Please Me'/'Ask Me Why').**

And then Monday, 11 February 1963 was over. The first LP from what would become the biggest and greatest and most influential band in the world was ready for remixing

---

* From 'Produced by George Martin', BBC *Arena*, 2011.
** They also recorded 'Hold Me Tight', which was left off the album. When George Martin first heard the band play the song 'Please Please Me' at Abbey Road he judged it far too slow, more like a plaintive Roy Orbison song than an exciting Merseybeat racket. The tempo was wrong. He asked them to rethink it: 'It badly needed pepping up,' Martin said later. 'Actually, we were a bit embarrassed that he had found a better tempo than we had,' McCartney conceded. The pepping seemed to work: it became their first number one.

and then a release 39 days later. In a few years, the recording of 'Strawberry Fields Forever' would require more than two dozen takes over five weeks. But the entire first album, excluding the singles, had taken just one day.

Mark Lewisohn, on the other hand, is taking rather longer to tell the story of that album and all the others in the Beatles' phenomenal seven-year recording history (only seven years – one has to pinch oneself every time one thinks of that). Lewisohn is the author of *All These Years*, a forensic and compelling account of the Beatles and their world. It may turn out to be a 30-year project. It was planned as a three-volume endeavour ending in 1970, but the author is now considering a fourth to accommodate solo projects and the aftermath.

'It was a stab in the dark,' he says. 'When I began in 2004 it was originally going to be a 12-year project, but . . . insanely bad judgement on that score.' The publication dates of the three volumes were once planned as 2008, 2012 and 2016. 'So this year ought to be seeing the conclusion of the series.' The revised timeline now suggests volume two in 2020 and volume three in 2028. 'And if I do a fourth one it will be into 2030-something.' When we met in 2016, Lewisohn was 57; a fourth title will take him well into his 70s. 'The usual parallel that Americans make is the series of books by Robert Caro on Lyndon B. Johnson,' he says. 'He still has one to do and he's 80-something, so he has a battle against time.'*

Lewisohn works from home in Berkhamsted, an ancient market town in Hertfordshire. When he sits at his desk he

---

* *The Years of Lyndon Johnson* will encompass five volumes; by 2015 Caro had published four of them, the first one appearing in 1982. We will meet LBJ again in the following chapter.

almost disappears among the books, music papers, tapes, boxes, filing cabinets and the rest of the gear, by far the greatest amassment of Beatles documents in private hands, so that a visitor has only one spot of four square inches to rest a cup of tea. Lewisohn's laptop is perched on a stand so as to free more space beneath it. And then there is the noise in his mind. 'It's like plate-spinning at the circus,' he says of the parallel timelines. In Volume One, 'there are simultaneous events happening in London, Liverpool and Hamburg, but in Volumes Two and Three the number of plates will multiply. While I'm off telling the Beatles' impact in Indonesia or New Zealand or Argentina, I could lose the readers with what's going on in London or Liverpool or anywhere else. I know that I'm stacking problems for myself all down the line in terms of weight of material and how to assimilate it all.'

I had come to talk to Lewisohn about Ringo's drumming, and how, over the years, he has been so maligned (to the point where Morecambe and Wise referred to him as Bongo). Lewisohn was a great supporter. 'He gave the Beatles what they always lacked,' he told me. 'There's no bad or even adequate drumming on any Beatles record. His fills were constantly imaginative and original. In terms of timekeeping he was a human metronome.'

But then I became more interested in Lewisohn's own rhythms. A 30-year project is a daunting thing for a fellow writer to contemplate; how does he arrange his days to handle the task? 'There's not enough time in the day to cover it,' he said. 'I try to do a double day every day – getting up really early and finishing as late as possible. I have lunch at the desk, and I have very few distractions.'

Of course, such considerations are apt. So much of the project is concerned with timing, and with the characters in the story aligning just so. So many events, Lewisohn writes in the first volume, 'have slotted perfectly into the puzzle' or are 'nothing less than a miracle of timing'. The occasion the Beatles met Little Richard was imbued with 'God-given timing'. When Brian Epstein sees the Beatles for the first time at the Cavern Club on Thursday, 9 November 1961 'right on cue . . . the tracks that had been running in parallel for so long finally converged'. Perhaps all histories find synchronicity and temporal coincidence in things that weren't that exceptional, or in things that would have happened anyway, sooner or later. But as Lewisohn attests in his introduction, 'throughout this history, the timing of everything is always perfect'.

Silent at last: Jean Thurmond greets her husband
after he finally stops talking.

Chapter Five

How Much Talking
Is Too Much Talking?

i) In the Time of Moses

Last year, on my fifty-fifth birthday, I received an email from a woman called Connie Diletti with an enticing offer. Diletti was the producer of an annual conference in Toronto called IdeaCity, a gathering of 50 speakers talking about big issues such as climate change, food science, and the possibility of Canada merging with the United States, and she wanted me to be a part of it. This year there was going to be a section about love and sex, and she asked whether I would talk about love letters (I had written a book about letter-writing, and my best examples were all about love in one way or another). I had never been to IdeaCity or Toronto before, and I had always wanted to see Niagara Falls nearby, and so I expressed genuine interest in attending. I emailed back, asking what the deal was: how many hotel nights would IdeaCity pay for? What was the story with the flights?

Connie Diletti's reply had all the sweeteners. In exchange for a 17-minute talk I was offered airfare, a five-star hotel, an HD video of my talk hosted on the IdeaCity site for ever, organised parties every night, and 'a special speakers' brunch on Saturday at Moses's home'.

There was more, but these were the salient points. The most salient of all was the fact that I was only required to speak for 17 minutes. Not my usual 45 with questions, and not the more rounded 15 minutes or even 20 minutes. Why 17, I wondered. Was this magical number arrived at after years of careful analysis? (IdeaCity was in its 16th year, a mere upstart compared to the 25 years of TED conferences, with which it bears comparison, but certainly old enough to have garnered a clear idea of when the audience tended to fall asleep.) Or was the 17-minute slot mine alone, with other speakers given what may simply have been equally random durations? Would Lord Lawson, another participant, be given only 12 minutes with which to deny global warming, his current specialty? Would Dr Amy Lehman be granted 28 minutes to talk about the abuse of malaria nets by the banks of Lake Tanganyika? Would the best speakers with the sharpest patter and the funniest slides – there was a university man due to talk about the science of icebergs – make their sessions just fly by, while others, speaking for the same time on 'the myths of garlic' or the 'rap guide to religion' seem interminable? And who was Moses?

When I arrived in Toronto three months later it turned out everyone else had precisely 17 minutes too. I learnt that TED talks were all intended to be precisely 18 minutes, a period that Chris Anderson, one of its curators, defined as the sweet spot: it gave the speaker enough time to be serious, but not enough to be academic; the 'clarifying effect' of concentrating a message into just 18 minutes worked equally for both the speaker and the audience, with neither party having enough time to get bored; and it was the ideal time for a talk to go viral online because it was about the length of a coffee break.

But at IdeaCity, the 17 minutes was, in the words of Moses, 'a bit of a fuck you' to TED. Connie Diletti told me that IdeaCity began in 2000 under the name TEDCity, in partnership with TED co-creator Richard Wurman (TED began in 1984). For a while, each speaker at TED and TEDCity had 20 minutes on stage, but when TED changed to 18 minutes and the organisation expanded and changed direction a little bit, Moses decided to go his own way by formulating the 'fuck you' element. (Plausibly, sometime in the future, a rival organisation, inspired by IdeaCity but wanting to better it, would just reduce the time again, to 16 or 15 minutes. Or even 8. It was all about essence, reducing it down like a good French stock.

Moses was Moses Znaimer, a Jewish Lithuanian septua-genarian media tycoon, a local combination of Rupert Murdoch and Hugh Hefner, albeit more liberal. He was a charmer, but I sensed that he hadn't got to his elevated pos-ition by being a charmer all the time. The television and radio stations and baby boomer cultural/political magazine called *Zoomer* outlined in the email were all his, and he also liked to surround himself with beautiful women and beautiful cars (he ran a DeLorean and a classic Jag). He also ran the show at IdeaCity, introducing each session and speaker, posing for photographs with each participant, and would act as the unofficial timekeeper. The official timekeeper was a prominent rectangular digital clock on the stage that began its countdown as soon as you opened your mouth. But the unofficial time-keeper was stealthier. As soon as you reached your 17-minute limit, Moses would appear on the side of the stage. If you exceeded it by a minute, Moses would slowly edge towards you, and if you went over beyond that, Moses would creep closer still, until he'd be standing beside you, ready to inter-cede with a witty and possibly deflating remark.

Fortunately I was on in the morning of the second day, leaving plenty of time to absorb the previous timekeeping of others and get unusually nervous. The event was held at Koerner Hall, a horseshoe-shaped venue seating more than 1,000. It was the home of the Royal Conservatory of Music, and so the sightlines and acoustics were both magnificent, as was the screen technology for your PowerPoint. Of course, this only served to crank up the nerves, as did the fact that it was being filmed and, as the initial email promised, 'hosted on our site forever'. The world could meet its slow and terrible end, quite possibly caused by one of the terrible ecological or humanitarian catastrophes described in an IdeaCity lecture, but my talk would still be up there, somewhere, being enjoyed by no one.

When you're speaking for almost an hour you have time not only to meander and lose your thread, but to pull it all together again before the end. If you miss something out in the first half, you can thread it back in during the last quarter, or perhaps even during the Q and A afterwards. But 17 minutes is unforgiving; there can be no longueurs, no recaps, no sidesteps. Besides, the audience had each paid $5,000 Canadian dollars to be there, so you better be hot.

My morning arrived. The lavish ring-bound programme stated I was due on at 10.01. Initially I assumed this was a misprint, but then I saw that other speakers began at equally precise and stupid times: 11.06, 1.57, 3.48. In the hour or so before I was due on I learnt that many speakers rehearsed their speeches down to the last twitch; they trimmed and trimmed until it came in at 16 minutes 30 seconds, allowing time for mid-talk laughter, gasping and breathing. I used to have a great fear of public speaking, something I traced back to my debilitating stammer at school. Words would simply take ages to come out, and some words, such as those beginning with 'st', I just couldn't say at all. The school environment is not a good place to work on such a handicap. Addressing the class was one dread, but it was nothing compared to addressing the whole school at assembly, something we were sporadically required to do. My other problem was that I liked to show off, and my stammer meant that I was doubly frustrated. My apprehensions continued when I was asked to publicise my first books, but gradually the anxiety eased, and my speech improved, and I began to look forward to book festivals. I liked the idea that I had conquered my fear. But now, watching others deliver perfect 17-minute sequences in smooth succession, my doubts returned.

Fortunately, the woman who was on at 9.31 a.m. – a talk about a new form of dating in which she would offer valuable presents to her friends if they set her up in a relationship that lasted (if it lasted until marriage she would reward the friend responsible for the set-up with a vacation worth $2,000) – mistimed her talk dramatically. She ran out of material after 11 minutes, and the rest of her session was spent answering tricky questions from Moses, such as 'it does sound a little cold-blooded, don't you think?' The man who was on after her and just before me, at 9.41, was a pro, and had a carefully ordered pile of cards and a funny set of slides. His topic was a gift to any audience members weary from the heavier issues of the day before, which had included 'Therapeutics for Age-Related Disease' and 'The Vegan Advantage'; now we were going to hear how the emergence of self-driving cars would be a boon to vehicular sex. He went down extremely well (ha ha).

Only now did I wish that I had rehearsed and timed things. I thought I began okay, if a bit washily. Before I came on, the producers had shown a brief clip of Benedict Cumberbatch reading a love letter from my book, and so I began by apologising that Benedict wasn't here to read it in person, which got a generous snigger. I then talked about how letters had told our history for 2,000 years and that tweets would make a poor substitute, not least to historians, and by the time I first glanced at the countdown clock I had already used up eight minutes. I had seventeen slides to show, and at this point had only clicked through two. I didn't quite panic, but I was aware that my brain was telling me several things at once, none of which I could share audibly: I was running out of time; they had paid for me to come all this way, and I wouldn't be worth it; Moses would encroach; I was about to be found out; why, with all this fancy technology, did the person in the control room not put my PowerPoint in 'Presenter View' so I could see which slide was coming up next? These were clear thoughts, and may have taken far less than a second to process, but I remember looking at the audience blankly for at least five seconds. (Neurophysiologists suggest we may be able to process information from visual stimuli in just 13 milliseconds; non-visuals connect faster still.)

The rest of the talk became an exercise in compression and how to maintain a sense of coherence in a limiting timeframe. As such, it was like life itself. Time had become my enemy. On the practical side I had hoped to inform and entertain and do a little pleading on behalf of the value of letters (terrible irony: letter-writing had ultimately been defeated by time and the speed of the alternatives), and suddenly I had nine minutes in which to flick through 13 slides and tell stories that usually took at least half an hour. There is a limit to how well one can shorten a story before it crumbles to nonsense. I had now entered into a dimension I couldn't remember being in before: a sad and immediate private battle against a clock. But the clock was only visible to me, and the audience was oblivious, although perhaps aware that I was talking faster and looking slightly frantic.

With three minutes to go I had eight slides left. I didn't have to show them all, or tell all my stories as intended, but I had a possibly funny line at the end that I was wholly reluctant to jettison. I scurried on. Air seemed to vanish from the hall. I now couldn't keep my eyes off the clock, and its pace was alarming. Moses made an appearance stage left and hovered. I zapped through the slides like a panicky boy listing over-learnt facts in a history exam. Then my time expired and the clock turned from green to red and started flashing. I said something like, 'I've got two or three very quick things to leave you with.' I glanced to my left: Moses trod water and politely stayed where he was.

I went about seven minutes over. I thought I'd botched the whole thing, but afterwards people were complimentary. Although this had been an extreme case, and self-imposed, the experience made me realise how destructive an over-concentration on time could be. Designed in this instance to provide a framework, a focus of concentration, it only succeeded in restricting those areas of my brain engaged in free thought and imagination. It was as if I was falling from my bike all over again, my brain automatically closing off all the pathways except those essential to not talking nonsense as fast as I could.

At the other extreme, could something be said for talking nonsense very slowly? What would happen if, as in the example that follows, the clock never flashed, and time looked as though it would never run out? What if one could go on speaking for ever?

ii) Talking It Over

If nothing else, the Democratic senator Strom Thurmond was a conviction politician; it just so happened that the thing he most believed in was keeping black people in their place. In practical terms, in the mid-1950s, this meant segregated schools, restaurants, waiting rooms, cinemas and public trans-port, and a judicial system that would turn a blind eye to lynchings.

But there *was* something else about Strom Thurmond: he

achieved lasting political fame not only by being the only US politician to sit in the Senate at the age of 100, but also by delivering, at the age of 54, the longest continuous speech in the history of American politics, and, as far as can be known, worldwide.*

The length of his speech came as a surprise even to his family and political aides, and when he rose to his feet at 8.54 p.m. on 28 August 1957 no one knew when he would stop talking and sit down again. After the first three or four hours, as the clock moved beyond midnight, few had either the curiosity or stamina to find out. But some dug in for the night, with a local hotel bringing in makeshift beds to the Capitol for those who wanted to doze through what Thurmond had to say. One of the things he said was (astonishing as it may seem to us now, not least from a senator with a long career ahead of him), 'I will never favour mixing of the races.'

At the beginning of the 1950s, the notion of civil rights was a highly pertinent issue, if not yet a focussed movement. But in the first half of the decade a growing sense of injustice collided with the flashpoints we now recognise as turning points: the murder of teenager Emmett Till in Mississippi; Rosa Parks refusing to give up her seat on the bus in Montgomery, Alabama, and the subsequent mass boycott; the politicisation of Martin Luther King, Jr. In 1957, following the prolonged violent fallout from the ruling of Brown v. Board of Education three years before, in which the legal segregation of blacks and whites in public schools was ruled

* He also achieved notoriety when he married his second wife, who was more than forty years his junior.

unconstitutional, President Eisenhower and his advisors rallied around the idea of a new Civil Rights Act. This would enshrine the voting rights of African Americans by removing barriers to registration (such as literacy tests and poll-tax requirements), as well as providing protection against supremacist intimidation – a move both humanely and consti-tutionally proper and, his administration hoped, politically advantageous. But there was one huge hurdle: the Southern Democrats had successfully blocked every attempted piece of civil rights legislation for more than 80 years.

No one would oppose it more than Strom Thurmond. Thurmond believed he was fighting a pro-constitutional campaign against the suffocating encroachment of federal control over American lives (he also managed to link deseg-regation with Communism).* He also believed that the system worked fine as it was: everyone in their place; an insignificant amount of protest; black people treated better than they were in the North; an incalculable improvement over the centuries of slavery; and boundless possibilities for domestic employ-ment as maids and menservants. At the heart of this belief was the feeling – genuinely held, not merely a lie that was told so many times that it assumed a level of truth – that both whites and blacks were 'happier with their own kind'.

He reasoned with his usually supportive allies, including Richard Russell, the senator from Georgia who led the Southerners' tactical response on reform issues, that they should not only vote against the bill but attempt to wreck it.

According to his distinguished biographer Robert A. Caro, the compromise negotiated by Lyndon Johnson was one of the most skilful pieces of operational politics in American

---

* His motivation for candidacy in the 1948 election was clear: to oppose the civil rights agenda of President Truman. Thurmond won four Southern states with 2.4 per cent of the vote; Truman won a shock re-election (at least according to the pollsters) against Thomas Dewey with 28 states and 49.6 per cent.

history. He managed to convince both sides that he was one of them; using midnight phone calls and cloakroom bonhomie, he persuaded everyone that the passing of the bill was inevitable, and that they alone would be the victors.

Johnson's own conviction that the bill should become law appeared to be above political self-aggrandisement. In later years he often spoke of the disgust he felt when his long-time cook, a black woman named Zephyr Wright, drove with her husband in his official car from Washington to his home state of Texas, but when she stopped for meals she could only eat at designated restaurants, and when she stopped to pee she would squat in the road.*

The biggest sticking point of the Civil Rights Bill, the amendment that would ultimately decide whether it would pass or fail, concerned the right to trial by jury. With an act designed to protect potential black voters registering to vote and then going to the ballot, there had to be a provision to prosecute those who held the law in contempt. Accordingly, one section of the bill gave the attorney general increased powers to protect civil rights with court orders. But in another section, a new amendment purposely declared that those charged with obstruction would be entitled to trial by jury; this was specifically designed to appease opponents of the bill, for with juries composed exclusively at the time of whites, the accused would see their acquittal as a certainty. The bill's proponents were outraged at the new clause, arguing it rendered the entire act useless, but there was more chicanery to come. Just before the amendment came to a vote, Lyndon Johnson appeased the liberals and unions with a further addendum, a guarantee that Southern states would permit black members of a jury to sit along whites; it was, after all,

---

* When, as president, Johnson signed the far-reaching Civil Rights Act of 1964, he gave her the pen that made it law: 'You deserve this more than anyone else.'

a bill to ensure equality of democracy. The amendment passed, and at the end of August 1957 the bill was ready for the decisive vote. And at this very moment, Strom Thurmond entered the debating chamber.

The filibuster – an act of sustained objection whereby a minority may wreck or at least delay an action proposed by the majority – is politics with time at its core. One may regard it as reassuringly constitutional and democratically essential, the equivalent of chaining oneself to the railings, the sole reason one entered politics in the first place. Or, if one has a busy day and a lot to get through and a belief in majority rule, it may also be regarded as rigorously *un*democratic, sheer bloody-mindedness from a picket line of crazies. To distinguish between the two, one often has to spend a lot of time listening.

Only later did it become clear how well Thurmond had prepared himself for a long session. Earlier in the day he had attended the Senate steam room to dehydrate; the lower the level of his body fluids, he believed, the slower would be his absorption of water, and the longer he would resist the urge for the bathroom. He filled his jacket with emergency supplies: in one pocket malted milk tablets, in the other throat lozenges. His wife Jean was in the chamber as he began to speak, and he would be grateful for the steak and pieces of pumpernickel she had brought in for him in foil.* His press assistant Harry Dent, later to become a key aide to Nixon in the White House, had noticed Thurmond gathering a lot of reading

---

* Thurmond's biographer Nadine Cohodas has noted that the precise duration of his speech would be as much a surprise to his wife as anyone: she 'had known her husband would not be home for dinner, but she had no idea he wouldn't make breakfast either'.

material that day, but assumed it was for research; in fact, much of what he had collected was soon to be part of his performance.

Standing at the back of the chamber, stocky and almost bald, addressing an audience of about 15, Thurmond began: 'There are mainly three reasons why I feel that the bill should not be passed,' he began. 'The first is that it is unnecessary.'* He then started reading election statutes from each of the 48 states, in alphabetical order, in an attempt to demonstrate that a grander federal law would be superfluous, and that further intervention would result in 'a totalitarian state'. Thurmond then argued the finer points of trial-by-jury legislation, expanding upon English military courts' martial precedents from the fourteenth to the eighteenth centuries, and taking particular interest in a case involving Charles 1 in 1628. In the course of the next few hours he would read the Declaration of Independence, Washington's Farewell Address and the Bill of Rights. Shortly before midnight, Everett Dirksen, a senator from Illinois, a Republican supporting the bill and presumably eager for his bed, noted to his colleagues, 'Boys, it looks like an all-nighter!' Paul Douglas, the other senator from Illinois, this one a liberal Democrat, later offered Thurmond a jug of orange juice. Thurmond drank a glass gratefully, but before he could refill it, Harry Dent, fearing a rush to the bathroom and thus the end to his marathon, removed the jug from his reach. Thurmond in fact enjoyed only one break from the chamber, as Barry Goldwater asked for an insertion in the Congressional Record, and Thurmond rushed to relieve himself.

Well before dawn, Thurmond's voice faded to a whisper

* For the full text of his speech see: http://www.senate.gov/artandhistory/history/resources/pdf/Thurmond_filibuster_1957.pdf

and a monotone. When one member asked him to speak up, Thurmond suggested he move a little closer. Others gently snoozed, including Clarence Mitchell, the chief lobbyist of NAACP (the National Association for the Advancement of Colored People) watching, or not, from the gallery. Thurmond began speaking about new levels of racial disquiet he believed had been brought on directly by the commotion surrounding the Civil Rights Bill. In previous months, he said, 'it was urged that property be made available to Negroes of means who wanted to build better homes away from congested homes in which Negroes tend to congregate. Subsequently, a fairly exclusive Negro residential section, near white neighbourhoods, was started. There were no objections. This sort of thing would be more difficult now, if not impossible, because the Negro is reluctant to cooperate . . . The Negro apparently has been led to believe the moon may be within his grasp; and lawless and more extreme whites have been aroused.'

Twice Thurmond almost lost the floor: once, when he sat down during an interruption (sitting down, even while speaking, was not permitted, and nor was leaning), and once when he bit into a sandwich in the cloakroom, forgetting that he needed to retain one foot on the chamber floor if he didn't want to be deposed. Fortunately Richard Nixon, the vice-president in charge of the Senate at the time, was consulting some papers and didn't notice Thurmond's absence (such was Thurmond's compelling performance).

So Thurmond grumbled on. At 1.40 p.m. he declared, 'I've been on my feet the last 17 hours and I still feel pretty good.' He was described by *Time* as 'a dull, droning speaker at best', the magazine noting that at 7.21 p.m. Thurmond broke the Senate record 'for long-windedness', beating out Oregon's Wayne Morse, the previous record holder who could only manage 22 hours and 26 minutes four years earlier when he talked against the passing of a law concerning state oil ownership.* (Morse himself had claimed the crown from Robert 'Fighting Bob' La Follette, who had spoken for 18 hours in 1908.** 'I salute him,' Morse said of Thurmond. 'It takes a lot out of a man to talk so long.'

After about a day, Thurmond received a strict admonishment from Harry Dent. His assistant had become increasingly concerned about his health and been to see the Senate doctor. He returned to the chamber with the instruction 'You tell him to get off his feet or I'm going to take him off his feet.' And then, heeding the advice, at 9.12 p.m., after 24 hours and 18 minutes, Strom Thurmond shut up.

In her biography, Nadine Cohodas reported that by the time he left the chamber his stubble had visibly thickened. Dent was waiting in the corridor with a bucket in case of dire need. Jean Thurmond was also waiting for him, and the kiss she planted on his cheek made the morning papers. But he was not acclaimed as a hero, even by his allies. Many of his Southern constituents couldn't understand why his fellow 'Dixiecrats' hadn't supported him and continued the filibuster in a relay (this was the common way with filibusters, or at least their threat: a daisy chain of objections that could tie the Senate up for weeks). But rather than champion him, his colleagues accused him of grandstanding. In attempting to wreck the bill at the end of a session, he risked destroying what the Southern Democrats believed was the best deal they

---

* See 'The Last, Hoarse Gasp', *Time*, 9 September 1957.

** La Follette ran two big filibusters – one in 1908, and one in 1917 as America was poised to enter the war (he argued against arming merchant ships against the Germans). His 1908 speech is primarily remembered for the glass of milk he drank during his oration: the Senate kitchen staff, apparently dismayed at having to remain open as La Follette droned on, conspired to lace his milk with bad eggs, and after more than 18 hours the senator declared himself too sick to continue.

could hope for, something they hoped would concede almost nothing. 'Under the circumstances we faced,' Richard Russell, formerly one of his closest allies, said, 'if I had undertaken a filibuster for personal aggrandizement, I would have forever reproached myself for being guilty of a form of treason against the South.'

Thurmond's effort was in vain: the following day the bill was passed in the Senate 60 to 15, and Eisenhower signed it into law on 9 September 1957. But filibusters have always been about more than just attaining victory; they are about passionate intent, and about intensity of belief; the greater the intensity, it is argued, the more voters and politicians should take note of a cause, for the more it will dominate the agenda. This was certainly true about civil rights, albeit not in the way Strom Thurmond intended.

Filibusters are about democracy in its purest form, the right of an opposing view to be heard above the din. They are about deep conviction, and this is one reason at least why they have prevailed against decades of opposition and continue to capture our imagination. But increasingly these days there is another view. It argues that less is more, that the filibuster is less a symbol of passion than a sign of pigheadedness and unconstitutional chaos. These days, in debating chambers as elsewhere in the world, we are seldom impressed by things that take a long time, except perhaps in the realms of under-water swimming and pornography.*

The term filibuster derives from the military and from

---

* For the long view see *Filibustering* by Gregory Koger (University of Chicago Press, 2010), and the lengthy article 'The Filibuster' by Catherine Fisk and Erwin Chemerinsky (*Stanford Law Review*, vol. 49, no. 2, 1997).

revolution. It originally described a man attempting to cause upheaval in a foreign state, usually for financial gain; the term grew in popularity after incursions into Latin America and the Spanish West Indies in the nineteenth century (the word has Spanish roots – *filibustero*, out of the Dutch *vrijbuiter*, the word that also spawned 'freebooter'.)

In current use, the term doesn't generally apply in debating chambers beyond the Senate; in the UK, for instance, such a performance is broadly known as a very long speech. The longest political speeches have of course claimed their own league table, though not every entry was intended as a delaying tactic. The list usually begins with Henry Brougham (about six hours on law reform in the House of Commons in 1828, two years before he became lord chancellor), Tommy Henderson (Independent Unionist speaking in Northern Ireland in 1936 for nigh-on 10 hours on individual spending budgets of government departments), and Sir Ivan Lawrence, the former Conservative MP (4 hours, 23 minutes in 1985 against a bill controlling the extent of fluoridation of water, the twentieth-century Commons record). European stars such as Green MP Werner Kogler speaking in Austria for more than 12 hours in 2010 was a mere blink when stacked up against Mustafa Kemal Ataturk (36 hours 31 minutes in 1927, albeit over six days). The most heroic filibuster of recent times was conducted by Wendy Davis in the Texas State Senate in June 2013, an 11-hour marathon successfully blocking the passage of more restrictive abortion laws. The senator afterwards revealed how she had been fitted with a catheter for her marathon, and her speech made her a star for a while, or rather a star again: two years before she had filibustered in the Senate against a cut in public-school funding. On both occasions, her speeches delayed rather than reversed the bills. But her stand was the thing – the provision of hope, scrutiny, visibility and voracious commitment.

What do most of these speeches have in common, beyond endurance and isolation? The *Charlotte Observer* put it well at the height of the civil rights movement in February 1960 (it *was* a movement by then): 'Here is a fight of words against time, of men against inevitability, of voices against the ebbing strength that portends eventual silence.'

In 2005, Andrew Dismore, then Labour MP for Hendon, spoke for 3 hours and 17 minutes to successfully defeat a bill proposing to give homeowners more powers to defend themselves against intruders. 'The aim is not to run out of steam,' he reflected some years later in the *Guardian*. 'You want to build up a tree of points that you wish to make. You must make them in a coherent order or the speaker could stop you. You are allowed to pause for three to four seconds, but it is risky to go any longer than that.' He said that a good support team is essential. 'You need your colleagues to make interventions when you are starting to flag. The best thing that can happen is that an opposition member tries to make a point. Ideally, over a three-hour speech, you would want 20–30 interventions. Arguing over the meaning of terms such as "could" and "might" is a useful delaying tactic, too.'

In Britain, as in America, the rules have tightened in recent years to ensure speakers remain on-topic; you can no longer read out a list of shellfish, as Dismore once did, or a recipe for fried oysters as Louisiana senator Huey P. Long did in a 15-hour filibuster in 1935, a feat that inspired an episode of *The West Wing*, in which a senator from Minnesota named Stackhouse protests a healthcare bill by reading out lists of ingredients for seafood dishes and creamy desserts.

Thurmond never forgave his colleagues for hanging him out to dry. But the real issue is, can we forgive Strom Thurmond? And to what extent can one forgive being on the wrong side of history? If voiced publicly today, his inflammatory comments would land him in jail. But his opinions were a product of the times, and popular too; certainly he would have regarded his views towards black people as more progressive than the English who had sent them to plantations in slave ships.

Thurmond's speaking record still stands. No one seems to have the stamina these days. Lesser filibusters still make news, because any test of endurance is a public spectacle, and we frequently enjoy seeing politicians suffer. But the application of the filibuster in the twenty-first century has dramatically changed, and an objector is rarely expected even to get to their feet; just the threat of filibuster is enough to register resistance.* To combat this, a process of 'cloture' must then be invoked, requiring that 60 out of the 100 senators be in agreement over limiting the length of a debate. Effectively, because of the vast number of filibusters threatened on any controversial or unpopular piece of legislation or presidential appointment, the Senate commonly runs on a three-fifths majority rather than a simple split of 51:49.

Thurmond was a product of his times. His denial of social justice paints him as a reactionary white supremacist, and that he was, albeit of the non-violent kind. His prejudice is not lessened or excused by what came after it, although what came after it is interesting.

---

* There are exceptions, and we may regard them as vainly glorious irrespective of our political slant: Wendy Davis in Texas, and Kentucky libertarian Republican Rand Paul speaking for almost 13 hours in the Senate on the use of drones for espionage (and in so doing deliberately delaying the appointment of President Obama's choice of John Brennan to run the CIA). Rand mentioned Strom Thurmond not long before he sat down, admiring the strength of his bladder.

In later years, Thurmond became a Republican, supporting Barry Goldwater's unsuccessful presidential bid against Lyndon B. Johnson, but he also edged moderately towards racial equality (he supported the appointment of black judges to the higher courts, albeit of a conservative hue). In this, he was also a product of his times; he would have been a lousy politician if he hadn't recognised the growing significance of the black vote. He would come to regret his most virulent outbursts, but he never publicly renounced his general views on segregation; he would, ten years before his death, make it clear to a biographer that he acted on a belief system that was perfectly acceptable to hundreds of thousands who supported him, and was based on strong democratic principles.

And times did change, or at least catch up with him. In 1971 Thurmond appointed Thomas Moss, an African American, to his Senate staff, and in 1983, he supported legislation to make the birthday of Martin Luther King, Jr a federal holiday (although his pronouncements seemed like apologia: 'I fully recognize and appreciate the many substantial contributions of black Americans and other minorities to the creation and preservation and development of our great nation.').

Any difficulty we may have in accepting an old shameful value system is usually a sign of healthy ethical improvement, and an undeniable corollary of progress. What was once considered acceptable is now disreputable, and hence banished. Beyond the fanciful time trials of Thurmond's most dramatic moment in 1957 lies a transformation in the lives of black Americans. What is an arguable case one day will, if it's worth arguing about at all, eventually be revealed as either visionary or anachronistic, and if we knew which way it would go we'd be both wise and wealthy, should we live that long.

In the days directly after Thurmond's filibuster, another

product of the times emerged in the energised dawn. As *Time* reported, the South had 'a new weapon'. The Reverend Dr Martin Luther King, Jr announced his 'get-out-the-Negro-vote drive', a campaign that included the establishment of 'voting clinics' to explain registration and the ballot, and an awareness-raising crusade that would enable 'Negroes to realize that in a democracy their chances of improvement rest on their ability to vote'. (Fifty-eight years on, in the last quarter of the Obama presidency, the black president spoke publicly about the possibility of ending the provision of the Senate filibuster once and for all; it was outdated, he said: 'The filibuster in this modern age probably just torques it too far in the direction of a majority party not being able to govern effectively and move forward its platform.')

And there is one more dramatic development in the story, another racial alteration of the legacy. Shortly after Thurmond's death in 2003, a woman named Essie Mae Washington-Williams came forward with startling news. She had been waiting a long time for this moment, but finally, at the age of 78, she could reveal herself as Strom Thurmond's illegitimate mixed-race daughter. Her mother was called Carrie Butler, a fitting name for a black servant of Thurmond's parents. Carrie was 16 when Thurmond got her pregnant. Thurmond had paid for his daughter's education and sent her family money while keeping her and his secret under wraps. Her published account of her life – she became a teacher in LA and had four children – was nominated for a Pulitzer Prize. She had frequent conversations with her father about race issues, a factor she believed broadened his understanding and softened his approach. She died in 2013, a fortnight after Obama was sworn in for his second term, at which time there were 43 black members in the House of Representatives, and one in the Senate. The sole member in the Senate was Tim Scott, a Republican from South Carolina, the place Essie Mae Washington-Williams was born, the state Strom Thurmond served for 48 years.

The most famous filibuster of all did not take place in the Senate or the House of Commons; it took place in Hollywood. In Frank Capra's *Mr Smith Goes to Washington* (1939) James Stewart plays a greenhorn who believes so passionately in exposing the corruption surrounding the building of a new dam that he speaks for more than 23 hours before collapsing. His female co-conspirator (Jean Arthur) cheers him on, while equating his chance of success to 'a 40-foot dive into a tub of water'. Smith comes prepared with a thermos and fruit, and threatens to stay 'until Doomsday' to get his way. Gleeful reporters rush from the chamber shouting 'Filibuster!' The most romantic among them calls it 'the most titanic battle of modern times. A David without even a slingshot . . .' Smith triumphs in the end, an outcome that surely came as a surprise to no one. It was the movies, after all, and the movies have always had their blissful way with time.

Harold Lloyd: hanging on for us all.

Chapter Six

Movie Time

i) How You Get to the Clock

The image of a man in glasses hanging from the hands of a clock above the streets of Los Angeles is one of the most enduring in all cinema. Symbolism simply doesn't get more tantalising. Harold Lloyd, the man on the clock, once said that the image came to him easily, but the tricky part was working out how he would get to be hanging there in the first place. This is how he did it.

*

Harold Lloyd was born in Burchard, Nebraska, in April 1893. The village was tiny, just a few wooden houses holding on against the high winds, and the place only made it onto the US map in 1881, when the Chicago, Burlington and Quincy Railroad came through. Trains made Harold his first money: his mother made popcorn, and he would put it in bags, hop on at his nearest station, work his way down each carriage of the train, and usually make it halfway before he was thrown off by a man called The Butcher, who had established his own train business selling sweets and tobacco. 'I made quite a bit of money for a youngster who had only half a train,' Lloyd remembered many years later. He also learnt something about the underdog. Though rather fragile in appearance, Lloyd was once a young amateur boxer; after a while he was heard to complain, obviously if understandably, that he didn't enjoy his face being punched by men who earned their money by erecting circus tents. Fortunately his face endured the onslaught, and his biographers note that he appeared extremely attractive to women, many of whom wanted to mother him.

Lloyd was initially interested in the theatre, but after his parents divorced and he moved to California with his father in 1910 he found that the money lay in movies. He developed three silent characters. His first two were rip-offs of Charlie Chaplin: Willie Work was a tramp with a sweet disposition, while Lonesome Luke had a trilby or a top hat, a walking stick and a downcast shuffling walk, and a greasepaint moustache comprised of two large dots. Lonesome Luke got Lloyd a lot of pratfall work, and he appeared in more than 200 silents, with a great many titles displaying a desperate desire for alliteration: *Luke Laughs Last, Luke's Lost Liberty, Luke Pipes the Pippins, Luke's Trolley Troubles, Luke Locates the Loot* and *Lonesome Luke, Lawyer*. And then there were ones with a militaristic bent: *Luke Joins the Navy, Luke and the Bomb Throwers* and *Luke's Preparedness Preparations*. Lloyd was often the naive bystander as an exciting and destructive new century rushes past. It was late 1916, early 1917. America was just about to enter the war. One of his films was called *Kicking the Germ out of Germany*.

Lloyd grew tired of Luke's limitations. It was only when he adopted his third persona, which he called the Glass Character, that he found a way of stepping out from Chaplin's shadow, and in so doing assured his wealth and fame. The Glass Character was rather like Lloyd himself – respectable and righteous, bashful but eager to impress. He dressed in the clean cut of the day, often wore a straw boater at a modest tilt, and although his eyesight was fine he donned round tortoiseshell horn-rimmed spectacles that somehow made him look both dim-witted and studious, like a tawny owl, and in years to come he would make the glasses fashionable. He was foolish but not a sucker, and you rooted for him, not least as he outfoxed those in authority and did crazy things to impress women. The glasses were lensless, and once on, they never came off, not even – or especially – when playing American football in his most successful film *The Freshman*.

In the mid-1920s, the peak of his fame, Lloyd was making around $30,000 a week, which is certainly equivalent to today's DiCaprio/Pitt/Clooney level, and he invested it in Los Angeles real estate. He spent $1 million on constructing Greenacres, a 16-acre estate in Beverly Hills from where he could see Rudolf Valentino's home and invite round his neighbours Charlie, Buster and Fatty. He made many more pictures than them, but time has not been kind to those movies; in later life, Lloyd estimated that about 70 per cent had been destroyed by their own flammability and a general disregard for their future worth. When sound came in the late 1920s, few dared to predict that silent movies would one day be the subject of nostalgia or academic study. They were just finished, something old in a speeding nation. Time has changed that view, but no one back then had the luxury of regarding large canisters of film as a potential library, much less a treasure trove. (The exact point at which a storage problem becomes an archive has yet to be calculated.)

Naturally, one of the pleasures of moviegoing is escape. Not just for a couple of hours in the dark, but for all time: movies may show us how to be free, and show the better, richer, redemptive way ahead – not an escape from reality, but an escape *into* reality, albeit the perceived reality of a story other than our own. The weightless promise of freedom featured strongly in those early movies, not least as each new mode of freedom came into view: the steam train, the hopping crankshaft car, the flight to the cities. For a while, even tall buildings must have seemed a thrill – the sky's the limit.

William Carey Strother was born in North Carolina in 1896, and as far back as anyone could remember he liked to climb. He was, in the vernacular, a 'builderer'. He began with trees, but Bill Strother just kept on going, on to church steeples and county courthouses and then buildering further and higher – the taller they would build, the higher he would climb. After a while he became The Human Spider, and it was the making of him. He would get $10 for his earliest 'professional' ascents and $500 at his peak.

Because $500 was a lot of money, The Human Spider soon found he had competition – from The Human Fly. In fact there were at least two Human Flies, and on one occasion the Spider and one of the Flies scaled the same building in competition on the same day. Strother won.*

The key to buildering was to plan every foot and hand placement at the bottom, much as a mountain climber would plan a route months before seeing ice. Once the groundwork was established, you could then add flourishes and tricks – pretend slips, gallant hat waves to the crowds, stunts with windows. Strother did a bit of charity climbing, and in 1917 he began raising Liberty Bonds to fund America's entry into the war. He didn't fight in the conflict, but he felt he faced comparable risks. 'It's dangerous business,' he said in April 1918, 'and death always climbs with you. In three years I'll have enough money to quit.'

But Strother never had enough money to quit; or rather, when he quit he hadn't earned enough money to retire. He

---

* Spider-Man the superhero didn't appear in Marvel Comics until 1962.

tried to make a living selling dog food and operating a guest-house, but then he hit upon something for which he had a calling. In her marvellous and disturbing book, *The Real Santa of Miller & Rhoads*, Donna Strother Deekens recounts how her distant relative found a new sense of worth by dressing up annually in a beard and velvet gown. Miller & Rhoads was a fancy department store in Richmond, Virginia, and in the middle of the century they made Bill Strother the highest-paid Santa in the world. Why was he so valued? Because his 'Santa setup' included entering through a chimney and allowing the children to see him comb his beard, and when he had done this he drew huge crowds to the tearoom to enjoy his 'Rudolph Cake'.*

In 1951, at the peak of his Santa fame, he told an interviewer from the *Saturday Evening Post* that he loved meeting all the children, but he still had a hankering for tall buildings. 'It makes you sweet inside when you look down and the crowd cheers. What is that word? Exult! I exult all over!' One day in 1922 he was up a tall building feeling sweet inside when Harold Lloyd strolled by.

'I was in Los Angeles, walking up Seventh Street, and I saw this tremendous crowd gathered round a building, the Brockman Building,' Lloyd told *Film Quarterly* in 1962. 'Upon inquiring I found that a Human Spider was going to scale the side of that building . . . Well, it had such a terrific impact on me that when he got to about the third or fourth floor I couldn't watch him anymore. My heart was in my throat and so I started walking on up the street.'

But Lloyd couldn't stop himself looking back to see if he was still there. The Spider progressed to the top, and Lloyd

---

* According to Phillip L. Wenz (a full-time Santa Claus at a Santa theme park in Illinois, and a charter member of the International Santa Claus Hall of Fame in Santa Claus, Indiana), Strother was among the first to properly do the whole Santa shtick, and in so doing put less rigorous Santas to shame. Strother took Santa 'to a level that included pure performance art'. I would so love to be making this up.

approached him afterwards about appearing in his next movie. But before filming could begin Strother was involved in a fall. So a new part was written for him, a role named Limpy Bill, and Lloyd began thinking that he would have to do a lot more climbing himself.

❦

To watch *Safety Last!* today, more than 90 years after it was made, is to experience a joy both intricate and soaring. Directed by long-term Lloyd collaborators Fred C. Newmeyer and Sam Taylor, this is, by most standards, a modern film: there is strong depth of character, a three-act structure and a climax that builds like a Beethoven symphony.

The film opens with a caption card: 'The Boy – He has seen the sun rise for the last time in Great Bend . . . Before taking the long, long journey.' We see Lloyd behind bars, saying goodbye to his mother and sweetheart. A noose hangs in the background, and a man who is probably a pastor arrives to console him. But we are deceived, the first of many deceptions: the next shot shows the reverse angle, and we are actually on a station platform, the bars marking the perimeter, the noose a device for messages to be gathered by speeding trains. Lloyd is travelling to the big city in search of fortune.

Lloyd promises to marry his sweetheart as soon as he becomes a successful businessman, but when we next see him, in a bare bedsit he shares with Limpy Bill, he is financially embarrassed; he has just pawned the gramophone.

He works in the haberdashery section of a modern department store. When Harold overhears a store manager announce that the business needs a publicity stunt to attract new customers and a thousand dollars is on offer for the best idea, he enlists Limpy Bill to climb the outside of the building.

But there are complications involving the police, and so Lloyd makes the climb himself. There are obstacles on every floor: nuts that fall on him and attract pigeons, entanglement in a net, some painters with a board. When he reaches the clock near the top and grabs a hand, he has us for all time.

Theatre managers asked for nurses to be in attendance before showing the film. '*Safety Last* Sends Audience Into Hysterics', one newspaper reported; 'Woman Faints As Lloyd Pulls Rare Thriller'. The *New York Times* concluded: 'When people are not rollicking in their seats at the Strand they will be holding on to the chair arms to keep them down.'

Safety Last! lasts 70 minutes (7 reels), but audiences found that time just froze. As with Orson Welles in the Viennese shadows, or Janet Leigh in the shower, life is temporarily suspended; the images lodge in our cortex. With Harold Lloyd dangling from a clock high above the city, our entire modern world just hangs there too.

You want a moral? When Lloyd makes it – OK, *if* he makes it, as there's some business with a rope and a mouse to get through first – his girl will be waiting for him at the top. At the end of the climb there is love: cinema has been telling the same story since the dawn of time.

ii) Oncoming Train

If it's true that audiences ran screaming from their seats when they first saw a train coming towards them in a Lumière Brothers film in January 1896, wouldn't that just have been a wonderful piece of publicity for early movies?

Before film could tell a proper story, it had to tell the story of itself. This story involved time and space: a five-second film of a man sneezing, workers shuffling from a factory, a couple kissing (a lengthy embrace, almost 20 seconds, the first time a censor was called), or a moving train. For what is cinema if not time made manifest?

When the train movie was first shown, the audience had a lot of clues as to what to expect. It was called *L'arrivée d'un train en gare de La Ciotat*. At the beginning of the film the way of the oncoming train had been carefully prepared – the crowds on the platform are standing back in anticipation and to ensure the camera had a full and clear view. Trains had been a feature of the French landscape for more than half a century. The only difference now was that a train would appear in the darkened basement room of a Parisian café.

Shown at the directors' intended speed, the film lasted only 50 seconds, only slightly longer than the sequence widely regarded as the first film ever, showing factory workers leaving the Lumière factory in Lyon after a day's work (it wasn't quite the first film, but it was probably the first film to deceive an audience – the sequence was shot several times and was filmed in the middle of the day; when they were done, the workers went back to work).

The fact that the train film *seemed* shorter to the audience was due to another trick, something that movies got right from the start – the concept of time speeded up. If a picture thrilled, if it captured the audience, if it was novel, then it swept away the notion of ordinary time. All other thoughts just vanished in the steam. And then there is the trick that time plays on memory: we may recall the train pulling in head-on, as if it would come hurtling through the screen, but that wasn't the film-makers' intention, and that wasn't the film. The train only moves towards us – rather sedately we see now – side-on. There is no threat to the audience's safety. The train is only in motion for less than half the film, and for more than half of that it is slowing down. For the rest of the movie the train just sits there hissing, and the action switches to disembarkation and embarkation and the usual platform mayhem. But history seldom recalls the station porter bustling along, or the man who looks drunk as he gets out of a carriage and staggers around.

Harold Lloyd was two when all this silent movie commotion began.* The first screen comedy, *L'Arroseur arrosé* (or *The Waterer Watered* or *The Sprinkler Sprinkled*), also by the Frerès Lumières, from 1895, gave away its entire plot in its title. It was humour the audience would recognise from vaudeville, and later from *The Benny Hill Show*. A man is watering a large garden with a long hose, a boy comes up behind him and steps on it, thus cutting off the supply. The gardener, not seeing the boy, is puzzled and looks into the nozzle. At which point, *mais oui,* the boy takes his foot off the hose and the gardener is drenched and his hat blows off. He sees the boy, grabs him by the ear, spanks him and resumes his duties.

The film lasted around 45 seconds. But it may also have been 40 seconds, or possibly 50 seconds. The timing of moving pictures in those days was anyone's guess. The standard length of a single-reel comedy was a little under 1,000 feet, but you could speed up the filming and slow down the playing, or vice-versa. Before automatic motors, much depended on the cranking skills of the cameraman during filming and the projectionist during showing. In the perfect standardised world, 1,000 feet of 35mm silent film shown at the accepted 16 frames per second would last 16½ minutes. But we live in a world where silent movies show too many people racing jerkily or dawdling aimlessly, and there is a reason for these

---

* The term 'silent movie' is a retronym, a word created to describe technological and societal progress. 'Black-and-white television' is also a retronym, as is the concept of the hardback book, the steam train and the analogue watch.

unnatural movements. Before sound and synchronisation, films were hand-cranked and hand projected, and the two often failed to match. *Robin Hood* (starring Douglas Fairbanks, 1922) and *Ben Hur* (1925) were both filmed at 19 frames per second, but the cue sheets provided by the studio requested a projection speed of 22 frames per second; *Monsieur Beaucaire* (1924, with Rudolf Valentino) was 18 and 24, while Keaton's *The General* (1926), made on the brink of talkies, was 24 and 24. Films with multiple reels would not always have the same rate over each reel, causing the projectionist even more problems. Get it wrong, and you could add minutes to a story that was never intended. But get it right, and you could alter the mood of the audience. In his study *Film Style and Technology*, Barry Salt refers to the 'expressive variations' performed by projectionists at a director's command: mood was romantically altered by decelerating a swishy ballroom scene or a kiss, and a person mounting a horse could also be slowed down to increase elegance and poise. A dream sequence or flashback, those other great cinematic devices, could also be elongated long after shooting was over. For certain moments, the man in the box behind you at the Odeon became as central to the creative process as a film's director or stars.*

---

* The first movie flashback occurred in 1908 in the film *Le fiabe della nonna*, a grandmother telling a story that then dissolves to amplify the details. Another dissolve and we're back in the present.

Barry Salt has also made a painstaking study of the varying length of film scenes through the decades (i.e. the time between cuts). Analyzing hundreds of movies, he found that the average length of a scene of an American movie with standard projection rates in the 1920s ranged from 3.5 seconds in *Don Juan* to 7.5 seconds in *The Magician*. But in European movies it ranged from 5 seconds in the French films *Eldorado* and *Poil de carotte* to 13 or even 16 seconds in the German films *Die Strasse* and *Scherben*. This may be one reason why European films are often maligned for their slow pace. In the 1940s George Cukor and Howard Hawks had extended average scene lengths to about 13 seconds. By the 1990s, Salt had spotted a big difference between the fast-cut pace of mainstream Hollywood action movies (2.2

There were other reasons why people and animals seemed to move in stop-go motion in black and white: the guileful manipulations of the cinema manager. In 1923, the year of *Safety Last!*, which lasted 6,300 feet, the cameraman and projectionist Victor Milner wrote in *American Cinematographer* that for a busy 8 p.m. showing he would hand-crank a 1,000-feet reel at the dramatic speed of 12 minutes, and in the afternoon, with business slouchier, he would 'project the same reel so slow that it took Maurice Costello [the first screen Sherlock Holmes in 1905] ages to cross the set'. The projectionist would receive these instructions daily, as would the musical director in the pit; the fuller the house and the greater the crush in the queue outside, the more the conductor and musicians would wave their hands, and the faster the audience had to be at reading the title cards.

Perhaps there was an artistic reason we projected ourselves this way: more vigour for the human race, a cleaner and more decisive look in an exciting age. The train coming through the screen – one stationary camera, one take with no edit – was too much like real life; ever since, reel life has helped us escape to an ideal. The film historian Walter Kerr has noted that Charlie Chaplin in *Modern Times* was 'filmed at a rate that puts springs on his heels and makes unleashed jack-knives of his elbows. This is how the films looked when they were projected as their creators intended.' Harold Lloyd's cameraman for many of his pictures was Walter Lundin, and his bespoke cranking of the camera could define the success of a movie: a chase was often slowed down to 14 frames a second to increase the apparent speed when shown; the slower he

---

seconds per scene for *Detroit Rock City* and 2.6 in *Deep Blue Sea*) and many literate indie movies in the same year (the average scene in Woody Allen's *Husbands and Wives* lasted 28 seconds, while in *Bullets Over Broadway* it was an astonishing 51.9; Richard Linklater's aptly named *Slacker* was 34.5).

went, the faster the cars and the trains.* This was at least one reason why Chaplin was Chaplin and Lloyd was Lloyd and you were you: not only were they able to form and retake their stories, but the cameramen and projectionists added dynamism to their every move. It was perfect comedic timing. In photography a comparable trick would later show itself in airbrushing and Photoshop; in music, Auto-Tune.

Everything changed with sound and motorisation. Only now was it possible to put a running time on the posters and promotional material. The first time a Harold Lloyd film was awarded a running time was in 1932, for the 96-minute feature *Movie Crazy*. But by then time had caught up with him, and filmgoers had new wonders and new idols: *Grand Hotel*, *Horse Feathers*, *Pack Up Your Troubles*, *The Mummy*, *Blonde Venus*, Greta Garbo, the Marx Brothers, Laurel and Hardy, Boris Karloff, Marlene Dietrich and Cary Grant.

When he was older, and wore glasses for real, and was said to be unchanged by all his fame and canny investments and was celebrated for his lasting marriage to his co-star Mildred Davis, Harold Lloyd looked back at his career with film historians. He said he was delighted to receive an honorary Oscar in 1953. It stung that he was too often critically ignored and only occasionally swam in the same genius pool as Chaplin and Keaton. He had made a slightly more successful

---

* Many early D.W. Griffith movies appear particularly jerky compared to those of his contemporaries because he deliberately instructed they be filmed at 14 frames per second; the film historian Kevin Brownlow has suggested that he was just trying to squeeze as much as he could into the one-reel 1,000-foot restriction imposed upon him by his film company Biograph. Slowness brought its own dilemmas. The heat from a projector's lamp would burn the film, and projectors carried a precautionary fire shutter which fell if the film was shown slower than 40 feet per minute.

artistic (if not financial) transition to the talkies than either
of them, although that's not saying much. Lloyd made seven
sound films, nine if you include the ones he made but didn't
star in. He made only five 'thrill' pictures, he said, and therefore hundreds of others that were, by definition, not so
thrilling, and he was occasionally a little peeved that, more
than any other film star before or since, he was principally
remembered not for one film, but for one stunt.

'That scary business in *Safety Last!* wasn't faked,' Lloyd
said in 1949, while promoting the rerelease of seven of his
old movies (not that he needed the money; he was thought
to be the wealthiest film star in America).

> I actually climbed that 14-storey building. What we did was put
> a wooden platform under me, two stories down, out of range
> of the camera, and shoot a sequence of me climbing a couple
> of stories, then stop and raise the platform for the next sequence.
> The platform was covered with mattresses but was only about
> 12-feet square and had no railings – if we'd had railings we'd
> have had to fasten the platform even further down, to keep the
> camera from picking them up. When I fell, I had to be careful
> to land flat on my back and not bounce. I *did* fall a couple of
> times, and was scared to death. That probably helped the picture.

Did time let him down? No, the opposite occurred: time
served. He got love and money and, in the most famous and
desperate image in all silent cinema, a vision of Everyman
successfully hanging on as time falls away. For now at least,
we get to shoot another movie.

One evening, in the spring of 2014, I phoned Suzanne Lloyd,
Harold's granddaughter. She had lived with Harold at his
Greenacres estate for her entire youth, and when he died in

1971, with Suzanne aged 19, she took over the ownership of his films and copyright licences, and ever since she has been saving her grandfather from the disintegrations of time by safeguarding his reputation and boosting his exposure. When we spoke on the phone she was about to launch a new range of merchandising – mugs, cell phone cases, the usual fan junk – all with the classic Lloyd images: Harold under a scrum in *The Freshman*, Harold with his hair on end from *High and Dizzy*, Harold on the clock. In a few weeks it would be Harold Lloyd 100, the centenary anniversary of *Just Nuts*, regarded as his first proper one-reel film. The logo was already at the foot of his granddaughter's emails: Harold dangling from his own giant glasses.

I asked her why she believed the clock image was so enduring. 'I think . . . I don't know,' she said. 'I think the movie had such an impact when it was made, and it was so thrilling, and it scared so many people. Even though some people don't know who he is, they see that image and they go, "Oh, we know that guy".' When she's not promoting his image, Lloyd is litigating against its use, and she talks of legal cases against those who have pirated his films and likeness without licence. The most common stolen image is Harold on the clock. 'People think they own it,' she said.

Despite being his granddaughter, Suzanne Lloyd used to call him Daddy. She sometimes still does. Her mother was Gloria, Harold and Mildred's eldest, but Suzanne describes her as 'very mentally unstable' and unable to take care of her. Her parents divorced before she was two, and she only saw her father at holidays. Her grandparents became her guardians, and so Harold brought her up as her own. As a teenager she looked after his old nitrate films, a messy job. She remembers her grandfather taking her to meet the Beatles after a concert. She says that whenever he got depressed he would put a big piece of paper on the wall and write on it in red pen: 'Why Worry?'

Suzanne Lloyd told me she was planning Lloyd film festivals in Europe, and she does much to popularise his thousands of stereoscopic photographs, containing images of St Paul's just after the Blitz and naked snaps of Marilyn Monroe and many other hot pin-ups, some of whom Harold is believed to have slept with.

I asked her about his timekeeping, wondering whether he was punctual.

> Oh my God, don't even get me crazy! Oh my God – punctual? My mother was so bad – she was always two hours late. So he used to go and lie to her, saying to meet two hours earlier than was needed. He was the most punctual person – unbelievable. He would stand at the bottom of the stairs and say, 'Train's pulling out of the station and you're going to be left behind!' He was on it, punctual, punctual. He was so in control, a good key issue with him. You knew he was in control.

He always wore the same watch, a Rolex given to him by Bebe Daniels, who was Dorothy in the first, silent, version of *The Wonderful Wizard of Oz* (1901), and appeared alongside Lloyd in several films, including *Lonesome Luke Leans to the Literary* (1916). His granddaughter said that Daniels was the first woman to break his heart, and he wore her watch until the end.

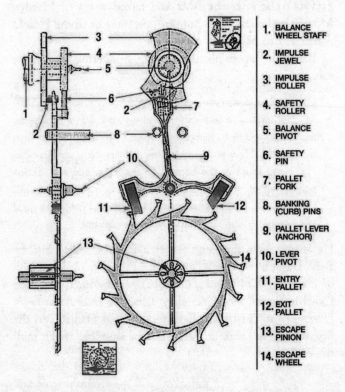

1. BALANCE WHEEL STAFF
2. IMPULSE JEWEL
3. IMPULSE ROLLER
4. SAFETY ROLLER
5. BALANCE PIVOT
6. SAFETY PIN
7. PALLET FORK
8. BANKING (CURB) PINS
9. PALLET LEVER (ANCHOR)
10. LEVER PIVOT
11. ENTRY PALLET
12. EXIT PALLET
13. ESCAPE PINION
14. ESCAPE WHEEL

Wheels within wheels: 'We never, ever, touch the movement with our fingers.'

Chapter Seven

Horology Part One:
How to Make a Watch

i) A Very Difficult Floor

'You will be able to do this,' an overconfident man in a well-lit room in a medieval town near the Swiss/German border tells me in the summer of 2015. 'I can guarantee to 99.98 per cent that you will be able to complete this by yourself.'

Before me on a low desk is a box of tools: a magnifying glass on a curled wire that attaches to my head and makes me look like an evil genius; a 'tweezer' that is heavier and sharper than the type used to sort stamps; a screwdriver with a head so thin it almost isn't there; a wooden stick topped with suede; a pink plastic twig the size of a toothpick; a blue plastic compartmentalised tray that looks like the lid on takeaway coffee. And then there is the instruction: 'If you lose or drop anything don't try to find it, it's a very difficult floor.' And 'we never, ever, touch the movement with our fingers. Why? Sweat. Your sweat will chew into the decoration of the movement roughly one to two months later, and then you can throw the watch away.'

Yes, I am about to sort-of make a watch. I will disassemble a standard movement by removing screws, bridges and cogged wheels, and then I will try to reassemble it using memory, dexterity and an instructor called Christian Bresser. 'Whenever we see golden springs we *please* do not take them out,' Bresser continues, pointing to a tiny part on the silver disc in front of me. 'A colleague of mine released this wheel, and he was not paying attention, and it was under full power, and the wheel went straight into his eye and blinded him. So it's always great to pay attention.'

Until they get complicated, making a mechanical watch is a fairly standard thing, for almost all are made upon the same principles. A coiled mainspring (powered by winding or other means) drives a collection of wheels, which in turn causes the oscillation of a balance wheel several times a second. This oscillation is regulated by another set of gears known as the escapement, the mechanism that turns the watch hands the requisite amount at a constant rate – the hour hand twice every 24 hours, the second hand once a minute. But before me on the table is, of course, something rather more complicated than this: 150 years of horological sophistication, an art so refined and intricate that a skilled watchmaker will squint and sweat and swear for 10 years to be worthy to build it. I have precisely 50 minutes.

The headquarters of IWC (no one calls it the International Watch Company any more) lies in Schaffhausen, some 40 minutes' drive north of Zurich on the banks of the Rhine, which has been a source of power, transport and inspiration since the company established itself in the late 1860s. For almost 150 years IWC has made elaborate and expensive timepieces for a discerning and loyal clientele, and its current range is not something a novice can usually make in 50 minutes. There is, for example, the Portugieser Minute Repeater, with its 46-hour power reserve, a Glucydur beryllium alloy balance, and a slide control that chimes the hour, the quarter-hour and the minute with two tuneful gongs (a mechanism that alone consists of around 250 parts), available in a platinum case and alligator strap for £81,900. There is the elegant Portofino, one for the ladies, perhaps, such as the Midsize Automatic Moon Phase with its 18-carat red-gold and 66-diamond case, with 12 further diamonds on the mother-of-pearl dial (beneath which hovers a ring displaying the Earth's movement through the heavens), retailing at £29,250. There's the Ingenieur Constant-Force Tourbillon, boasting an invariable amplitude of balance and thus near-perfect accuracy, a 96-hour power reserve, a double moon phase display for the northern and southern hemispheres, and a countdown dial to the next full moon, in platinum and ceramic at £205,000.

And then there's the model that made the company famous during the Second World War, the stark Big Pilot's Watch, a massive simple dial with a huge glove-operable crown and an inner case with protection against magnetic fields and sudden drops in air pressure. First constructed in 1940, a revised model now has a recommended list price of £11,250. (Being Swiss, and interested in both money and neutrality, IWC sold its pilot watches to the RAF *and* the Luftwaffe, and both were grateful as they calibrated the best way to shoot each other out of the sky. Due to a navigational error in April 1944, Schaffhausen was bombed by an American pilot; the town suffered much damage and lost 45 lives, although the bomb that hit IWC fell through the roof and failed to detonate.)

All these watches are very attractive. The most attractive thing about them is that they are not flashy or overbearing, and none of them, unlike many other watches at the top end of the market, resemble a Swiss Army knife. If you're going to wear your money on your wrist, then it's nice if you don't cause offence while you're doing it. IWC prides itself on making watches for purists, which may explain why the company is not as famous as some of its rivals and occupies an upper-middle tier in Swiss *haute horologie*, not quite at the altitude of Patek Philippe and Breguet, but certainly high enough to merit its own museum. The story it tells there is, predictably enough, one of glorious innovation and expansion: the building of its current factory on the site of a monastery orchard in 1875; its first wristwatch movement in 1915; the first automatic winding mechanism of 1950; the automatic diver's watch of 1967 with pressure resistance to 20 bar; the world's first titanium-cased chronograph of 1980, designed by F.A. Porsche.

No one at IWC will give me even a rough estimate of how many watches it has made during its lifetime, or even how many it has made in the last year; it has become increasingly sensitive about such things since 2000, when it became, in exchange for 2.8 billion Swiss francs, part of Richemont, the luxury goods conglomerate which also owns, among others, Montblanc, Dunhill, Jaeger-LeCoultre, Vacheron Constantin and Cartier. But the company entertains visitors with many other statistics on its guided tour, such as the 659 parts required to make one of its magnificent Grande Complications, which is 453 parts more than there are bones in the human body.* The tour involves the donning of white coats and plastic blue shoe covers, time in sealed air-pocket anterooms to minimise dust in the labs, and signs that read:

---

* Reading the first draft of this chapter, my editor made a simple note in the margin: 'How is this even possible?' The answer lies in the tiny screws, springs, plates, wheels and jewels, but also in the weights on the edge of the balance wheel, the ratchets that mediate the power supply, the interconnected barrels that create an energy reserve, and the pallet fork attached to the escapement wheel that causes the ticking sound. The greatest wonder of all is that this is a *mechanical* movement, much of it adapted from pocket watches created in the seventeenth century. The precision tooling and some of the fitting may be done by machine, but the design and final assembly are done by brain and hand. In all the talk of the absurd cost of these timepieces, and the ingenious madness of the gimmickry, one is often left dumb-struck by the beauty of the engineering. 'How is this even possible' indeed.

'These demonstrating watches are complicated, fine mechanical masterpieces. Your guide would be glad to show you the functions of these watches, please do not try it yourself. Thank you for your understanding and have a nice day!'

Along the way I saw men and women building layers of the less sophisticated models with manuals at their side; these are not the skilled artisans I would encounter later, but production-line staff employed after a few weeks' training. (There is a careful distinction between 'watch assembly' and 'watchmaking'. Watch assembly primarily involves piecing together parts that may have been assembled elsewhere, often manufactured by other companies, parts shipped in crates and compiled, much as one might make a car or any other intricate factory product that may, despite this intricacy, be learnt by heart. Watchmaking is another art altogether, something it would take years rather than weeks to learn, and requires not only steely patience and concentration, and a deep understanding of mechanics, but also practical inspiration; anyone can paint by numbers, only the few paint like Cézanne, Monet or Renoir). I then passed drilling and milling and polishing machines and swathes of lathes, and photographs of brand ambassadors Kevin Spacey and Lewis Hamilton. There are framed displays of IWC's involvement with worthy causes and glamorous ones, including the education of underprivileged children in France, the Tribeca and London film festivals, and the protection of the giant iguana in the Galapagos Islands.

I ended up in the Grande Complications lab where they produce the Portugieser Sidérale Scafusia, ten years on the drawing board, the most elaborate watch in the company's history. Not only a constant-force tourbillon, not only a 96-hour power reserve, but also a display for sidereal time, which differs from solar time by a little less than four minutes each day, and will help the wearer 'find the same star each night in the same position' (the underside has a celestial chart showing hundreds of stars, which may, during production, be aligned to the customer's personal location in the universe). The watch will make you feel important and insignificant at the same time, and will be accompanied by a bill for about £500,000.

One of those responsible for this great feat is a German named Romulus Radu. Radu is 47, and has been with IWC for his entire career, but works at eye level to his desk, so that on first meeting he looks like a child. He needs to keep his back and shoulder straight, he says, 'otherwise it would be like working for eight hours at a kitchen table'. He wears plastic pink gossamer caps on three fingers to improve his grip. He says he also works on the perpetual calendar, a watch offering a day/month/year display lasting 577.5 years. I asked what would happen to it *after* 577.5 years (self-destruction perhaps, or reversion back to a Casio?), but the answer was as inevitable as it was absurd: in the year 2593 the display will have to be corrected by one day, and 'your local IWC boutique will be able to help with this'.

'Not everyone has the hands for this job,' Radu observes as he works on the base of a tourbillon. I suggest he must also have a particularly robust psychological constitution for the work he does.

'Yes.'

'Because,' I say, 'I think I'd just go mad.'

'Sometimes I go mad too, but only sometimes.'

I look at the parts in front of him and his dashboard of screwdrivers, the thickest head thinner than a baby's finger-nail, and wonder how long he could concentrate without wanting to throw everything out of the window.

'Everyone has a bad day,' he says, 'but usually I can work for two or three hours on one part before I need a break.'

A coffee break?

'I have one in the morning and an espresso at lunchtime. One has to be careful.'

Suddenly, looking at Radu's work, I'm presented with the best reason to buy a watch when I don't need one – because it is a masterpiece. Having simplified and mastered time more than a century before, the master watchmakers of Switzerland, Germany, France (and, until the 1950s, England) have had plenty of time to make adjustments. So they have *complicated* things.

In May 1873, the American magazine *Watchmaker and Jeweller* carried an advertisement announcing the successful foundation of a company 'with the object of combining all the excellence of the American system of mechanism with the more skilful hand labor of the Swiss'. IWC, founded five years before, was finally in business. The ad showed a palatial factory, which hadn't actually been built yet, and a guarantee that its watches were 'the least liable to get out of order'. The products – initially elaborate pocket watches on chains or brooches – came in 17 patterns and boasted stem-winding systems not requiring a key. They were offered at prices 'that defy competition'.

IWC's founder, Florentine Ariosto Jones, had trained as a watchmaker in Boston before the Civil War and moved to Europe not long after its conclusion (he may have been injured in the fighting; some accounts suggest this is why we have only one adult photograph of him). Jones was in his mid-20s and perceived an opportunity: the possibility of applying advanced industrial techniques to the cottage-style special-isation of the master watchmakers of Geneva and Lausanne. Rather than make every watch from scratch, a base model could be established with interchangeable and replaceable parts using milling machines to make screws and escape wheels, and imported workbenches to make case decorations. The Americans (namely Jones and his associate Charles Kidder) would bring the production line, while the Swiss would provide something they are still famous for: the finishing school.

Despite his enthusiasm, Jones met mostly resentment and obstruction; the skilled French-speaking locals didn't take kindly to the disruption of working practices that had served them since their earliest clock manufacture 400 years before. He received a warmer welcome in the German-speaking north of the country; the inhabitants of Schaffhausen particularly liked the prospect of 100 new jobs.

IWC's initial output was disappointing: Jones told his creditors he would produce 10,000 watches a year, yet by 1874 the company had sold barely 6,000 in total. The Swiss banking shareholders loosened Jones's control, and only nine years after the company's formation he was sent back to Boston (his watchmaking and engineering exploits continued, but he died in his mid-70s in some poverty). Today, his name lingers in IWC's hushed museum and one of its conference rooms. And it was here, in the Jones Room, that my own expertise in watch production came to the fore.

One reason IWC will today let a complete novice make a complete fool of himself on the banks of the Rhine is to show why a £205,000 watch is actually worth £205,000 – in other words, how damn near unattainable the mastery of a master watchmaker is. Not that they'd actually let me loose on one of their top marques, of course. In front of me on the desk is the hand-wound Calibre 98200, at 37.8mm the largest the company has to offer, produced exclusively for watch-making classes. My assignment entails removing 17 parts and then reappointing them again, to the point where the watch won't yet function fully (there are neither hands nor a complete power train), but a few wheels and pinions will at least inter-connect and be directed by the rod and crown. With less than an hour to complete the task, it's construction for simple-tons. 'We have two ways of holding the screwdriver,' my instructor says, lining up a zinger he has used a thousand times before. 'The right way and the wrong way.'

The removal and reconstruction entails repeatedly flipping the dial side and the underside. The easy part of the work – the bit that compares favourably with rewiring a plug – consists of screwing in bridges, the sections that hold the layers and complications in place. Rather trickier is the task of inserting the toothed-rim barrel encasing the mainspring beneath the minute wheel, and aligning a 0.15mm pivot with the jewels. (I was working with synthetically engineered rubies. These low-friction jewel bearings – used particularly in gear trains and anti-shock mechanisms – have traditionally given watches a hallmark of quality; the more of them one had, the greater the supposed accuracy, longevity and security of the movements. Without additional complications a trad-itional mechanical watch is replete with 17 jewels, but a multi-tiered IWC confection may demand as many as 62. The term 'complications' is used for anything in a watch superfluous to telling the time, such as a feature showing the phase of a moon.)

Making anything really small tends to be extremely expen-sive, at least at prototype and the final manual pass. In the watch industry, the precision of the tiny parts is one reason for the great cost (even the tiniest screw costs eight Swiss francs; actually *because* it is such a tiny screw). Then there is the relentless endurance with minimum lubrication, an add-itional reason that men admire these watches so much. But the major contributory factors are human and old-fashioned – the wisdom, handed down through centuries, required to make something beautiful and functional from an otherwise inanimate assemblage of metal and stones. 'It's the worst thing to say,' Bresser tells me, 'but it's the God complex, or the Frankenstein complex. You have the white overcoat, and you're creating life.' Midway through my attempt to do something similar, as I'm tweezering the arresting pin, he says, 'If you drop it, you're not actually a watchmaker so I'm not going to hurt you.'

As I tried not to drop screws on the floor, I considered a new challenge, and you may attempt it too: try to name just one famous living master watchmaker. No rush: very few people beyond the inner circles can do it, and the craft has always been happiest hidden.* But these craftspeople – almost all of them men – are surely worthy of our attention. Christian Bresser, for example, is 43. He tells me he once wanted to be a fighter pilot. As a boy growing up in Jamaica and then Florida, his main hobby was building toy models. He had little interest in watchmaking until taking an apprenticeship at a German goldsmith's in his late 20s. 'I realized it's a very emotional thing. Certain early watches I built I look on as my kids.' In 2000 he went looking for a job at several Swiss companies, including Rolex, Omega and Zenith, and he found them 'shiny shiny' but lacking the smaller family environment he experienced at IWC (the company employed about 500 people then; now it's more than 1,000). One of his tasks at interview sounded familiar: disassembling and assembling a watch. The difference was, his involved rather more delicate parts, and the movement had an inbuilt fault he had to detect. 'When I

* Historically the task becomes a little easier. There was, after all, an Abraham Louis Breguet (1747–1843), born in Switzerland and apprenticed in France. And there was Antoni Patek, a Pole, who met the Frenchman Adrien Philippe in 1845 and formed a company six years later. But there is no Monsieur Hublot, for example, and no Mr Rolex (or at least not in the realms of horology; it's marketing, like Häagen-Dazs).

began I had the watchmaking vocabulary of a 10-year-old,' he says. Today his talent is split between making perpetual calendars and double chronographs, and marketing and educating. He holds his basic watchmaking class on a regular basis, as much a sales exercise as one of horology: the novice visitor feels good about completing a simple process, and this enriched appreciation of pinions and pivots will lead, within the hour, to the glittering baubles in the gift shop.

The gift shop is situated next to the museum, and both suggest that, on the practical level, IWC is still run on tracks laid down almost 150 years ago: the efficiency of the mechanised production line combined with the meticulous mastery of the finishing line. But the museum, with all its display of ingenuity, falls rather short of telling the whole story of IWC and its enduring message of weathering storms. The company has survived many challenges and fluctuations: in watch trends and currency markets, changing labour demands and work practices, as well as fierce and brilliant competition from 300 or so other Swiss watchmakers, Chinese knock-offs; and now, in the second decade of the twenty-first century, it is facing a whole new type of competition – from, of all things, a *computer* company.

The weather from Cupertino hangs as heavy over Schaffhausen as it does over the rest of Switzerland, but the threat from the Apple Watch is about something bigger than a single product. This is the prospect of total digital connectivity, the challenge of how far and how soon we are prepared to control everything in our lives from our skin, either with it (the smartphone) on it (the smart watch) or under it (chips ahoy). No one has the answer to this yet, but no one in Switzerland can afford to ignore it, just as they couldn't really afford to ignore the impact of quartz.

Unlike the impact of quartz, which was a new cheap way

of doing the same thing, the smart watch does a great many new things too, with timekeeping decidedly the least important. When the Apple Watch began to appear on people's wrists in 2015, many felt disappointed: it didn't seem to do much that an iPhone couldn't do, except on a smaller scale. It notified you of incoming calls and email, just like the phone, and it could store your travel documents and pay for your coffee, and monitor your fitness workout. The beautiful flapping butterfly screensaver on the matt-black face was for some, with more money than sense, more than enough to justify the purchase, but for others, not least in the mechanical watchmaking industry, the butterfly signalled chaos. The Apple Watch (and its cheaper Android competitors from Samsung, Pebble and elsewhere) was a potential signifier of doom. Up to the middle of 2014, the response from Switzerland to Apple and its clones had been either muted or dismissive, a complication it would barely acknowledge; but things have changed, not least because the grand old masters were in downturn.

At IWC the opening gambit is called IWC Connect. This is not a watch but a strap, available initially just for its pilot watches, and the strap contains a big button. Press this and turn it, and you have a link to your phone and apps and health features and email notifications. The device is a discomfiting nod to the microprocessor, the antithesis and sworn enemy of traditional *haute horologie*; its position on a strap is the Swiss way of embracing the digital advance while distancing itself from both its inelegance and its threat. An IWC watch will not, in the foreseeable future, offer an MP3 player or camera, much less a biannual upgrade of its operating system, preferring to tick on beautifully, and mechanically, waiting until the storm passes, hoping that it does.

ii) Just What Is It About the Swiss?

How did this unassuming, landlocked country come to dominate an industry that it didn't establish? How did it move from a mastery of dairy production to a mastery of dairy production and miniature precision mechanics? And how did it refine the idea of charging tens of thousands of Swiss francs for an object that often kept time less accurately than an object costing £10? (Or how, when the Swiss exported 29 million watches in 2014, did this figure account for only 1.7 per cent of all watches bought globally, but 58 per cent of their value?)

In 1953, when Eugène Jaquet and Alfred Chapius published their vast and authoritative volume *Technique and History of the Swiss Watch*, they were slightly vague on the issue of provenance. The first watches – first round and then oval-shaped, and worn as large necklaces – appeared around 1510, initially in Germany, the Netherlands, France and Italy. A small trade developed in Geneva a few decades later, thanks largely to artisans employed as goldsmiths; filigree and enamel work, and experience with intricate engraving tools, enabled craftsmen to turn their attention to miniature mechanics. Jaquet and Chapius found records for 176 goldsmiths working in Geneva in the sixteenth century, and their emergent watch-making skills were almost certainly aided by the arrival of Huguenot refugees from France. The earliest watches necessitated a certain bulkiness, for they accommodated a cone-shaped pulley mechanism known as a fusee to distribute the wound power as evenly as possible (rather than just running at full force at the start of a cycle and weakly at the end of it). The balance spring (the wound hairspring that holds the power in a mechanical watch), was probably developed independently by the Dutch mathematician Christiaan Huygens and the English philosopher/scientist Robert Hooke in the mid-seventeenth century, and it greatly improved this control (and thus the timepiece's accuracy). Before this the earliest watches dared tell only the hour, for their precision was often compared unfavourably to a sundial; the minute hand, also developed by Huygens and first utilised by the English clockmaker Daniel Quare, appeared only around 1670.

The first signs of the Swiss exporting their wares came in 1632, when a watchmaker from Blois named Pierre Cuper II travelled to Geneva to commission 36 watches from Anthoine Arlaud; the order was required to arrive at Marseilles within a year. Other orders for watches made by Arlaud's son Abraham and a certain Jean-Anthoine Choudens came in from Constantinople a few years later. It appeared that the Swiss had already established a reputation for superior quality and decoration: the Genevese were also masters of enamel cases. By the 1690s there were watchmakers in Basel, Berne, Zurich, Lucerne, Rolle, Moudon, Winterthur and Schaffhausen. Neuchâtel also became a prominent centre for skilled craftsmen fleeing religious persecution elsewhere in Europe, and Neuchâtel established what was probably the first watchmaking school, taking on apprentices in their early teens, valuing the importance to the canton, if not the country, of a watchmaking infrastructure. But it was La Neuveville in the Jura that lays claim to being the first city of horology; along with winemaking, the production of pocket watches became its principal occupation.

None of which quite explains why it was Switzerland, rather than Germany or France, that gained the pre-eminent sterling reputation. But this is because the pre-eminent sterling reputation emerged primarily in the twentieth century. Prior to this, several other countries were just as prominent. Companies such as Breguet, Cartier and Lip in Paris, A. Lange & Söhne and many small firms based in Glasshütte in Germany – all produced prized specimens and established reputations. And in England, which could justifiably claim to be the innovative centre of clock and watchmaking in the seventeenth and eighteenth centuries, the choice of premier craftsmen was long: Edward East, William Clay, Thomas Mudge, John Harrison, Richard Bowen, Richard Towneley, the Frodsham family, Thomas Tompion and S. Smith & Sons in London and Cheltenham ('Watchmakers to the Admiralty') – all names now forgotten beyond the catalogue and the museum, mainly due to the habitual English practice (the railways, industrial manufacture, the national football team) of underinvestment and shrugging neglect of important concerns in which the country once led the world.*

The Swiss just surely kept on going, occasionally buying up some of the best firms elsewhere in Europe, benefitting from the free trade movements of the mid-nineteenth century, and forming trade bodies and certification targets that increased the industry's reputation for quality and honesty. In the nineteenth century, workshops expanded into mechanical manufacture that made full use of newly reliable escapement mechanisms and the tourbillon (invented respectively by Mudge in London and Breguet in Paris).** The development of increasingly flat watches saw pocket watches develop into wristwatches; a watch on the wrist was particularly useful when riding. The Swiss also made full use of developments in winding, adopting early the stem and crown we have today as a replacement of the previous winding by key. The export trade set great store by all these improvements.

---

* In its catalogue of 1900, in which pocket watches were offered from £3 to £250, Smith & Sons claimed that 'Its lifetime, in comparison with the Swiss, is treble.' It made a special point of its 'non-magnetizable watches', which would not be in any way affected, as others have 'all too sadly' proven to be, when exposed to railway travel or any proximity to electricity.
** The tourbillon mounted the escapement and balance wheel in a rotating cage, thus limiting the detrimental effects of gravity on performance.

By 1870, the Swiss watch industry was employing at least 34,000 people and making an estimated 1.3 million watches a year.

And then there was war. Switzerland's watchmakers flourished because of their country's neutrality, and IWC was not alone in making wristwatches for opposing sides during the two world wars.* But peacefulness, even as it aids concentration at the workbench, does not in itself explain the exquisite Longines or Ulysse Nardin, just as it does not explain the cuckoo clock.** The most intriguing thing about Orson Welles's memorable speech as Harry Lime in *The Third Man* is its flat inaccuracy:

> What the fellow said – in Italy for 30 years under the Borgias they had warfare, terror, murder, bloodshed, but they produced Michelangelo, Leonardo da Vinci, and the Renaissance. In Switzerland they had brotherly love, they had 500 years of democracy and peace, and what did that produce? The cuckoo clock!

It is one of the few lines in the screenplay not written by Graham Greene. And it is not true: the cuckoo clock was first made in Germany, which has not enjoyed 500 years of democracy or peace.

These days, the qualities that make a watch Swiss are classified legally, and are as closely regulated as champagne or Parmesan (the description on watches is always 'Swiss made' or just 'Swiss' rather than 'Made in Switzerland', a tradition dating back to 1890). To qualify, a watch must meet certain strict criteria (or, according to the Fédération de l'industrie horlogère suisse FH, where this classification originates, a

---

* Switzerland's military engagement effectively ceased with the end of the Napoleonic Wars in 1815, but during the revolutionary period production was hugely disrupted.
** But of course nothing will ever explain the cuckoo clock.

watch must adhere to 'The new requirements stipulated by Swissness'). To classify as 'Swiss Made, a watch must a) have a Swiss movement, b) have this movement incorporated in a case that is made within Switzerland and c) be checked and certified in Switzerland. To classify as having a Swiss movement, a watch must a) have this movement assembled within Swiss borders, b) have this movement inspected and certified in Switzerland and c) include components with a minimum of 60 per cent of 'Swiss value' (this is up from the 50 per cent set by law in 1971). These laws do not appear to unduly trouble websites such as perfectwatches.cn, which offer Chinese replica (i.e. fake) Rolex Daytonas for £370 and Breitling Navitimers for £127.

Perhaps the prominence and reputation of the Swiss watch may be best examined outside Switzerland, say in Australia. Here, for example, a man called Nick Hacko has been trying to make a watch that will be as robust and reliable as anything Geneva or Schaffhausen could offer, but assemble it in Sydney and sell it more cheaply, without the marketing hoopla. This is a feat that has become very difficult to achieve.

Hacko, bullish in build but mild in temperament, is not only a watchmaker but also a watch repairer and a watch dealer – he calculates he has sold more than 9,500 Swiss timepieces and repaired 17,000 – and in all roles he has recently come to admire and loathe the Swiss in equal measure. When I walked into his office in mid-February 2014, pretty much the first thing he did was hand me a black T-shirt emblazoned on the back with a huge amount of text (the typeface was ubiquitous Swiss Helvetica). The T-shirt was a tract more than a garment, and if you met someone wearing it at a party you would probably move away fast. It read, in part:

> Yet another corporate monopoly forcing independent traders out of business . . . Swiss watch brands are working to ensure that any repair work is carried out exclusively in their workshop, on their terms. Support our campaign. Sign the petition. Save the time.

'Here – have two!' he said, as he gave me another. One was medium, one was large. 'You're probably between them,' he said.

English is not Nicholas Hacko's first language. He was born in Yugoslavia in the early 1960s to a family of watch repairers, and he began fixing his own mechanisms when he was 12. He left not long after the outbreak of war in 1991, first to Germany and then, in 1994, to Australia, where he arrived, aged 31, with the most basic repair tools and 20,000 Australian dollars, most of which went on the bond securing his first shop. 'I worked really hard,' he remembers. 'It takes about ten years to build your reputation.'

His current shop has the feel of an office, occupying a suite of rooms on the fourth floor of a building in Castlereagh Street, Sydney's equivalent of Regent Street. Directly below him are showrooms selling Dior, Cartier, Rolex and Omega, but he is dismissive of those who are swayed by such glitz. 'A repairer is always looking from the inside out,' he says, 'But most collectors are all about looks. They love a brand name.'

Hacko is the P.T. Barnum of the dissenting watch world, a flamboyance particularly visible in an arena of the taciturn and retiring. He has 10,000 subscribers to his free newsletter, with another 300 paying for more specialist content. He describes himself and his breed as 'a person who knows he is always right. A watchmaker talks a lot, complains even more, yet himself hates time-wasters. If you haven't seen one in real life, think of Tom Hollander, just a bit shorter and less handsome.'

The wall of glass-fronted cases along one side of his office shimmers with exquisite items, but the visitor's eye is drawn to the solid boxes nearer the entrance – an array of watch-winding machines that move gently back and forth to imitate the action of an arm in daily motion. 'These are not for lazy people,' he explains. 'If you have a collection of automatic watches that are wound by being worn on the wrist, you need to keep them turning with power. It's also a nice way to show them off.'

The watch he is making is called Rebelde, the Spanish word for rebel. It is a manual piece with a large crown, wide at 42mm and heavy in surgical-quality steel, and it has an arresting face, an unusual mixture of roman and Arabic numerals. Hacko designed and commissioned all the components himself, and the watch is a product of one simple thing: it 'was not conceived as a brand to showcase the watchmaker's genius, or even to fulfil a need for a mechanical timepiece,' he explained on his blog. 'It was born simply out of necessity for physical survival.'

'The big picture is this,' he tells me. 'Watchmaking began who knows where. But we know when it moved to Switzerland for mass production and to America for cheap mass production. And then the Japanese started making fantastic stuff. But what has happened recently is more clear – the Swiss are operating a closed shop.' He refers to the arguments on the T-shirt, specifically the unavailability of spare parts. 'The worst thing of all is that they don't admit why they're doing it. They're being greedy, but they don't say "it's to protect our sales", but that independent watch repairers outside Switzerland can't be trusted to do a good job. But these are the same repairers who have been keeping the Swiss industry alive for a hundred years!'

The Swiss policy has led, he says, to a great many experienced craftsmen struggling for their livelihoods. His watch is a protest at the freeze-out, and, by sharing the drawings and each stage of production on his blog, an attempt to inspire the next generation of watchmakers. Six months after I met him, his watches were ready for market. Six months after that he had sold almost 400, at prices ranging from $2,500 (stainless steel) to $13,900 (rose gold).

Hacko's passion for horology occasionally verges on the suffocating (he talks about long-suffering wives bored by watch talk, and of chronic haemorrhoids from sitting down all day) but his obsessions have won a great many supporters. One day he wondered whether it would be possible to send a wristwatch – the same wristwatch – to every country on earth, and subscribers to his email bulletins have pledged to help him find out. The watch in question is a Davosa, a Swiss brand from the Jura mountains with its roots in the 1860s. The watch had to be worn ticking on land at 340 places, including tiny specks in the Pacific, Central Kiribati, Western Kiribati, North Korea, South Sudan, and of course both polar regions. Ideally there should be proof (a local newspaper or landmark in the background), and if the watch was lost, or otherwise not returned to Hacko, then the challenge would be over.

Hacko was confident of success, but estimated that it could take between 5 and 12 years to complete the task. 'Yes, we are in this for the long haul!' At the time of writing, the watch has already visited the Philippines, West Malay, Singapore, India, Pakistan and, fittingly for Hacko, Serbia, Bosnia, Croatia, Montenegro and Slovenia. And it has touched down in Switzerland and taken off from Switzerland.

I envied that watch. After my visit to IWC at Schaffhausen I was sitting in a departure lounge at Zurich airport, obligatory Lindt selection box at my side, surrounded by huge illuminated IWC adverts promoting a spirit of adventure and manliness at extremes both high and deep. Soon it would be time to set my clock back an hour, but there was a delay on the Heathrow flight: the departure board said 'Wait in lounge'.

After 30 minutes or so, the board had the same message, except now other Swiss flights were also delayed. And then all the Swiss flights were cancelled. We went to the desk and were told to wait for further announcements, and everyone started checking their phones for flights on other airlines. It was already about 7 p.m., and there weren't many flights left that evening. Then there was an announcement to proceed to the transfer desk at another terminal, and about 100 people started running, including those who clearly hadn't run for a while. We were told there was some sort of technical fault with the onboard computers, although it wasn't known why they all began to malfunction at once. Two or three couples at the front of the queue were transferred to a BA flight, but the rest of us got vouchers for hotels in town. We ran to cabs to beat fellow passengers to the rooms at the Best Western, and we used our meal vouchers to eat something filthy in the hotel bar.

At 6.30 the next morning we reassembled for the minibus, but at the airport the early flights had again been cancelled. One tries to be philosophical in these situations, and I reflected on all the ironies – Switzerland, of all places, home of perfect timing, watch shops almost every inch of the airport, and all these lives delayed, all this time wasted – but after a while it all just got extremely annoying. The next flight at mid-morning was definitely set to go, the mysterious computer problem all fixed apparently, although inevitably one asks oneself whether you really wanted to fly on that first one out, knowing what one does about the bugs one encounters when upgrading the operating system on a phone. And then a woman at the departure desk told us the precise reason for the delay. It was a leap second.

The day before was 30 June. Every three or four years the Earth's rotation becomes sufficiently out of sync with our atomic timekeeping (known as Coordinated Universal Time or UTC) that it becomes necessary to make an adjustment.* (Measured by an atomic clock, which is accurate to one second in 1,400,000 years, the regular day consists of 86,400 seconds. But the Earth's rotation, which is affected by the gravitational drag of the moon, is very gradually slowing down, so that NASA scientists estimate that the solar day lasts on average about 86,400.002 seconds.) If nothing was done to correct this anomaly, after hundreds of thousands of years we would find that sunset occurred at noon. The addition of an extra second is usually made on 31 December, and it comes with warnings suggesting the possibility of doom. The more digitally connected we all are, the more our lives may be affected by an adjustment to universal time: when the last leap second was added in 2012, Qantas grounded 400 flights to accommodate its computer network's failure to compute. The National Institute of Standards and Technology at Maryland, which maintains a weighted average of atomic clocks from around the world, joined with the US Department of Homeland Security to issue a set of guidelines about the extra second, and included the information that during the

---

* UTC is composed of International Atomic Time (a scale composed of the readings of about 400 atomic clocks around the world) coordinated with Universal Time or Solar Time, which is based on the Earth's rotation. UTC is the time standard accepted by most countries in the world and is maintained at the Bureau International des Poids et Mesures (BIPM) in Sèvres, France. It stands as official legal time, an important standard to have, when, for example, your insurance policy renews or expires.

transition atomic clocks, and those guided by them, would display the time (approaching midnight on 30 June 2015) as 23 hours, 59 minutes and 60 seconds, something one rarely sees. Alternatively, digital clocks might display 'multiple 59 or 00s . . . or even just freeze the time for one second.'*

There have been 26 leap seconds added since the Earth was synchronised with UTC in 1972, and for years there has been dissent about the need for such a thing at all. The Americans tend to be against it, citing possible complications, like the threat of Y2K or grounded planes at airports. The British are definitely in favour, not least because it upholds a link with our very first, and most fundamental method of timekeeping, the sun and the stars.

Of course, I only learnt these details later, after I had spent my last hours in Switzerland alternately bored and fuming, a tiny cog in a vast mechanism. I was part of the atomic clock, a temporal tourist at best, a life of electromagnetic transitions in atoms of caesium. We do not, after all, run the world with our beautiful ticking discs. My watchmaker Christian Bresser may have felt he was playing God, but what a delusion that was. It wasn't the Sun around the Earth, it was the Earth around the Sun.

---

* It also included this advice: 'Manual intervention may be required on some cesium and rubidium atomic frequency standards, as well as some quartz standards . . . Historically, leap second changes have created significant operational problems. All coordinated time scales will be affected by this adjustment.'

Roger Bannister: at the end of the race lay the start of the story.

Chapter Eight

Roger Bannister Goes Round and Round

In the 1970s I won an end-of-year form prize at my school in Hampstead, and my reward was a £10 book token to spend on any book I fancied.

My prize was to be presented on Speech Day, a sub-Etonian tradition in which we all had to wear cricket trousers and sit in the main hall through interminable accounts of the sports teams and drama department and staggering Oxbridge success, and in which everyone you hated got a prize presented from someone you'd never heard of. This person usually had only the most tenuous link to the school and always spoke about the challenges of life ahead and making lemonade. In an effort to impress my mother and the school and the prize-giver on the day, I went to the local bookshop and chose *The Jews in the Roman World* by Michael Grant, a volume I'm yet to open, let alone read. I don't think anyone was impressed, least of all the prize-giver, who was the school old boy Roger Bannister.

But obviously I was impressed with him. Bannister was not one of the boring speakers I had feared, but a true old boy, and a Boy's Own hero. He had been a legend for almost 20 years, and although I can't remember if he spoke that afternoon about his sub-four-minute mile (maybe just in passing; he was probably sick of it, and everyone knew the story pretty well), he was by far the most famous person I had ever met, if you can call a handshake a meeting. Forty years later I met him again, and at that point he was *only* talking about it, four minutes of once-fluid time that had been frozen, stretched, amplified, revised, memorised and mythologised. In the years since he broke the record in 1954, many people had run the mile a lot faster. The difference between him and the ones who came after was that his run was timeless.

At our second encounter, Bannister was promoting his new autobiography *Twin Tracks* at the Chipping Norton Literary Festival. It was 60 years since his astonishing run on a track by the Iffley Road, Oxford, but for our benefit he was still breasting the tape. 'Somehow I had to run that last lap in 59 seconds . . . time seemed to stand still, or did not exist. The only reality was the next 200 yards of track under my feet. The tape meant finality, extinction even.'

He was speaking at the Methodist Church Hall. When the event was over I asked him how he felt about living the same four minutes repeatedly; I could think of no one else in a similar position in any field.* He said he had long tried battling against it. 'Once,' he said, 'I would rather have been known also for my achievements as a researcher,' but he was now content. 'I don't think many people had the life I've enjoyed for four minutes' work!' He was joking about the four minutes' work. He had become obsessed about the time, and it had dominated his life for two years.**

Everyone gasped and delighted at Bannister's story, for it was still one of those tales that took to the air like a Spitfire. The thrill lay in the amateurism of the whole effort, and the

---

* Of course there will be hundreds: people reliving glories and disasters; memories of accidents and errors of judgment; even the pop star endlessly replaying their huge but unrepeated chart success, Terry Jacks or Norman Greenbaum on a greatest hits tour.

** Ever since he failed to win a medal in the 1,500 metres at the 1952 Helsinki Olympics (he came fourth).

tang of the Pathé newsreel. He spoke of how he had trained *in his lunch hour* to knock 3.7 seconds off his previous best mile, and how, because he was working as a doctor at St Mary's, Paddington, he did an early shift on the day of the race, before boarding a train to the meet at Oxford on his own. He remembered how, worried about the force of the wind only 30 minutes before race time, he wondered whether the record should be attempted at all; he recalled his pacing partners Chris Brasher and Chris Chataway becoming increasingly impatient with him. And then there was the wonder of the Tannoy announcement from his friend Norris McWhirter: 'Result of Event Eight – One Mile. First, R.G. Bannister of Exeter and Merton Colleges, in a time which, subject to ratification, is a new Track Record, British Native Record, British All-Comers Record, European Record, Commonwealth Record and World Record . . . Three minutes . . .' and the 3,000 spectators drowning out the rest of the time with cheers.* The time was 3 minutes 59.4 seconds.

The most intriguing thing about Bannister's timing was psychological. Runners had been trying to beat the four-minute barrier for decades before Bannister and his chums came

---

* Norris liked his records, gaining fame on the television series *Record Breakers* and editing *The Guinness Book of Records* and its offshoots with his twin Ross. The McWhirters would often take Bannister to race meetings in their car, and Bannister says he was sometimes unsure which McWhirter was which. Norris was also known for his politics, which combined reactionary Conservatism with libertarianism; were he still alive he probably would have been an ardent UKIP supporter. He died on 19 April 2004 and had dined with Bannister the previous evening; at the end of the meal, in the presence of Sebastian Coe and others, he repeated his famous timing Tannoy announcement from 1954.

Ross McWhirter was assassinated by the IRA in 1975 after he had offered a reward for information leading to the conviction of IRA members connected with past bombings.

along, and every few years they drew a little closer. Walter George had run 4:12 and ¾ in London in 1886, a record no one believed would be broken. In 1933, New Zealander Jack Lovelock ran 4:07.6 at Princeton. During the war the pace increased dramatically, as if it was now or never: in July 1943 the Swede Arne Andersson managed 4:02.6 in Gothenburg, and a year later in Malmö hit 4:01.6. A year after that Gunder Hägg, another Swede, also running in Malmö, achieved 4:01.3, and there the record stood until Roger Bannister sharpened his spikes almost nine years later. When Bannister arrived in Oxford for the big race, several athletes would have been wishing him ill, believing that 1954 was *their* year instead, not least the American Wes Santee and the Australian John Landy (both were clearly upset when reporters rushed to tell them that Bannister had beaten them to it).

But the strange thing was, once Bannister *had* done it, they all could do it. Landy ran an astonishing 3:57.9 in Turku less than seven weeks later. Bannister then ran another sub-4 minutes in Vancouver, and the following year Laszlo Tabori, Chris Chataway and Brian Hewson all ran under 4 minutes in London. By 1958, the record was held by Herb Elliott of Australia with 3:54.5, and by 1966 American Jim Ryun managed 3:51.3. In July 1981 Sebastian Coe ran 3:48.53 in Zurich, but his time was beaten only a week later in Koblenz by his great middle-distance rival Steve Ovett with 3:48.4. Two days after that, in Brussels, Coe reclaimed the record with 3:47.33. In July 1999 the Moroccan Hicham El Guerrouj ran 3:43.13, and there it stands, yet to be broken, as surely one day it will. The current record, explained by a combination of improved diet, stricter training at altitude and physical constitution, would have left Bannister about 120 yards behind at the finish.*

* The women's record, achieved in 1996 by the Russian Svetlana Masterkova, stands at 4:12.56.

This is half of the story of sport, of course. A limit is reached, a limit is exceeded; what seems impossible one year is suddenly possible every year after. Norris and Ross McWhirter's efforts at *The Guinness Book of Records* and associated television programmes were predicated on such improvements. Before sport became a subject for record books, there was just the realisation that humans (upright, no tail) were rather slow compared to things they tried to catch: the kangaroo managed 45 mph, the cheetah 85 mph, the spine-tailed swift 220 mph. Before steam and motorisation, humans probably managed about 35 mph on ice sledges and horses. For a while the fastest human by accident was probably Frank Ebrington, the occupant of an uncoupled carriage as it sped down the Kingstown–Dalkey (vacuum-pumped) atmospheric railway near Dublin, at an estimated speed of 84 mph in 1843. The first to exceed 100 mph were the crews testing the Siemens & Halske electric engine on a track near Berlin in 1901. While the fastest humans in history were the crew of Apollo 10 on re-entry into the Earth's atmosphere: 24,791 mph.

Roger Bannister was running at an average of 15 mph. But Bannister's four minutes had another brilliant layer on top of the speed: the time itself. Four minutes was a perfect time for those not terribly interested in sport – long enough to keep you hooked, not so long that you got bored. A mile in four minutes was something we could feasibly imagine running ourselves, even though everyone before Bannister had failed to do so. Four minutes was the length of a 78 rpm record, or a long pop song, or, today, a view on YouTube without major commitment.

'Now, ladies and gentlemen, we have an extremely special lot for you here. As I'm sure you've all seen, Christie's are hugely honoured to be offering you this – possibly the most important, iconic, um, piece of sporting memorabilia, *British* sporting memorabilia, that Christie's has ever offered. Of course – Roger Bannister's running shoes, he broke the record back in 1954 on the 6th of May, the Iffley Road running track. We're delighted to be offering them . . .'

Time passes, and the auction house or charity shop always benefits. It was now September 2015, 61 years and 6 months since the race, and an auction titled 'Out of the Ordinary' was getting into its stride. Bannister's shoes were lot 100, and the auctioneer had already dispensed with a collection of 21 novelty biscuit tins and a Victorian brass and steel working mechanical model of a canal dredger. There was also the pine door from the studio of the illustrator Ronald Searle, signed by, among others, John Peel and Stephen Hawking.

Bannister's shoes each weighed 4½ ounces and looked like kippers – thin, black and smoky brown, off-white string laces and six primitive spikes on each. They were displayed in a Perspex case at the side of the auctioneer's podium, but when it was their turn an assistant with white gloves removed them and held them in front of her face. Photographers stepped forward to record the moment. Potential bidders were given a saleroom notice with an amendment: 'The title for this lot should read "A Pair of English Black Kangaroo Leather Running Shoes" and not as printed in the catalogue.' The catalogue described them in exactly the same way, except without the kangaroo. (How many people in the room thought 'it was the kangaroo that gave him the extra spring in his step' is impossible to say.)

There was another amendment too: 'It should also be noted that the footnote stating that Sir Roger Bannister had retired from professional athletics should in fact read amateur athletics.' The catalogue estimate was £30,000–£50,000, but this was noble guesswork. The shoes had never been sold before.

'As you can imagine, ladies and gentlemen, we've got a lot of interest in the lot, so I'm sprinting right along there to 45 to 48 to 50 to 55 to 60 thousand pounds. I already have offered 60 thousand pounds. Any advance at 60 thousand pounds? Who's going to bid me 65 thousand? Sixty-five, here it is. Sixty-five, Kate, thank you. At 65 thousand pounds. Who's coming in next? Sixty-five thousand. Seventy thousand at the back of the room, thank you, sir. At 70 thousand, Kate, come back to me.'

Kate and her colleagues were at the side of the room on the phone with bidders. 'Seventy-five thousand. Eighty thousand. Eighty-five. Eighty-five thousand pounds. Ninety-five. Ninety-five thousand. A hundred thousand pounds, thank you, sir, back of the room, 100 thousand pounds. Against the telephones, 100 thousand. A hundred and twenty thousand, 130 thousand pounds. A hundred and forty thousand. A hundred and fifty thousand, quite right too.' And so it continued: 'A hundred and eighty thousand pounds, new bidder. Having a think at the back of the room. There it is, 180 thousand with Kate.' The shoes went for £220,000, and there were cheers and applause when the gavel came down. Kate's anonymous bidder had won after just under three minutes, and ended with a bill, including commission and tax, for £266,500. When interviewed before the auction on why he was selling up, Bannister just said 'it was the right time to part with them'. He was failing, he had carer bills and children and charities to consider. Sixty years ago as an amateur he would have been fatally compromised by benefitting from his ancient and noble sport. Now, of course, in the era of systematic Olympic Soviet doping and Paralympians standing trial for murdering their girlfriends, anything went, and quite right too.*

---

* Bannister's famous day had featured in auctions before. There were at least three

When Bannister withdrew from the track in 1955, he dedicated himself to medicine. His specialty was the autonomic nervous system, and to explain what this is, Bannister is fond of quoting an American physiologist named Walter Cannon: 'It is that part of the nervous system which Providence in its wisdom decided should be outside the range of voluntary control.' Bannister and his colleagues spent years analyzing cerebral circulation, ocular nerves, the lungs, heart, bladder and digestive system. One of his most engaging investigations was into the causes and purposes of fainting (or, medically, postural hypotension) due to emotional stress (caused, perhaps, by the sight of a needle or blood or sudden bad news). Many of Bannister's experiments took place on a motorised tilting table he had seen being wheeled out of Great Ormond Street: he strapped patients onto the table with a seatbelt, and he measured blood pressure and other cardiac functions as they moved from horizontal to vertical. Back issues of the *Lancet* feature Bannister's research into all manner of autonomic disorders, but his greatest legacy is the work conducted to revise Brain's *Clinical Neurology*, the classic textbook of how to diagnose and treat disorders ranging from epilepsy to meningitis. The book later became known as Brain and Bannister's *Clinical Neurology*, and by the time the seventh edition came out in the 1990s he had included advances in

---

stopwatches that recorded the time of 3.59:4 (some reports have five), and one of them is in a glass case with other Bannister mementos in the gallery at Pembroke College dining hall, where he served as master for eight years. The watch held by the chief timekeeper Charles Hill had been bought at auction by novelist Jeffrey Archer for a little under £9,000 in 1998, and then resold by Archer in June 2011 to benefit the Oxford University Athletics Club; at the second auction the winning bid was £97,250. Another stopwatch used on the day by W.J. Burfitt came up for auction in May 2015 and surpassed its estimate of £5,000–£8000 to reach £20,000. At Chipping Norton I asked Bannister about the watch he wears now. He said he didn't really know what it was, and when he examined his wrist he wasn't much the wiser, and the maker's mark was difficult to read. 'I don't think it's a famous make, but it always keeps good time.'

molecular genetics and the neurological complications of Aids. But in the fourth edition, published in 1973, one of Bannister's largest revisions concerned what was then still described as Parkinsonian disease or *paralysis agitans*. The degeneration of neurons was always progressive, Bannister observed, although the rate of deterioration varied considerably. There was a wide range of drugs to limit the tremors, but nothing yet to reverse or halt the process. More than 40 years later our understanding and treatment of Parkinson's has advanced considerably, but the outcomes are still familiar. Parkinson's is a disease that, whatever the severity and variety, slows you down; it distorts one's motor system and it may radically affect one's perception of time. The fact that Bannister is now himself afflicted he calls 'a strange irony', but I'm unsure if the irony derives from the source of his work or the source of his fame.

Bannister received his knighthood for services to medicine. He has advised governments on health policy, and in 2005 he was given the first lifetime achievement award by the American Neurological Association for advancing our understanding of degenerative disease. But I think everyone came to see him in Chipping Norton because we were interested in that other thing.

Over the years, Bannister had clearly had enough of repeating himself; it was like running round a track. One great day, one truly famous thing, one perfect outcome that entailed being held aloft by other men. The achievement would never be bettered, no matter how the modern mile time shortened, and autonomic neurology would only get you so far at the dinner table. A broken record can never be unbroken. I asked Bannister whether running 3:59.4 had in fact been as much of a curse as a blessing, and immediately

I felt embarrassed for having asked him, an insufferable boy who once won a form prize at the school and never really got over it. He must have been asked about the burden almost as often as he had been asked about the glory. But he was gracious and patient in response, and he had a Pixar-style uplift. 'No, it was an honour,' he said. 'It seems to inspire younger people to think that nothing is impossible.' (As he had written in 1954 – and in 2014 – 'We shared a place where no man had yet ventured, secure for all time, however fast men might run miles in future.') So he told the story again. What he could not do was tell the same story in a new way. Time usually imposes embellishment (the fish that got away grows bigger over time), but not here. Here it is always 6 p.m. just off Iffley Road on 6 May 1954, and Bannister, in his mid-80s, is relying on certainties. In 1954, in his first account of the race, 'Those last few seconds seemed never-ending.' He wrote how

> The faint line of the finishing tape stood ahead as a haven of peace, after the struggle. The arms of the world were waiting to receive me if only I reached the tape without slackening my speed . . . Then my effort was over and I collapsed almost unconscious, with an arm on either side of me . . . I felt like an exploded flashbulb with no will to live.

And his newly published account in 2014 had changed primarily in its grammar: 'The faint line of the finishing tape stood ahead as a haven of peace after the struggle. The arms of the world were ready to receive me only if I reached the tape without slackening my speed . . . Then my effort was over and I collapsed almost unconscious, with an arm on either side of me . . . I felt like an exploded flashbulb.' The biggest difference was, being older and nearer his end, he now had 'a will to live'. But there was one other slight modification. Those last five yards before the tape had seemed to him to stretch out so far that race time and stopwatch time appeared to be at odds, a new elastic consciousness. Sixty years ago he wrote: 'The last few seconds were never-ending.' In his new book it was: 'Those last few seconds seemed an eternity.' Same difference, perhaps, but the change of phrase was meaningful to him, for he's been living those last few seconds his entire life.

He signed about 20 books, and when he left the church hall he walked slowly with a stick, and a car was waiting to run him through the Cotswolds to his home.

Nick Ut: 'I have very important film.'

Chapter Nine

Vietnam. Napalm. Girl.

i) The Split Second

A few photographers somehow manage to shoot one master-piece after another. Henri Cartier-Bresson did it. So did Robert Capa, Alfred Eisenstaedt, Jacques-Henri Lartigue, Elliott Erwitt, Robert Frank, Gisèle Freund, Ilse Bing, Robert Doisneau, Mary Ellen Mark, Garry Winogrand, William Eggleston and Vivian Maier: so much stunning, innovative and memorable work. Nick Ut wasn't like that. Nick Ut took one photograph.

Strictly, he took more than one photograph, but only one photograph anyone remembers. It's the only photograph of his that anyone wants to talk about or buy. It's a photograph that built and almost suffocated a reputation all at once, and one that won him the Pulitzer Prize. It may even have hastened the end of a war. The image is so powerful that when Leica want to remind people of it in advertisements promoting their cameras, the photo isn't used at all. Instead, there are just three words in white type on a black background: Vietnam Napalm Girl.

The story is justly famous too. At about 7 a.m. on 8 June 1972, a 21-year-old Vietnamese photographer named Huỳnh Công Út set off for Trang Bang, a small village north-west of his base in Saigon. It was a familiar journey. Nick Ut, as he was known to his American colleagues, had been a photo-journalist with the Associated Press for five years, taking up the trade not long after his brother, also with AP, had been killed on assignment. (Some would have it, in pure tragic narrative, that in searching for the perfect photograph, Ut was avenging his brother's death.)

Just after noon he was among a small group of other journalists and US troops on Highway 1 leading to the village when he saw two planes dropping bombs and shortly afterwards he saw people fleeing and running towards him in distress. One of the planes had also dropped napalm. His first instinct was to photograph them, and professionally he was in luck. Two of the other photographers present were loading new film, but Ut had enough film left in his Nikon and his Leica.* He used the Nikon with a long lens to pick up the huge dark cloud over the village, and then switched to the Leica as the people neared. He first took photographs of an elderly woman holding what appeared to be a dead baby. And then he saw a small group of children running towards him. There were five in all. He saw that one girl, screaming with her arms outstretched, had shed her clothes, and the burns were visible on her skin. And then Nick Ut took his picture.

The children stopped a little further up the road and were surrounded by troops and journalists. Ut remembers that the naked girl kept shouting the words '*nóng quá!*' (too hot!'). His second instinct took hold: he stopped taking photos; he had to help them get to hospital. The girl, whose name was Phan Thi Kim Phúc, and who clearly needed help the most, was given water and then wrapped in a soldier's rain poncho. Ut accompanied them to the closest hospital, where Kim Phúc, drifting out of consciousness, was judged too sick to treat. Although still alive, she was taken to an area she believed later to be a morgue.

---

* When Ut's photo is printed at full frame, which it originally wasn't, the large figure to the right of the frame is clearly another photographer struggling to reload.

Nick Ut returned with his pictures to his agency bureau in Saigon. He remembers being asked by the darkroom technician, who was a skilled photographer himself, 'Nicky, what do you have?' Ut replied, 'I have very important film.' But compared to the speed at which the events of the previous few hours had just occurred – the bombing, the unfolding tragedy, the photos, the rush to hospital – the next few seemed to take an eternity. His films, eight rolls of high-speed Kodak Tri-X 400, had to be developed and fixed in a hot dark room, requiring continual movement of the negatives through the chemicals. They were then hung up to dry in a cabinet fitted with hairdryers, and several pictures were made up into 5×7-inch prints. It was clear from the start that one picture, negative 7a, was something exceptional. As a viewer one tends to focus on the girl, but it is an extremely busy photo, with two distinct lines of activity and a road that not only frames and directs one's view into the story, but also invites us to consider the burning horror beyond. There are five barefooted children running towards us, all related. On the left of the frame is a boy in such distress that his huge gaping mouth resembles something we would normally only see in a *Peanuts* strip. Behind him, at the back of the group, is the youngest child, the only one not looking towards the camera, momentarily distracted perhaps by activity behind him. Then there is Kim Phúc, a burn clearly visible on her left arm, running in what appears to be a thin strip of water. Behind her, a boy seemingly holding hands with a slightly older girl, and behind them a line of soldiers and photographers in uniform, distinctly set back from the young chaos, almost oblivious, as if this was a common occurrence. Later, the children in the photograph would be identified from left to right: Kim Phúc's younger brothers Phan Thanh Tam and Phan Thanh Phouc, and her cousins Ho Van Bon and Ho Thi Ting. When Horst Faas, the AP bureau chief in Saigon with 10 years' experience in Vietnam, looked at the image for the first time that after-noon he reportedly said, 'I think we have another Pulitzer here.'

But there was a problem: the same element that gave the picture its terrible force was also the thing that might make it unusable in the newspapers: AP, and most of the world's media, had a strict rule about not printing full-frontal nudity. The immediate thought was that the image couldn't be sent. Faas argued with his head office in New York that rules were made to be broken, and it was agreed that the image would not be cropped to show Kim Phúc alone or in close-up. And then the radio-wave transmission began, a 14-minute line-by-line process for each image if the lines held up, which they rarely did. The picture was first sent to AP in Tokyo, and then via land and submarine wire channels to New York and London. And from that point the story wasn't about speed any more. For a short while, the world waking up to that photo hung in suspended time. Everyone drew breath.

Television pictures from the day's events, taken by ITN and NBC, had got there first with the story, but it was Nick Ut's photo that burned into the memory. The initial shock – which was the same as Ut's original shock as he clicked the shutter, 'Oh my God. What happened? The girl has no clothes' – immediately turned to outrage. *This was unforgivable inhumanity. The war had to stop.* A single image taken in a fraction of a second (and it is always the personalised image of a few that amplifies the suffering of millions), brought the story home. It helped, as it always does, that the victims were children, innocent and bewildered. Yet it would be three more years before the war in Vietnam drew to a close.*

---

* Ut's image wouldn't be the only, or first, great photograph from Vietnam. Other 'marmalade droppers' (so-called because their impact causes the morning newspaper reader to mishandle their toast) included Eddie Adams' photograph from 1968 of a Viet Cong suspect being shot in the street at the beginning of the Tet Offensive

When AP entered the famous photograph for the Pulitzer Prize that year it had a title: 'The Terror of War'. When it won, in the 'Spot News' category, Ut was still in Saigon. On 8 May 1973, 11 months after the napalm attack, the photographer's name became famous to the outside world, and the subject of a historic photograph himself when he was captured being embraced and kissed by the American news reporter Edie Lederer not long after the news came through. They were in an office of some sort, with Lederer side-on and Ut smiling directly at the lens. The photographer in this case was another AP man, Neal Ulevich, who was on the spot to mark what was assumed to be the end of the story. In the AP files the key source words accompanying the picture are: Standing Kissing Congratulating Embracing Smiling.

When I met Nick Ut in Germany in May 2014 he ran through his story in brief without much prompting. It is what he's been doing for forty years. Now in his mid-60s, he is a short and stocky man, hair almost entirely white, articulate eyebrows and a mouth that is either smiling or about to. He now lives

---

(another photo which won a Pulitzer), and the photograph by Malcolm Browne from 1963 of the Buddhist monk Thich Quang Duc engulfed in petrol flames in protest against the repressive US-backed regime of Catholic Ngo Dinh Diem. (If you ever need an example of how war photographers tend to think differently from you and me, how about this: shortly before his death at the age of 81, Browne was asked by *Time* magazine in 2012 what he was thinking when he looked through his viewfinder at the burning monk. He replied, 'I was thinking only about the fact it was a self-illuminated subject that required an exposure of about, oh say, f10 or whatever it was.')

The preponderance and impact of single images – the fraction of a second that outlives a generation – was one reason why Vietnam became the last American war in which those in authority allowed the press to roam and report freely. In future, accredited reporters would be obliged to be embedded with the military. Too often, of course, 'embed' is another word for 'control'.

in Los Angeles and was still working for AP. He did all sorts of things – news, politics, celebrity – and still went where he was sent.* I took a picture of him posing with his Leica camera, and the grin broke wide – almost incongruously so, given the fact that he was standing in front of an enlargement of his famous photograph backlit by a light box.

Nick Ut was in a birthday mood, as was everyone that day. We were at a place called Leitz Park, on the outskirts of Wetzlar, a small town about an hour's drive north of Frankfurt, to celebrate Leica's 100th anniversary. At an exhibition showing what Leica could do, Ut's photograph hung alongside other photos that could also be summed up in three words: 'Sailor Nurse Kiss', 'Spain Falling Soldier'. Almost all of the photographers named in the opening paragraph of this chapter, many of whom regarded their Leicas as extensions of their bodies, were also represented with enlargements on light boxes, and some of them, including Elliott Erwitt, were also in attendance as paid Leica ambassadors. We were really here for a joint celebration: a century of steady technological advance for an inspirational piece of machinery, and those single brilliant moments – that ecstatic kiss – that the machinery made possible.

Unlike the rest of Wetzlar, which can trace its roots back to at least the eighth century, and is predominantly made from timber and brick, Leitz Park is mostly steel, concrete and glass, part of it in the shape of a grooved-rim lens. The site had recently become Leica's gleaming new headquarters, a 15-minute drive away from its former home at Solms. It incorporated a factory, a museum, an exhibition space, a café

---

* On 8 June 2007, for example, 35 years to the day since he photographed Kim Phúc, he was on assignment to photograph Paris Hilton at a court appearance. 'Two tearful girls in the throes of terror,' the *New York Daily News* noted as it reported on the coincidence. 'Nobody cried for Paris Hilton,' Ut said wisely, 'but everybody cried for Kim Phúc'.

and, of course, a shop, where you may try to resist buying a Leica insulated mug, a Leica umbrella and a USB stick that slots into a rubber key ring shaped like a Leica. That day there was a four-hour auction too, at which a small wooden shop display stand with a Leica logo reached £4,650; an advertising poster went for £8,235; and Elliott Erwitt's Magnum press card signed by Robert Capa reached £20,900. Then there were the cameras, topping out at £465,000 for an early motorised model from 1941 that was capable of taking 250 photos on a single roll of film (the camera of choice on German bombing raids, which went some way to explaining its rarity).

All of Nick Ut's most valuable gear had already been snapped up by the Newseum in Washington DC, where you may see his Leica M2 with the 35mm Summicron lens from June 1972. His situation reminded me a little of Roger Bannister's – a lifetime of work distilled into a split second. And then other absurd similarities suggested themselves. Like Bannister, Kim Phúc is also running – running away, but also into a new and famous future; it is the running that saved her. And you could find a thousand runners breasting the tape at a finish line the way Ut has frozen her in time.*

He told me he keeps in close contact with Kim, who is now married with children of her own and lives in Canada (she defected with her husband during their honeymoon in the early 1990s). She is a goodwill ambassador for UNESCO and heads a foundation that provides support to child victims of war. Ut says she still suffers pain from her burns but is kept strong by her Christian faith. She says she is happy

---

* When I met Ut in Wetzlar, the camera around his neck was a newish digital model, with a shutter speed of up to 1/4000th of a second. The M2 model he used in June 1972 could shoot up to 1/1000th of a second.

being known as 'The Girl in the Picture'.* She calls him 'Uncle Nick'.

Ut also spoke of a long-standing misinterpretation surrounding his photograph. Some reports have suggested the napalm attack from two South Vietnamese planes on Trang Bang that day was misdirected, but he disputes this. When they re-entered the village a while later, American troops found many dead Viet Cong, the intended target. Ut thinks that the pilots had assumed that the previous civilian inhabitants – Kim Phúc and her family among them – had already fled. He said that most people called the photo 'Napalm Girl', but he still preferred to call it 'The Terror of War'.

The story of Leica cameras, like the famous images they've made of the world, is one of good judgement matched with good timing. Many factors in film photography have focused on speed – the shutter, the film transport lever, the time it takes to load a roll as the world rushes by. The digital obsessions – the speed of processing, the number of frames per second – are not that different. But the Leica story is the one that made it possible for a photographer to be at the right place at the right time in the first place.

Between 1913 and 1914, an asthmatic amateur photographer named Oskar Barnack was getting tired of lugging a tripod and cumbersome bellow-type camera around his local German forest. He had began his career as an optics engineer at Zeiss, and, not long after he moved to rivals Leitz to specialise in

---

* For more on Kim Phúc's life story see cbsnews.com/news/the-girl-in-the-picture. See also 'How the Picture Reached the World' by Horst Faas and Marianne Fulton on digitaljournalist.org, and 'Remembering Vietnam' on vanityfair.com, 3 April 2015.

precision microscopes, he wondered about substituting the heavy and fragile glass plates he used for each photograph with a radically smaller negative, leading to a camera so small it could fit in his pocket. Barnack thought of using movie film; he had seen a similar idea at Zeiss using a negative of 18×24mm, but the images it produced were awful. And then he had one of those perfect moments: what if he turned the film on its side and doubled the width, so that it now measured 24×36mm? His first metal prototype camera was designed so that the film could be threaded through horizontally (unlike cine film in a movie camera). The results were astonishing. The tiny image withstood enlargement to the size of a postcard, and he had found the ideal aspect ratio of 2:3. The next part of the story was equally enchanting: the number of frames on his first rolls of film – 36, the industry standard – arose from the length of Barnack's outstretched arms, the maximum number he could manage in one unspooled strip. Not quite true, alas: his arms were longer than that, and the first spools of cine film could take 40 shots.

Barnack gave his camera a lens previously milled for microscopy and started taking photos of his children and the Wetzlar streets (tourists now come to snap from the same spot where he took a picture of a large timbered building that still stands today). But the most important early photos were taken in 1914 by Barnack's boss Ernst Leitz II, who took Barnack's second prototype on a trip to New York and on his return pronounced it worthy of 'keeping an eye on'. The camera's name was initially 'Liliput', and then 'Leca' for LEitz CAmera. Those who tried it called it revolutionary.

The war intervened, and the first commercial models only appeared in 1925. They were not an instant success; purists dismissed them as toys and struggled to grasp the novel concept of producing a big picture from a small negative (Leitz also made enlargement apparatus). But by the end of the 1920s the camera's worth had been re-evaluated, and early adopters praised its portability and ease of use. Political artists André Breton and Alexander Rodchenko immediately saw the potential of what they called a 'fixed explosive' – the dynamic freezing of motion in a world of upheaval. Documentary photographers could meet the huge demand from the flourishing news magazines by shooting the world from the hip. And in 1932 a prince of photography put his 'eye of the century' to the viewfinder, and the world changed yet again.

ii) 'I am Muybridge and this is a message from my wife'

Henri Cartier-Bresson immediately saw his Leica as a weapon. He had been big-game hunting in Africa and, using a vocabulary that has been part of the photographer's lexicon ever since (loading, shooting, capturing), compared the Leica to his gun. He particularly admired the instantaneity of his camera – the way the reflex of the shutter recalled the reflex of a rifle. His targets were often ordinary Parisians, and no one has ever taken a more inspirational portfolio of images (his only competitor in this field is Robert Frank, whose pictures for his 1958 book *The Americans* were also shot on a Leica). After the Second World War, much of which he spent as a prisoner of the Nazis, Cartier-Bresson adopted a less confrontational though no less exacting approach, something he would much later compare to the more graceful sport of archery.* He became the medium's first superstar, and by the time he co-founded the Magnum photo agency with Robert

---

* In 1958, Georges Braque had given him the inspirational book *Zen in the Art of Archery*, an early form of questing spiritual mindfulness first published in Germany many years before Robert M. Pirsig's *Zen and the Art of Motorcycle Maintenance*.

Capa and others in 1947, his work was already hanging in the Museum of Modern Art in New York.

In 1952, he also became linked to the most famous phrase in the history of photography, although the phrase wasn't actually his. The term 'decisive moment' appeared as an epigraph to Cartier-Bresson's introduction for a new collection entitled *Images à la sauvette* (roughly: *Images on the Run*). It was taken from the memoirs of a seventeenth-century Frenchman named Cardinal de Retz, and the full quote was 'There is nothing in this world that does not have a decisive moment.' 'A' decisive moment is somehow less definitive than 'the', but the change was made when the collection was published in America and the phrase was used as the main title. The term and notion was now famous, but what did it mean? In Cartier-Bresson's definition it refers to 'the simultaneous recognition, in a fraction of a second, of the significance of an event as well as of a precise organization of forms that gives that event its proper expression'.

The influential critic Clément Chéroux, writing in *Henri Cartier-Bresson: Here and Now*, explains that the phrase 'fertile moment' had already appeared in the preface to another collection of photographs that Cartier-Bresson had taken in India. He also suggests that the term has been overused to describe Cartier-Bresson's work. While many of his classic shots from the early 1930s are masterpieces of timing (the man jumping over water at Pont de l'Europe, say), only his reportage for Magnum in the late 1940s and '50s truly merits the description. It certainly doesn't suit his Surrealist, political or portrait work, and 'the majority of the late (contemplative) images could have been taken several seconds before or after the moment they were actually shot'.

And perhaps one man had found the true meaning of the phrase many years before. In the 1860s Edward Muybridge won early acclaim for his magnificent photographs of Yosemite, huge panoramas involving a precise assemblage of multiple glass plates. The vista was huge, and if anything flew or ran while the shutter was open it would appear as a blur or smudge. But then Muybridge found a way to quicken the shutter to such a degree that it seemed he was freezing time. Men would jump and cockatoos would fly and he would catch them in midair. A woman would pour water from a bucket and he'd capture a solid form before it hit the ground.

His most famous work began in the spring of 1872, when he was 42, precisely 100 years before Nick Ut opened his shutter on the terror of war. Edward Muybridge took a series of photos of a trotting horse named Occident, and the story of the shoot – photographed to settle the question of whether all four legs were off the ground at the same time (they were!) – is one of the most romantic treasures in art (there is no evidence that the question ever became the subject of a wager). Muybridge was tracking locomotion on the minutest scale, the impossible wonder of a mechanical eye perceiving what the human one could not. But the horse had almost been his undoing too.

These days, it's not just photographic historians who adore Muybridge, but neurobiologists too, albeit less for his pictures than for his rage and obsessions. His unique vision may have sprung from an artistic temperament born less from patience and skill than from a near-fatal accident. In June 1860, Muybridge, who was then a successful book-seller and bookbinder and had yet to pick up a camera, was due to take a steamer from San Francisco bound for Europe. But he missed his connection, and instead a month later he booked a passage on a stagecoach to Missouri, from where he hoped to take a train to New York and then travel on to Europe. But he had barely reached Texas when the horses bolted and crashed the stagecoach into a tree. At least one passenger died, while Muybridge was thrown out and suffered a serious head injury. Muybridge said he had little recollection of the accident, but during his recovery he noticed that his sense of taste and smell had both deteriorated, and that each of his eyes now detected a slightly different image, causing him to see double. He sought help first in New York and some months later in London, including a consultation with Sir William Gull, a physician to Queen Victoria, who, apart from advising his patient to get as much fresh air as possible, could offer little in the way of explanation or clinical diagnosis.

But modern brain specialists have a more exacting view of the events. In 2002, a psychology professor from the University of California, Berkeley, named Arthur P. Shimamura, published a report in the journal *History of Photography* entitled 'Muybridge in Motion, Travels in Art, Psychology and Neurobiology'. He presented an intriguing thesis: contemporary reports of his accident and its after-effects were consistent with damage to an anterior section of the frontal lobe known as the orbitofrontal cortex, an area of the brain concerned with creativity, inhibition and expression of emotions. According to Shimamura, evidence from a friend of Muybridge suggested that 'prior to his accident, Muybridge was a good businessman, genial and pleasant in nature; but after the accident he was irritable, eccentric, a risk-taker and subject to emotional outbursts'. This may have been both good and bad, leading to all sorts of further calamity, as we shall see, but also liberating his perceptive abilities. 'Shutting off one's orbitofrontal cortex – from time to time – may actually enhance one's creative expression.'

In July 2015 the *Journal of Neurosurgery* published an article by four clinicians at the Neurological Institute in Cleveland, Ohio, suggesting there may even have been a simple inspiration, conscious or not, for so much of Muybridge's work to come: 'Although he had no memories of the days preceding the accident or the event itself, he had a sense of time being stopped and suspended with his near-death experience. He was moving fast and suddenly time stopped.'

Beyond the obvious symptoms, there are two clues that all may not have been right with the man. The first is that he kept changing his name. He was born Edward Muggeridge in Kingston upon Thames, on the south-west fringe of London, in April 1830. He would switch to Muggridge and then Muygridge in the 1850s, before finally settling on Muybridge in the 1860s. Towards the end of his life he also changed his first name to Eadweard (although when he was photographing coffee production in Central America he also briefly became Eduardo Santiago).

The other notable thing about his personal life is that he killed a man. In 1872, at the age of 42, as his career in California was entering its first full bloom, Muybridge married his 21-year-old studio assistant Flora Shallcross Stone, and their first child, named Florado, arrived two years later. In October 1874 Muybridge discovered that he wasn't the father. To brighten the time when Muybridge was taking photographs out of town, Flora had occasionally stepped out with a man named Harry Larkyns, described subsequently in the newspapers as 'gay, dashing and handsome', which were rarely adjectives passers-by would have applied to her husband. The affair was betrayed by a photograph, possibly one of Muybridge's own. When, in October 1874, Muybridge visited the home of a midwife to settle a bill he turned over a photograph of what he thought was his child to find the inscription 'Little Harry'. Muybridge reached for his Smith & Wesson, travelled to the ranch where Larkyns was staying near Napa Valley and greeted him with the phrase 'I am Muybridge and this is a message from my wife.' He then shot him.

In the murder trial that followed, the jury brought home an unexpected verdict: not, as one might have anticipated, of guilty but insane, but of justifiable homicide. Muybridge was judged to be quite within his rights to kill someone who had made his wife pregnant, and so the photographer skipped out of the courtroom to continue his mission to freeze time. As the psychologist Arthur Shimamura observed, the others in the story fared less well: Flora became ill and died five months after the trial; Florado was shipped off to an orphanage; and Larkyns stayed dead.

In her exciting book about Muybridge, Rebecca Solnit takes the temperature of society at this time and finds it red hot. 'The experience of time was itself changing dramatically during Muybridge's seventy-four years, hardly ever more dramatically than in the 1870s. In that decade the newly invented telephone and phonograph were added to photography, telegraphy and the railroad as instruments for "annihilating time and space" . . . The modern world, the world we live in, began then, and Muybridge helped launch it.'*

Paradoxically, his most famous photographs enabled us to see familiar things for the first time. Published in 1887, his *Animal Locomotion* was the culmination of his work over 15 years, 11 volumes in all, with almost 20,000 images arranged on 781 large composite collotype prints. If his photographs weren't yet considered art they were instantly acclaimed as

* *River of Shadows: Eadweard Muybridge and the Technological Wild West* (Viking, 2003).

science: Muybridge demonstrated his work at several leading scientific institutions, including the Royal Academy and Royal Society in London, and the photos on show took the word 'animal' in its loosest form, for as well as pictures of horses, baboons, boars and elephants there were children running to their mothers, naked wrestlers, a man throwing a baseball and a woman pretending to smack a child.* After first using six cameras arranged in a horseshoe to take images of a subject from different angles, he was soon experimenting with a battery of 12 cameras lined up in a row, a wire triggering each shutter release as the subject trotted by. For most of his non-equine studies in *Animal Locomotion* – a woman climbing stairs carrying a water jug, or two women disrobing – he used cameras fired a fraction of a moment apart by an electrically preset clock.

The whole project was sponsored by the University of Pennsylvania, whose interest was sparked by the possibility of obtaining photographs for medical training – or, as one correspondent put it, to show 'the walk of diseased people, paralytics etc'.** The enterprise was also open to individual supporters, and those who subscribed early were offered a chance to deliver an animal of their choosing to be photographed at Muybridge's studio. It's unknown how many guest animals turned up, but the most commonly featured subject

---

* His achievements would find echoes not only in photography and film-making, but in many other realms of science and art: Edgar Degas, Marcel Duchamp, Francis Bacon, Sol LeWitt and Philip Glass have all acknowledged an artistic debt.
** Muybridge had fallen out with the sponsor of his first photos of equine locomotion, Leland Stanford, the former governor of California. (Stanford owned Occident and other horses photographed by Muybridge in the 1870s.) Stanford had made his money from the railroads, and when he wasn't racing horses he directed much of his wealth to philanthropic causes: part of Stanford University now stands on the site of the Palo Alto farm at which Muybridge conducted many of his horse studies. More far-sighted biographers of Muybridge have thus made a direct link between the pioneering technology of his photos and Silicon Valley.

in Muybridge's photographs is Muybridge himself, often naked, engaged in activities ranging from sitting down and sprinkling water to 'stooping for cup and drinking'. He has a lean body, a long pointed white beard and a sense of exhibitionism that viewers may feel extends beyond scientific exploration into rampant narcissism.

The photography historian Marta Braun has written that Muybridge's motion studies are not always what they appear to be. Occasionally the photos are presented out of sequence, and often they have been treated in some way – cropped, enlarged, and pieced together 'into deceptively cohesive patterns . . . *Animal Locomotion* is a project whose every element had been subject to manipulation of one kind or another.' In attempting to make or confirm a point, Muybridge has presented the viewer with a different image to the one seen by the camera, a benign fraud (and a certain suggestion, very early on, that if the camera doesn't lie, the photographer often will). Just as it purports to reveal a moment of true life, the darkroom instead offers distortion. He cropped and enlarged and edited in the tradition of all classic storytelling. If you are looking for the beginning of the fantastical and unreliable world that is American film-making – in fact *all* film-making – you will find it here.

Muybridge displayed his photos on an object he called the zoopraxiscope, a wooden box projecting an illuminated spinning glass plate. It was a revolving magic lantern able to trick the eye. Muybridge meticulously placed his motion studies sequentially on the plate (initially as painted silhouettes and line drawings), creating the impression of movement when the disc spun at speed. It was a primitive movie projector, and it made the world's head spin too. Muybridge referred to one of the earliest versions of his invention as 'a scientific toy', but it turned out to be rather more than that: his photographs dissected time, and then his machine reassembled it.* Muybridge also patented a new, quicker shutter system, and his ability to capture a fraction of a second in time would soon, for the price of a camera, be available to all. But a faster shutter speed could only help you so much: you still had to be there to click the button at the perfect moment, and you still had to be a talented soul to make art. This held true whether you were Muybridge in California, Cartier-Bresson in Paris or David Burnett on a highway not far from Saigon.

David Burnett was the man who didn't get the picture. He was working in Vietnam for *Time*, *Life* and the *New York Times*, and he was standing right by Nick Ut at about noon on 8 June 1972 when Kim Phúc and her family ran by. Unfortunately, he was one of the two photographers loading his film at the time. As he explained in the *Washington Post* magazine in 2012, on the 40th anniversary of the event, those born into the era of digital photography might find it hard to understand what operating a film camera was like, 'that there was, necessarily, a moment when your finite film would end at frame 36, and you would have to swap out the shot film for a fresh roll before being able to resume the hunt for a picture'.

The hunt for a picture – surely something Cartier-Bresson would have understood, as if the perfect photo was out there in the wilds somewhere, and you just had to find it. And in those other brief moments, when you were changing a film, Burnett knew that 'there was always the possibility of *the*

---

* Several pieces of Muybridge's equipment, as well as his scrapbooks and more than 150 of his *Animal Locomotion* prints, may be seen at a permanent exhibition near his birthplace at the Kingston Museum. He returned to England in the 1890s and died in 1904, and on his gravestone they got his name wrong: Maybridge.

picture taking place. You would try to anticipate what was happening in front of your eyes, and avoid being out of film at some key intersection of time and place . . . there are plenty of stories about those missed pictures.'

On that particular day and time, Burnett was changing film in one of his Leicas, which he remembers as 'an amazing camera with a reputation for being infamously difficult to load'. He saw the plane come in with the napalm, and then faint images of people running through the smoke. As he was still fumbling with his camera, he saw Nick Ut put his viewfinder to his eye. 'In one moment . . . he captured an image that would transcend politics and history and become emblematic of the horrors of war visited on the innocent. When a photograph is just right, it captures all those elements of time and emotion in an indelible way.' Not long afterwards, but too long afterwards, Burnett had reloaded his film and he remembers Ut and his driver taking the kids to the hospital. When he next met up with Ut at the AP office a couple of hours later he remembers Ut stepping out of the darkroom holding a still wet print of his picture.

When he reflects on that day now, Burnett's clearest memory is 'the sight, out of the corner of my eye, of Nick and another reporter beginning their run toward the oncoming children'. This was a new picture: Ut actually running *towards* the children. Burnett says he often thinks of that day and how unlikely it was that one picture from a relatively minor skirmish became one of the most important images from any war. 'For those of us who carry our cameras along the sidewalk of history for a living, it is comforting to know that even in today's digitally overloaded world, a single photograph, whether our own or someone else's, can still tell a story that rises above language, locale and time itself.'

Car plant circa 1930: a driver in Germany awaits his airbag.

Chapter Ten

The Day Shift

i) We Will Crush, Squash, Slaughter Yamaha!

A few years ago I decided to learn how to make a car. The Mini was approaching its fiftieth birthday, and I was in the middle of writing about its turbulent history when I realised I couldn't hope to understand the production process unless I became a part of it. So at 6.15 a.m. one Monday in November 2008, I drove to the BMW plant at Cowley, on the outskirts of Oxford, where the Mini is made, and entered the security gates with dread in my heart.

It was still dark, and it was my first day of basic training. There were two other men on my course, and both had some experience of making cars. I had no experience of making cars and could barely manage to add air to my tyres on a forecourt. I was told I would be thrown in at the deep end, and it would be physically exhausting, but I probably wouldn't have too much trouble mastering the actual procedure if I followed simple instructions. The most important of which were to a) take pride in my work, b) not slow down the production line, and c) not do anything wrong that might result in a court case. The worst thing would be to do something wrong and not tell anyone about it.

My training – which was not specifically designated as a test of my aptitude but clearly was – involved working on two of the car's most critical components. The first entailed bolting on the rear subframe to ensure that the wheels and rear brakes wouldn't suddenly surprise a driver one day by falling off into the road, and the second entailed securing the electrical connections for the airbag control box, which, if secured correctly, would prevent the driver and passenger flying through the windscreen in the event of a collision (and if not, wouldn't). Mike Colley, the vehicle assembly manager, began his instruction with the news that the plant contained a quiet room, situated very close to the training room, 'should you want to go and pray'. He explained the basic layout of the plant and then projected a slide on the screen behind him. 'These are some scrivets found left in a car.' (The picture showed some small secure fasteners, nominally a cross between a screw and a rivet but really more like a screw and a Rawlplug). 'OK, they wouldn't make a lot of noise; however, if you've just spent £20,000 on a brand-new vehicle, the first thing you're going to do is have a good look around it to see where everything goes and what sort of space you've got. If you lift up the boot and the little panel where the toolkit is, and you find a couple of scrivets there, you're not going to be best pleased.' I felt that scrivets would be the least of my problems, and I was sure that any purchaser of a car in which I had fitted the airbag control panel would feel the same.

Colley said that as with most production lines, the key elements were safety, efficiency, accuracy and production flow: a successful day was one in which everyone employed on the production line would deliver precisely what was required of them in precisely the time allotted. Every piece of welding and bolting and installation of, say, the window electrics, had to be delivered in the tiny window before the next bit of welding and bolting and installation passed to the worker waiting a few metres up the line. Everyone would have their own responsibilities, and if everyone lived up to the standards expected of them a car would roll off the production line every 68 seconds.

Unless someone pressed one of the stop buttons. An 'andon' button, named after the Japanese word for lantern, was situated on a pillar every ten or fifteen feet down the line. The button halted production and sent a siren to the manager's office indicating that someone wanted help. 'They will come down the line, see the light and say, "Andon! Andon!" and you will say, "Yes, I couldn't get that bolt on," or whatever.'

The problems with stopped time on a production line were obvious: a reduction in efficiency and income, and an increase in stress for those charged with keeping things moving. Ian Cummings, a process improvement manager, told me that the stress made him think that he had the hardest job he could imagine anyone doing. Even on a day when no one pressed the stop buttons, success relied 'on other people all coming to work at the right time and in the right frame of mind'. Sometimes Cummings wished that people could be more like machines; the problem with staff was that they introduced variability into the process. Absenteeism put a big spanner in the works, or rather didn't, and not everyone was punctual. A three-minute warning buzzer sounded at the start of every shift, after which the line would begin to roll. You were permitted to leave the plant to visit Tesco or Burger King on your lunch or dinner break, but if you weren't back on time, 'It's no good saying, "The queue was massive and I was starving", because the line will start without you and you will miss five or so cars.'

When the first Mini was sold in 1959, no one – not even its egomaniacal designer Alec Issigonis – would have dared suggest the car would last 50 years or become such a global success. No one used the word 'icon' outside the walls of a church. The twenty-first century Mini (strictly a MINI, to distinguish it from its predecessor the Mini) is a very different car to the one that became one of the great British symbols of the 1960s (it's now owned by BMW for a start), but even in its pumped-up, heftily priced modern state it is a product that is clearly doing something right; it was in tune with the times then, and a combination of skilful engineering and marketing ensured that it was in tune with the times now. On the day I turned up for training, 53 new cars really were coming off the production line every hour, an extraordinary thing for such a complex bit of machinery, not least because each car had a highly customised order sheet that had been drawn up by a purchaser in a showroom only about eight weeks before. About 800 cars were completed each weekday, and because of the immense choice of alloy wheels and wing mirrors and roof decals and a hundred other options, it could take a great many days before the build sheet of any two consecutive cars on the production line was identical. As a customer, there was only one option you couldn't choose: the option that someone like me wouldn't be given responsibility for the installation of your rear brakes.

A man named Richard Clay, the vehicle assembly manager, turned up to provide guidance on bolting on the rear subframe. This was lifted onto the car by robot, and it was our job to fit the lateral arms and the anti-roll bar. 'You have sixty-eight seconds to do your process.' The other two trainees sighed a little, as if they could do the task and still have time to go shopping. 'If any of these fixings were not secured correctly it would leave the car unfit to drive or render it immobile,' Clay said. 'This could lead to serious injury or loss of life and damage to corporate image. And these things could lead on to court cases. It's all bad things.'

Assembly involved the complex but highly regulated process of scanning and tooling known as IPSQ – International

Production System Quality. Every car has a programmable and traceable electronic history, with barcode scanning that checks every new stage in the build process. As the car progresses along the line, a system known as DC tooling checks that the fixings are correct in their torque measurements and signs it off for that part of the build. The strength of critical fixings is measured in newton metres – with about 150 newton metres required for the subframe but only perhaps 2 for an airbag crash sensor. 'Don't let go of the trigger too early,' Richard Clay said. 'Put this bit over the roll bar, locate the stabilisers, sit the bolt here on the lower arm – it's easier if you hold it into your body, make sure it bites. And then just the same on the other side.'

The first job we were required to do was to scan a vehicle's personal identification number (VIN) on or below the bonnet. At the end of the line, all the processes are stored in the computer, and so if something is wrong they know what to fix in the rework areas. In common with most factory production systems, Mini operates on the principle that everything should be 'right first time'. There was one further piece of advice: 'Please do not use the scanners as hammers. They cost £400 each and £150 for the batteries. If you're on a process that needs something pushed in, please ask for a little mallet that will be provided to you.'

After the rear subframe work we moved to the other end of the room where there was a bench with electrical connections – the airbag sensors.

'We will time you on this,' Clay said, 'but it's not a question of pass or fail. It's to show you that the task has to be performed at a certain speed on the line and you can't just clown around. A non-connected connector can cause a rework of half a day just to find the loose connection, and the whole car has got to be stripped and everything taken out. So if you can't make your connection properly at the start, make sure you tell somebody. And please keep all the lubricants away from the electrics – they do not mix.'

As soon as we start I become aware that the others are much, much faster than me. Some things just won't go in, or need special techniques I don't have. Clay says things to the other people like 'Good' and 'Oh, that's good'. He says nothing to me. On the tape recording of my efforts I can just hear myself above the machine noise, 'I'm having trouble with this one!'

Rather than one minute and eight seconds it takes me just over eight minutes. 'Eight minutes!' Clay says. 'Not the worst. It once took a guy fourteen minutes.' That guy was not currently working at the plant. Of the 2,400 'associates' who were, I guessed that all of them were faster than me at the things that mattered here. After lunch I try it again. The tips of my fingers are sore and chafing. I knock it down to just over five minutes. The cars of the future are being held up all the way down the line.

Much of what the British managers were teaching me at Cowley had been learnt from the Germans running BMW production lines in Munich, and much of what the Germans in Munich had learnt came from the Japanese at Toyota City. When it came to timing at work, the Japanese were the envy of the world.

The principle of Right First Time was just one component of a much broader principle of production known as Just-in-Time (JiT). Originating at Toyota in the 1960s, JiT was as much a karmic philosophy as a practical one: in utilising this revolutionary production system, the worker and the factory became almost indistinguishable; the product that resulted – be it a widget or an ocean liner – resulted from the quest for ideal industrial harmony. The concept relied upon the elimination of waste and excess stock, a streamlined logistical supply chain, a highly flexible and motivated workforce, self-contained but interlinked production units, and every possible attempt to eradicate the possibility of mistakes. Clearly, not all of these involved time in terms of minutes and hours, but the aim was to combine all these elements within the most symphonically well-proportioned timeframe to create a plant working at full efficiency, capacity and profitability. The key was the elimination of waiting and a frictionless flow. The goal, as at the Mini plant, was to maximise profit by eliminating errors and unpredictability; in effect, this entailed making humans interact as smoothly as oiled cogs. Machines do not return late from Burger King, and they do not push the andon button, and only when programmed to do so would they use scanners as hammers.

JiT achieved its ultimate and most visible level of 'leanness' at Toyota in the 1980s, and although there is evidence of the practice at Japanese shipyards and other factories before this, it was the car manufacturer's methods that would be most influential throughout the West in the last three decades of the century (not least at that bastion of automation, Ford).

A further innovation at Toyota had a similarly influential effect. Just-in-Time strategies on the factory floor had enabled the company to produce cars many times faster in the late 1970s than was possible a decade before, but the customer was only benefitting marginally from the increase. The sales division at Toyota had not made a comparable improvement in leanness, and it could still take almost a month for orders to be registered, financed, transmitted to the factory and delivered. Management at the company realised something that seems obvious to us today: patience was not a virtue that many consumers held dear. In 1982, when Toyota combined its manufacturing and sales divisions, it established a far more cohesive computer system that streamlined the old method of customer orders being conducted in batches, a method that bottlenecked vital information and wasted much time. Analysing the results of this move a few years later in the *Harvard Business Review*, George Stalk, Jr, the senior vice-president of the Boston Consulting Group, observed that Toyota had expected to cut the sales and distribution cycle time in half: from four to six weeks to just two to three weeks across Japan. But by 1987 the cycle had shrunk to eight days, including the time required to make the car. 'The results were predictable,' Stalk writes. 'Shorter sales forecasts, lower costs, happier customers.'*

But Just-in-Time is only one example of how the Japanese manipulated the concept of industrial time and gained a global advantage before the rest of the world caught up by copying it. For another glimpse we should leave the car industry for a moment and look at the lessons learned in the motorcycle industry. The battle between the Honda and Yamaha motorcycle divisions in the early 1980s was so fierce, and the outcome of the battle so decisive, that it became an industry fable. It even had a shorthand moniker: the H–Y War.

The conflict began in 1981, with Yamaha building a new factory that it claimed would make it the biggest motorbike company in the world. Honda, which currently held that position, predictably did not react kindly to the claim and did several things to ensure it wouldn't happen. It cut its prices, ramped up its marketing budget and galvanised its workers around a new war cry: '*Yamaha wo tsubusu!*', which translated as 'We will crush, squash, slaughter Yamaha!' At the root of this proposed devastation lay an entirely new approach: after sweeping structural changes, Honda was able to dramatically increase the speed at which it introduced new models and turned around its stock.

* 'Time – The Next Source of Competitive Advantage', by George Stalk, Jr, *Harvard Business Review*, July 1988.

Within the space of 18 months it introduced or replaced 113 models, improving its manufacturing time by 80 per cent. In the same period Yamaha managed only 37 model changes. Some of the changes to Honda's new machines were cosmetic, but there were also many engine and other technical improvements, and the intent was clear: we have everything any biker could ever need, and we will react faster than any of our competitors to changes in new technology and fashion. The fear of obsolescence that concerns the modern consumer was thus allayed, and Honda not only succeeded in seeing off its immediate competition, but also its other rivals Suzuki and Kawasaki. (In a humiliating climb-down, Yamaha's president announced, 'We want to end the H–Y War. It is our fault. Of course there will be competition in the future but it will be based on a mutual recognition of our respective positions.')

Other companies learnt from the examples of both Honda and Toyota. Matsushita cut the manufacturing time of washing machines from 360 hours to 2; companies making white goods in the US managed comparable improvements. 'For any company in any industry, the key is not to get stuck with a single simple notion of its source of advantage,' Stalk wrote in the *Harvard Business Review*. 'The best competitors, the most successful ones, know how to keep moving and always stay on the cutting edge. Today, time is on the cutting edge. The ways leading companies manage time – in production, in new product development and introduction, in sales and distribution – represent the most powerful new sources of competitive advantage.'*

---

* This time-based innovation has ensured that Japanese and other Far Eastern manufacturing companies continue to produce televisions and products from plastic injection moulds in one-third of the time required in the US, and time has become a more critical measurement than the traditional financial indicators of success. The lead in technical innovation and design may have swung from Japan to the digital industries of Silicon Valley, but the most efficient mass manufacture – from the latest phones to the most lavish books – is commandeered by plants in Asia.

At the Mini plant at Cowley, the influence of Honda and Toyota was everywhere. All the Just-in-Time advances in response times and inventory reductions and streamlined factory layout were evident, as was the ever-increasing variety of models and customisable options. A huge investment in plant capacity and expertise in 2000 meant that production increased from 42,395 cars in 2001 to 160,037 in 2002, and it would keep growing to meet demand from – of all places – Japan. The consumer, increasingly keen to buy better faster, benefitted from greater choice and keener delivery times, and BMW, Mini and the staff on the outskirts of Oxford were the beneficiaries in terms of increased orders, output and profit.

But a runaway success will quickly become a runaway disaster without a decent set of brakes. One reason the Mini was such a hit was because owners trusted the manufacturing as much as they loved the marketing, and the managers trusted the staff not to let the manufacturing slip. And thus was I cruelly exposed. Because of my very poor speeds on the electrical connections for the airbag control box, the people in charge of the assembly line thought it best that I wasn't let loose on real moving cars. There were customers all over the world waiting anxiously for their Minis, and they didn't want the production slowed by even five minutes, or the possibility of things wired up in a way that, somewhere down the line, could lead to court cases.

ii) The Boss from Hell

Before the joke went out of fashion, people in business were fond of describing a management consultant as someone who borrowed your watch to tell you the time. And once it was true.

A century ago, the pioneer of management consultancy, a man named Fredrick Winslow Taylor, hit upon a way to jump-start industrial production in the United States by going into an underperforming factory with a stopwatch and timing what he saw. Mostly what he saw was a combination of indolence and inefficiency, and his solutions were straightforward and exacting. He calculated that the fastest time a specific task could be performed was usually much faster than the time it *was* being performed. He called the slack working practice 'soldiering', and informed factory owners that if their business was to flourish, all would do well to adopt his new and precisely timed practices. Inevitably, his recommendations did not endear him to workers or their unions; from nowhere, they suddenly appeared to have a new boss from hell. Taylor talked of the pride a fully occupied worker would take in the newly optimised working day, while his detractors accused him of caring little for the physical or psychological effects of his new methods. But his ideas took hold, particularly when factory owners saw their production double and profits multiply within a couple of years.*

Taylor's theories were shaped at the Midvale Steel Works near his birthplace in Philadelphia. Rising through the ranks between 1878 and 1890, Taylor managed to meet the huge demand from the railroad and munitions factories by boosting efficiency and eliminating waste; he almost trebled output.

---

* The concept of equating time with money was something that would have been familiar in Rome 2,000 years ago. The phrase 'Time is Money' was popularised by Benjamin Franklin in *Advice to a Young Tradesman, Written by an Old One* (1748, collected among his memoirs). A few years later he offered a further explanation, recalling his days as a printer in London in the 1720s. 'He that is prodigal of his Hours, is, in effect, a Squanderer of Money. I remember a notable Woman, who was fully sensible of the intrinsic Value of Time. Her Husband was a Shoemaker, and an excellent Craftsman, but never minded how the Minutes passed. In vain did she inculcate to him, That Time is Money . . .'

He achieved similar success at a paper mill and another steel works, and added to his family wealth with a new steel-cutting technique he pioneered with his associate Maunsel White. In the words of his biographer Robert Kanigel, the people he worked with saw 'the world speed up before their eyes'.

Taylor would never use the words 'human', 'cog' and 'machine' in the same sentence. He initially called his principles 'task management', later adopting the title 'scientific management'. But as his methods spread rapidly through American industry and then to the far reaches of the world, most people just settled for 'Taylorism'. His defining manifesto was published in New York in 1911, a grandstanding hustings-style appeal to make the nation great again. The pamphlet was accompanied by an illustration showing a hand grasping a stopwatch – a persuasive notion of grand destiny underpinned by empirical science.*

His monograph – and we should remember that it was written more than a century ago – opened with an assertion that may strike today's reader as familiar: 'We can see our forests vanishing, our water-powers going to waste, our soil being carried by floods into the sea; and the end of our coal and our iron is in sight.' But the biggest waste was rooted in human inefficiency. This, in Taylor's estimation, was a blunder that could only be corrected by great imagination and scientific training. 'In the past the man has been first; in the future the system must be first,' he claimed, arguing that 'the great men' once thought essential for the future of all prosperous

---

* Conserving national resources was a sensible wish; it became a prescient necessity when the US entered the war six years later. But the desire to make the country great again may have appeared a tired political slogan even then. The belief of a better past is clearly a compelling one, but whether the past was better in the days of Taylor and Roosevelt in 1911 or in the mind of Donald Trump in 2016 is difficult to say.

industry could now be superseded by ordinary men schooled in modern methods.

By modern methods Taylor meant his own. 'Among the various methods and implements used in each element of each trade there is always one method and one implement which is quicker and better than any of the rest,' he wrote. 'And this one best method and best implement can only be discovered or developed through a scientific study and analysis of all of the methods and implements in use, together with accurate, minute, motion and time study. This involves the gradual substitution of science for rule of thumb throughout the mechanic arts.'

His 'science' was observational and data-driven. Workers would be studied in situ performing their daily tasks, and Taylor would go around with his stopwatch marking the smallest of details: how long it took to 'set tire on machine ready to turn . . . Rough face front edge . . . Finish face front edge . . . Rough bore front . . . Finish bore front.' He was fascinated with the ideal time it would take to fully load a shovel, and precisely how much that shovel should carry for optimal efficiency; when the amount was known, he ordered new shovels just for the task. No one had measured these kind of tasks in such detail before, or given such a high-handed purpose to doing so. After the temporal breakdown, each machinist would be given an instruction sheet and management guidance on how best to accomplish the task using as little 'foot-pound' as possible.* Each worker was then

---

* The 'foot-pound' measurement was a rough gauge of expended energy, as applicable to hands as to feet; at one stage it was called 'human horsepower'. Taylor's work on time would soon be extended by Frank and Lillian Gilbreth, whose application of psychological and spatial work methods resulted in the more refined 'time and motion' studies of the workplace. Broadly speaking, the Gilbreths introduced a more human element into the study of labour management, more concerned with the holistic potential of human capital (rather than just output), and thus paving the way for more modern forms of personnel management and 'human resources'. They

rewarded with a slightly higher wage if the tasks were performed satisfactorily within Taylor's new guidelines. In a crude sense it was the start of the methods we have seen in post-war Japan; 'Just-in-Time' was Taylorism mechanised, supersized and rehumanised.

How original was Taylor's focus on time in the workplace? It was certainly novel in its rigour and rhetoric, but it contained several elements that those schooled in English factories would have recognised from a century before. As early as 1832 Charles Babbage published *On the Economy of Machinery and Manufactures*, a work that suggested how the best placement and use of spinning and weaving looms may yield the greatest results, and also how a division of the workforce should separate unskilled manual labour from those with greater ability, and pay them accordingly. Babbage, best remembered today as the father of programmable computing, acknowledged that he was merely advancing the earlier thinking of the Italian political economist Melchiorre Gioia, and both of them were digesting the eighteenth-century free-market manifestos of Adam Smith. But it was the detail in Taylor's work that set him apart, and his ruthless polemic.*

Taylor diagnosed something that his predecessors had not: a disease of national laziness. He claimed that American and English sportsmen were the best in the world, eagerly straining every sinew for victory. And then they went to work

---

also applied their time and motion methods to their family of twelve children, as detailed in their biographical novel *Cheaper by the Dozen*.

* E.P. Thompson's famous essay 'Time, Work-Discipline and Industrial Capitalism' (*Past and Present*, 1967) contains a fascinating survey of the distribution and use of clocks and other timing mechanisms in the workplace. He suggests that a surprising number of labourers in industrial England at the start of the nineteenth century owned pocket watches, perhaps their most valuable and prized possession. But these were often banned from cotton mills and other factories. Rather than workers controlling their output by their own time, it was time itself that was the master; owners would put the clocks back in the evening to artificially lengthen the working day.

and shirked. His definition of 'soldiering' had two branches: the natural and the systematic. The first was symptomatic of the human condition, 'the natural instinct and tendency of men to take it easy'. The second was institutional, a belief that working faster than your fellow worker was disloyal and disruptive, favouring the management over one's own class; there was a feeling too that working faster would ultimately lead to less employment.* In 1903, in a paper entitled 'Shop Management', Taylor gave the example of a man who lived his life at two different speeds.

> While going and coming from work [he] would walk at a speed of from three to four miles per hour, and not infrequently trot home after a day's work. On arriving at his work he would immediately slow down to a speed of about one mile an hour. When, for example, wheeling a loaded wheelbarrow, he would go at a good fast pace even up hill in order to be as short a time as possible under load, and immediately on the return walk slow down to a mile an hour, improving every opportunity for delay short of actually sitting down. In order to be sure not to do more than his lazy neighbor, he would actually tire himself in his effort to go slow.

Ultimately the key to efficiency lay not in the strict enforcement of new rules, but in education and coercion. Antagonism between management and worker should be replaced by an understanding of the virtuous circle: increased production would lead to a lower price for a product, and thus greater sales, more profits, higher wages, and ultimate expansion and greater employment. That this was not already self-evident at the beginning of the twentieth century, Taylor thought astonishing. 'There is no question that, throughout

---

* Taylor suggested that 'soldiering' in the United States translated as 'hanging it out' in England and 'ca canae' in Scotland.

the industrial world, a large part of the organization of employers, as well as employee, is for war rather than for peace, and that perhaps the majority on either side do not believe that it is possible so to arrange their mutual relations that their interests become identical.'

War and soldiering of a different sort would soon under-line the need for maximum production in a way Taylor's tracts never could, although his death in 1915 robbed him of the satisfaction of witnessing it. In the century that followed, Taylor's reputation has risen and fallen. In 1918, the American Academy of Arts and Sciences acclaimed him as 'the legit-imate successor of James Watt', suggesting that his work would 'equally transform society'. Others have regarded his methods as suffocatingly hierarchical; the layered application of additional supervisors within a new management structure was just the thing that monolithic companies would later attempt to shed as the century reached its close.

Despite his stated hope for harmony, Taylorism led to much workforce discontent; staff turnover at the factories employing his methods increased substantially, and railroads and steel mills ground to a halt in protest. And by all accounts Taylor was not a pleasant man to do business with, displaying many of the traits – bullishness, self-aggrandisement, profanity – he claimed that management should avoid. Justifying his exacting division of labour, he once commented that a man who was 'physically able to handle pig-iron and is sufficiently phlegmatic and stupid to choose this for his occupation is rarely able to comprehend the science of handling pig-iron'.

Taylor's 'science' has long been ripe for parody, although the work most commonly held up as the great satire of inhumane industry, Charlie Chaplin's *Modern Times* (1936), is as much an attack on the Ford-style assembly line as it is on Taylor's management techniques. Chaplin plays a bolt-tightener making an unspecified product for the 'Electro

Steel Corp'. At the very start of the film (after the credits presented over the face of a large clock), a scene of herded sheep merges with a crowd of workers exiting a subway station, and the suggestion of 'lambs to the slaughter' is clear. Chaplin is billed simply as 'A Factory Worker'. The automated meal he's fed while strapped to a chair consists of metal nuts from malfunctioning parts. His manicured boss twice issues instructions to make his conveyor belt go faster.*

Henry Ford always maintained that Taylorism and Fordism had practically nothing to do with each other, and this was almost true; Ford drew more influence from another successful branch of American industry, the abattoir. (The car production line only started rolling after Ford moved to new premises in Detroit in 1913, which was around 70 years after one of the earliest conveyor-style assembly lines started at the works of Richard Garrett & Sons, a company making portable steam engines in England in the 1840s.) But there were a couple of similarities between Taylor and Ford: both wished to restore pride and prosperity to American manufacturing, and both threatened to legitimise – through science and the appetites of the market – the dominance of the machine (be it the machine of management or the machine of steel) over the power of the individual.

Taylor's greatest critics cite this as Taylor's greatest ill. His considerations of time and profit greatly changed the way many large industries were geared through the middle of the century (not least in the booming manufacture of stop-watches), but the rigidity of the system had detrimental effects

---

* Although Chaplin claimed that *Modern Times* was a meditation on the Great Depression and the soullessness of the jobs that survived it (the factory sequence only occupies the first quarter of the film), the fact that many viewers made a link with Ford was to be expected. Chaplin visited Henry Ford and his son Edsel at their Highland Park site in Detroit in 1923, and there is a photograph of them standing in front of a large machine that would not have been out of place in the movie.

on prosperity and industrial relations in the longer term. It was one of the reasons why Japan forged ahead after the war, and why the Japanese system was widely adopted elsewhere in the world in the 1980s.

If he is remembered at all, Frederick Winslow Taylor is recalled primarily as a pioneering and influential maverick. His biographer Robert Kanigel writes that he enjoyed a far more varied and aesthetic life than the one he proposed for the majority of his workers. He always stayed in the best hotels, drew large royalties from his innovations in steel cutting, and worked when it suited him. Often he seemed not to understand the quantity of negative disruption his schemes left in their trail. But there is something else he bestowed beyond just a coercive top-heavy management theory and strict bean-counting. 'Taylor bequeathed a clockwork world of tasks timed to the hundredth of the minute,' Kanigel wrote in 1997. 'He helped instil in us the fierce, unholy obsession with time, order, productivity and efficiency that marks our age. Foreign visitors to America often remark on the rushed, breathless quality of our lives. Taylor – whose life, from 1856 to 1917, almost exactly coincided with the [American] Industrial Revolution at its height – helped make us that way.' Kanigel notes that when John Sculley, one-time chairman of Apple, delivered his address at an economic conference organised by President-elect Bill Clinton in Little Rock in 1994, Taylorism was specifically mentioned as a system from which the modern world should be liberated.

In its place, a new shackle. Our digital world would have astonished Taylor, but by the time modern business came to be controlled by computers he would have been shocked by so much else as well. He could not have foreseen the rise of

Asia, nor the ideal of the eight-hour day, nor indeed the place of women in the workforce. But then again, nothing dates as fast as our perception of the future. In 1930, the economist John Maynard Keynes predicted that in a century we would work only 15 hours a week and wouldn't know what to do with ourselves the rest of the time.* Certainly we wouldn't need our professional time-management books or advice on how to reclaim 18 extra 'me minutes' from every day. Instead, we would spend all our time at the movies and be afflicted with something known as 'the problem of leisure'. And how, I wonder, is that particular problem working out for you at the moment?

---

* One of Keynes's other predictions is, however, proving difficult to dispute. 'In the long run,' he said, 'we are all dead'.

Buzz Aldrin and his Omega: still lost in space.

Chapter Eleven

Horology Part Two: How to Sell the Time

i) Vasco da Gama Special Edition

A Timex arrives in the post. Four days earlier I had seen it advertised in a magazine, and I justified my purchase with the thought that if I buy this model for £59.99 I won't then be tempted by one of the other, and frankly ridiculous, watches advertised on the other pages of the magazine, almost all of which cost thousands of pounds more. It's a Timex Expedition Scout, made in the USA, chunky and wide at 40mm, a size that's all the rage at the moment, a thick beige nylon strap that looks like canvas, and a design that owes much to the military. It's not a complex thing: a quartz analogue movement, only one old-fashioned time-setting crown and no ugly stopwatch buttons or moon-phase nonsense, no see-through crystal backing that lets you glimpse the movement (probably because on this Timex all you'd really see is a battery), a second hand that purposely jolts with each second rather than skimming over the face, a brass case made to resemble polished steel, no jewels whatsoever, a small date indicator that must be corrected at the end of every February, water resistance to 50 metres, Arabic numerals, buckle clasp, a trademarked Indiglo feature that lets you press the crown and see the whole watch illuminated in aquamarine, important for night glances and dangerous missions. But I do not perform dangerous missions; I do not need the deep-water resistance either, or the bizarrely loud noise from the movement that means the watch has to be put in a drawer overnight to dull the sound, thus rendering the Indiglo feature unusable. So why did I buy this watch? More significantly, why does anyone living in the twenty-first century ever need to buy another watch of any sort ever again?

These are not the sort of questions to trouble the watch industry or its marketing departments. Indeed, the watch industry's busy marketing departments are the *answer* to the questions. I bought a watch, and so will millions of others, purely because of marketing: we are sold the need to keep and display time at every turn, and the more we don't need to buy a watch, the more pervasive the sell. Readers of high-end magazines will be familiar with a process, a nego-tiation, which involves turning over forests of paper before reaching the contents page. Open the *New York Times* and the paper appears to be ticking. Along with a bit of perfumery, jewellery and cars, the selling of watches is keeping print journalism alive.

In the first few pages of a recent *Vanity Fair*, in order:

1. '"Tradition" is too conventional for the work we under-take. We sculpt, paint and explore. But sculptors, painters and explorers we are not. There is no word for what we do. There is only a way. The Rolex Way.'

2. 'The Vallée de Joux. For millennia a harsh, unyielding environment; and since 1875 the home of Audemars Piguet, in the village of Le Brassus. The early watch-makers were shaped here, in awe of the force of nature yet driven to master its mysteries through the complex mechanics of their craft.'
   (The text appears on a manipulated photo of a dark forest illuminated by a full moon.)

3. 'In homage to the European explorer and his need for utmost precision, Montblanc pays special tribute with the Montblanc Heritage Chronométrie Quantième Complet Vasco da Gama Special Edition featuring a full calendar and a blue lacquered constellation around the moon phase, which shows the exact same night sky above the Cape of Good Hope as Vasco da Gama observed it in 1497 on his first journey to India. Visit and shop at Montblanc.com.'

(Accompanied by photo of man with a shoulder bag about to get onto a helicopter.)

These advertisements are designed to snare the general reader. The advertisements for those already ensnared – the horological connoisseur, those who already have many watches and are looking for something else to add to the glistening pile – go far deeper. They have to: only a wartime spiv would consider wearing more than one watch at a time, and so the others languish in a case or vault or winding machine, redundant in all but sparkle and investment potential. Besides, having more than one watch on the go simultaneously is unnerving: one watch provides us with the confidence that we know the time accurately; two watches, each showing a slightly different time, surely shatters this illusion. And then there's the cost: spending tens of thousands of pounds on an item that was once essential but is now redundant requires, one would imagine, a fair bit of persuasion. And so these advertisements must appeal to a different side of our nature, and they do this by becoming plainly absurd and overreaching. I once attended a watchmakers' convention, and I provided my email address on the registration document, so of course I continue to receive emails from many exhibitors selling their newest wares. I always open them with delight:

Dear Simon GARFIELD

Franc Vila is pleased to present you the FV EVOS 18 Cobra Suspended Skeleton in texalium. Please find enclosed the PR kit and discover this new timepiece.
Best regards,
Ophélie

I couldn't wait to open the attachment, not least to find out more about texalium, a substance so new that it didn't yet have an entry on Wikipedia. 'Oh time, suspend your flight,' the PR kit began; this is for me, I thought. 'Taken from the famous poem by French writer Alphonse de Lamartine, these words wonderfully sum up the new Cobra with its suspended skeleton movement . . . In order to appreciate the inner mechanical workings, the timepiece has eliminated the dial and replaced it with the glass for a better view of the movement. When our regard stops at the skeleton movement, it is like magic. Time becomes suspended as if by enchantment.'*

Or perhaps you prefer the Harry Winston Opus 3, a 'symphony' designed by Vianney Halter, just 14 when he joined the Watchmaking School of Paris in 1977, a digital piece inspired by a calculator. It took two years just to construct the prototype, with 250 components, including 10 stacked and overlapping discs, 47 numerals rotating on their axes at different speeds, displaying the hours, minutes, seconds and date through six different windows or 'portholes', two rows of three, a blue number displaying the hours in the upper windows on the left and right, black for the digital minute in the lower windows also on the left and right, a red number

---

* The Cobra, released in July 2015 and limited to 88 watches, is 57mm in width, which is enormous, and reflects the trend for increasingly muscled-up medallions. Its maker Franc Vila is Spanish and self-taught, and, according to Ophélie, 'leaves nothing to chance'.

for the date in the centre column read vertically. A masterpiece of timekeeping, but also ugly and cumbersome and obviously unnecessary, in an edition of 25. Price on request. (About one million pounds.)

I also received an email from a French atelier, Louis Moinet, established 1806, and inventor of the chronograph (or stopwatch). LM's new watch was also an old watch, boasting a dial made from fossilised dinosaur bone. This Jurassic Watch, all mod cons inside, was between 145 and 200 million years old on the outside. The dinosaur in question was discovered in North America and has been authenticated by a dinosaur museum in Switzerland. It's a diplodocus, one of those with a long neck and tail, and also a herbivore, which would please the horological vegetarians.

This was another reason for buying a watch: the ability to wear something historic. Modern marketing does well when attached to narrative storytelling. These days, even eggs in supermarkets have a story to them – where they were hatched, the proud heritage of the chicken. In horology, the modern masters of this narrative are the owners of a company called Bremont, based in Henley-on-Thames, Oxfordshire, England. Bremont has made a name for itself by including tiny pieces of historic objects within its timepieces and then advertising the shit out of them with a narrative description worthy of Robert Harris.

Formed in 2002 by two Englishmen (Nick and Giles English), the company has its roots in beautifully crafted aviation pieces, but it adores a bit of derring-do too. So for its Codebreaker chronograph of 2013 it featured three elements of the Bletchley Park story in one model: the crown held a bit of pinewood from Hut 6 (which concentrated on cracking Enigma machine ciphers). The case, in either stainless steel or rose gold, featured a section of a Bletchley Park computer punch card on its side. And the back of the case incorporated a thin slice of a rotor from an original German Enigma machine. Starting at around £12,000.

Reflecting an earlier period of British ingenuity, another watch features a tiny section of timber and copper that fought the Battle of Trafalgar in 1805 (the English brothers pounced on Nelson's HMS *Victory* during routine maintenance and did a deal with the owners). And then there is the Bremont watch incorporating a bit of stuff that changed our lives – the first heavier-than-air powered flight by the Wright brothers on 17 December 1903. Orville and Wilbur flew four times in one day near Kitty Hawk, North Carolina, and one may have assumed that their plane, the *Wright Flyer*, would soon become one of those untouchable historical objects from which no part could ever be sold or recycled, like the HMS *Victory* or Hut 6 at Bletchley. But no. Until 1948, the *Wright Flyer* was on display at London's Science Museum, and it now resides in the Smithsonian's National Air and Space Museum in Washington DC.* But sometime between the first flight and the first public display in 1916, the brothers removed the muslin covering the spruce wings and replaced it with other, fresher, cleaner material. Bremont bought the original muslin from the Wright brothers' family, and now here it is on the back of the Bremont Wright Flyer Limited Edition, a tiny speck of woven fabric under glass. They are very beautiful objects, grand history on one's wrist, and, writing as a Timex owner, I would actually like one of those watches. But not, perhaps, for £29,500.

---

* The plane spent far more time in transit in crates on trucks and ships than it ever did in the air, a battle for its display comparable to that being waged over the Elgin Marbles. It spent the first 13 years after its flight crated up in a shed in Dayton, Ohio, then went to a brief airing at the Massachusetts Institute of Technology in 1916, then went on holiday for a few weeks in 1917–19 to various expositions and engineering shows, and all the while it was the subject of dispute between Orville Wright and the Smithsonian about whether the plane was actually the first to fly.

And then there is heritage, advertising's guilt card. Centuries of craftsmen have ruined their eyes making these objects for you, so surely you, a person of taste, are not going to abandon this fine tradition now by buying something from the Argos catalogue. We have been making these priceless timepieces here in a tiny workshop in Berne since before the moon began, so surely it's time you added one to your collection. And then there is Breguet, or '*Breguet depuis 1775*', where the quotes in its lush, *café-crème*-coloured advertisements trade off its literary connections. 'A dandy on the boulevards . . . strolling at leisure until his Breguet, ever vigilant, reminds him it is midday.' (Alexander Pushkin, *Eugene Onegin*, 1829.) Or: 'He drew out the most delicious watch Breguet had ever made. Fancy, it is eleven o'clock, I was up early.' (Honoré de Balzac, *Eugénie Grandet*, 1833.) These days we'd call it product placement: 'A fine gold chain hung from the pocket of his waistcoat, where a flat watch could just be seen. He toyed with the "ratchet" key which Breguet had just invented.' (Honoré de Balzac, *La Rabouilleuse*, 1842.) In quoting the masters (there are other ads in the series: Stendhal, Thackeray, Dumas, Hugo), and listing its most famous customers (Marie-Antoinette, Napoleon Bonaparte, Churchill), the brand tempts us by association: a timeline of the distinguished to which we may add our notch, given the dosh.

ii) Welcome to Baselworld

These days, very few watch advertisements feel the need to address the issue of timekeeping, or any of the other topics that would have occupied the thoughts of our grandparents, such as reliability or the length between service intervals. Instead, the advertisements tell principally of wonder and adventure, often in the form of humankind against the elements or humankind achieving ultimate goals – a watch to wear when competing in the America's Cup, a timepiece to wear when you've won seven Grand Slams. In the promotional world of poetic astronomy and harsh, unyielding environments, accuracy is a given, and the accuracy is far beyond what anyone may require on their wrist. In fact, no one needs a watch to tell the time at all these days, for we may tell the time in a hundred other trusted ways. What began at the church and town hall, and then moved to the factories and railways, has now, by act of transistor, atomic physics and satellite, been made infallible and omnipresent. The world – the computing world, the navigational world, the money world, the entire industrial world and our exploration of the universe beyond – all of it depends on accurate timekeeping, but none of it depends on anyone looking at their watch. And yet we do this still with conditioned regularity, to the point where the world's largest tech company decided recently that it had to make a timepiece of its own. And to the point where, when the world's most renowned makers of timepieces gather in Basel each year to launch their fabulous new wares at an airport-size trade fair called Baselworld, they do so in an atmosphere of unfettered jubilation and wealth, and in the knowledge that, despite selling us something we already have and therefore don't need, it is also something we will happily buy for ever more. Why? Because some men want jangly stuff to define their status, and have done since the time of Henry VIII. Suited and moneyed men don't get away with wearing much jewellery these days, not least when they are posing up mountain and beneath lake, so a watch solves all desires and expectations. Early in 2015, Sebastian Vivas, the man who runs the museum at Audemars Piguet, admitted that he wasn't afraid of the Apple Watch, but what really scared him was the day when men accepted they could wear gemstones 'without a time-keeping pretext'.

As with music and fashion, the design of a watch will always be subject to the vagaries of taste: one decade we covet heavy chronographs, the next it is superfine elegance. But the surprise is that, even in the digital age, watches themselves have proved to be – or are sold as – perennial tools of necessity. But still, why the watch? Surely there's an answer beyond salesmanship and consumerism and showing off: 'My salary and bonus affords me this absurd piece of jewellery, and I believe the adverts when they tell me this is a way of expressing my unique personality and displaying my appreciation of the finer things.' The science historian James Gleick has observed that human anatomy meets data processing only twice – in the brain and in the wristwatch. He observed this in 1995, writing that watches had recently expanded their ability – albeit often in a clunky box-like form – to carry altimeters, depth finders and compasses, and 'announce your appointments . . . monitor your pulse and blood pressure . . . store phone numbers . . . play music.'* Today, our ability to over-engineer and miniaturise has reached new levels: a small object once obsessed with displaying only one important thing can now also display 56 less important things.** Once you had to wind it twice a day, and the snob value was

---

* The *New York Times* magazine, 9 July 1995.
** The record for the number of complications is indeed 57. The record was broken in September 2015 with the unveiling of a new timepiece from Vacheron Constantin, the Tivoli. This is a pocket watch, Victorian style, and is able to simulate the chiming sequence of Big Ben, a Hebrew perpetual calendar with a special notification for Yom Kippur, the length of the night, equinoxes and solstices, among other things. The previous record was claimed by Franck Muller with its Aeternitas Mega 4. The AM4 still claims the title of most complicated *wristwatch*, with its 1,483 components and 36 complications, 25 of them visible. This has a *grande sonnerie* capable of playing the chimes of the clock at Westminster Cathedral, a Gregorian calendar, a moon phase with an error of only 6.8 seconds per lunar month. The Franck Muller brand is justifiably proud of its achievement. Under the heading 'Masterpiece', it blurbs, 'This watch inspires countless emotions as an exceptional timepiece and is simply unique in the eyes of lovers of the art of fine mechanics and luxury watch makers.' It costs $2.7 million.

in its precision: the closer it was to the church bells, the more you crowed. Nowadays, in a busy world, winding takes too much time, and so the task is taken away from us, the horological equivalent of the dishwasher; you need merely shake your arm in normal day-to-day activity, and the spiral mainspring will power the drivetrain automatically, and the hands will turn with sure precision.

But there *is* another reason for the proliferation of the wristwatch beyond our innate desire to preen. Telling the time has, since sometime in the fifteenth century, been the way we display our mechanical and technological mastery. A watch may be something to show off to a colleague at work, but may also represent something grander, something astronomical: we have achieved this magnificent feat of engineering, and in so doing we have aligned our stars and gone some way to mastering the very nature of time itself. What began as a pendulum and evolved into an escapement has now become a tiny, light and elegant contraption to regulate a frantic world. The world we have made, accelerating almost beyond our control, was created in large part by the clock and the watch – the ability to take our destinies inside, away from the universal cues of the heavens. A watch of precision may still suggest that we are nominally in charge. But does a more expensive, rarer, thicker, thinner and more complicated watch suggest we are more in charge than others, or more in charge than before? The advertisers would have it that way.

Baselworld has chosen its name well. It is indeed a world of its own, held each March in a multi-tiered exhibition hall of 140,000 square metres, and most of the big brands have created a nation state within it. When I visited in 2014, for example, Breitling had built a huge rectangular tank containing hundreds of tropical fish above its stand, for no other reason than that it could. And it wasn't a stand, it was a 'Pavilion'. Elsewhere, Tissot and Tudor had giant walls of flashing disco lights above their wares, while TAG Heuer had placed one of its watchmakers at a bench at the front of its pavilion to demonstrate how doubly difficult it was to build a watch while being watched. Just as motor racing fans love the occasional crash, TAG Heuer aficionados stand around waiting for their man to drop a screw on the carpet.

I crushed my way into the Hublot conference with José Mourinho, then still the Chelsea manager, the company's latest brand ambassador. Every watch company needs its ambassadors: the fact that they do not usually wear the watch while achieving their greatest feats is not a major consideration. Lionel Messi and Cristiano Ronaldo have signed for Audemars Piguet and Jacob & Co. Alongside Mourinho, Hublot also has Usain Bolt. Breitling has John Travolta and David Beckham, Montblanc Hugh Jackman, TAG Heuer Brad Pitt and Cameron Diaz, Rolex Roger Federer, IWC Ewan McGregor, and Longines Kate Winslet. Patek Philippe, ever keen to market itself as a brand with longevity and cross-generational worth, has shied away from asking, say, Taylor Swift or other shooting stars to represent its interests. Instead, it celebrates its client list from another era, starting with Queen Victoria.

Mourinho has just flown in to Basel from the Chelsea training ground at Cobham. He is wearing a grey raincoat over grey cashmere knitwear, and he accepts his watch with light applause and a short speech about how he has been part of the 'Hublot family' for a long time as a fan, but now it's all been made official (i.e. he's received his bank transfer). His watch is called the King Power 'Special One', almost the size of a fist, 18-carat 'king gold' with blue carbon, a self-winding Unico manufacture Flyback Chronograph with 300 components, 48mm case, all the mechanics exposed on the dial side, blue alligator strap, a skeleton dial, a power reserve of 72 hours, an edition of 100 and a price of $44,200. Just like Mourinho, the blurb says, 'The watch is provocative . . . the robust exterior hides the genius below.' Astonishingly, it's both stunning and hideous at the same time. Call for availability.

The strangest thing about the Hublot King Power was not that it looked like an armoured tank, but that it didn't keep very accurate time. When the popular American magazine *WatchTime* conducted tests on an earlier model, it found it gained between 1.6 to 4.3 seconds a day, which is not what you'd expect from a Swiss watch costing so much. My Timex Expedition Scout does better, losing about 18 seconds a month, or about 4 minutes annually. Four minutes annually, in the scheme of things, is nothing. You can run a mile in that, but it takes longer to stroll the length of the Baselworld carpeted walkways. Because I only had Timex money and not Hublot money I spent most of my time at the fair looking at the marketing, the thing that had brought me here in the first place. I particularly liked the text for the Mondaine Stop2go, which, as with most Mondaine watches, modelled itself on the Swiss railway clock. But this one was designed to run fast for 58 seconds and then stop at the top of the dial for two seconds before moving on again. It was an unnerving thing to see on the watch itself – time really standing still – but I was also thrown by the accompanying tagline: 'What does two seconds mean to you?'

At the Victorinox Swiss Army stand was a man who said that his watches reflected the same attributes as its knives, being both functional and reliable. This year the brand's 'hero' watch was the Chrono Classic, 'all about the long and the short' in its ability to house both a perpetual calendar and a chronograph capable of timing a hundredth of a second. But this would have been all rather too conventional for the people milling around the MCT stand marvelling at its Sequential

Two S200, a watch that had clearly had enough of conventional timekeeping by hands, and instead promoted hours 'indicated by four generous blocks, each composed of five triangular prisms'. The hour 'appears in a remarkably readable manner through an open "window", while the others are hidden by a segment turning counter-clockwise every 60 minutes'. There is clearly no point asking 'why?' with a watch like this, anymore than you would ask 'why?' with a Picasso.

Although the majority of the brands were aimed at over-achieving men, overachieving women were also welcomed with promotional baloney. At Hermès, the Dressage L'Heure Masquée 'affords a permanent opportunity to make the "great escape" and to seize only the moments that truly count'. Fendi took 'fur towards peaks that have not been explored for almost a century . . . a precious strap in two-tone mink'. The Crazy Carats watch revealed 'three different types of gemstones according to the mood of the moment'. At Christophe Claret, the Margot resembled a daisy, 'a unique and patented compli-cation that will steal women's hearts: a world first! A push at 2 o'clock and the watch springs to life, as though abandoned to nature's whims, by hiding one petal, sometimes two, impos-sible to say.' And then there was Dubey & Schaldenbrand, and its Cœur Blanc. This displayed two hands in a ring of diamonds, which 'seem to float on the dial, as though nothing holds them there but their own power of seduction'. They 'embrace the caseband, form one with the attachments, twinkle like stars on the crown, and come to a dazzling conclusion on the buckle of the strap'.

I also came to a dazzling conclusion: these watches all had one thing in common beyond their cost, intricacy and madness. Everywhere I went, all the watches showed roughly the same time. Not the accurate time, because that would have been too difficult: what *was* the correct time in this airless pristine hall of fake pavilions? Why spoil the illusion of this moneyed weightlessness by imposing a stricture on it? Instead, almost every watch on show was stuck at around ten past ten. Why then? A watch set at 10.10 appears to be 'smiling'; it leaves the face free at 3 o'clock, the usual position for the date; it forms a pleasant and balanced appearance, ensuring the hands do not overlap and do not obscure the manufacturer's name at the top of the dial. Timex sets its promotional watches to 10.09:36, although adverts from the 1950s show 8.20; this was consciously flipped to avoid its watch faces looking downcast and frowning. These days, there is a conscious effort to ship all its customer watches also set at 10.09:36, for a setting six seconds earlier at 10.09:30 would obscure what it calls its 'secondary language' of features, including the Indiglo illumination and the water pressure depth. Mondaine has chosen 10.10 precisely; Rolex favours 10.10:31; TAG Heuer 10.10:37; the Apple Watch has gone for 10.09:30 on both analogue and digital faces (and it used to always show 9.42 a.m. on its iPhone ads, the time Steve Jobs first unveiled the phone in California). In 2008, the *New York Times* conducted a pop-scientific survey of this trend, finding that all but three watches in Amazon's bestselling 100 men's watches were set to roughly 10.10, while it found a rare exception from Ulysse Nardin in its magazine: its watches were set at 8.19 (a company executive explained the Swiss manufacturer was not trying to change the world, it was merely a clearer way of displaying its calendar. No such problem obscuring the day/date in the middle of the face at Rolex, although here there were other rulebooks: in the Rolex world it was always, and perhaps always will be, Monday 28.

12:06

At the Timex stand it was all about lifestyle. There were photos of beautiful people sitting around campfires with the straplines 'Wear it Well' and 'Get Outside' and information about the brand's 'Fall Lookbook'. These campaigns were obviously very different from those surrounding the brand when it began in the 1950s, when the television advertising entailed strapping a watch to the end of an arrow and shooting it through a pane of glass (tagline: 'It takes a licking and goes on ticking'). Another advertisement was titled 'SHOCK!' and featured a man with a mallet: 'Timex watches successfully withstand forces equivalent to being thrown against a concrete wall!' But my favourite advert wasn't an advert at all, it was just brilliant PR: in May 1981, the front page of the *Boston Globe* reported that a man from New York had swallowed his Timex whole when confronted by a mugger on the violent streets. The watch was removed from the man's stomach five months later, and the surgeon was delighted to report that although the time was a little imprecise, what with all that darkness and swill, the watch was *still ticking*.

After my stroll I went into a large hall for the opening press conference. A grand procession of dignitaries was followed by something akin to a re-enactment of victory at Troy. The speakers had each endured vast amounts of *toilette* and *coiffure*, and they each had their own piece of good news: the fair this year is the biggest, the brightest, the brashest and the most unashamedly boastful watch and jewellery show there has ever been in one place, so hoorah for us, and lucky you to be a part of it. There are, apparently, 4,000 journalists present at the fair, which is almost certainly more than covered two world wars. About a tenth of them are in the hall for the opening speeches and the slide presentation, and many of these are from the Far East with interpreters in their ears. The PowerPoint says: The value of Swiss watch exports are up 1.9 per cent on the previous year, a value of 21.8 billion Swiss francs in 2013. The trend is inexorably upwards: exports are SF8.6 billion higher than five years before. The trend for cheap Swiss watches is down – a 4.5 per cent decline in watches valued up to SF200 – but at the upper end, the end that counts, it's all good: a 2.8 per cent increase in watches costing SF3,000+.

That was in 2014. A year later, the mood had changed and darkened. There was a cloud over Switzerland, and the threat from Apple Watch was only a part of it. There was also global financial insecurity to contend with. The Swiss franc was strong, which meant prices looked more expensive. Demand in China and Japan was down, and the market in Hong Kong had all but disappeared. Fluctuations in the rouble had hit Russian orders. The Richemont group had reported something unfamiliar in its recent profits: a flat line, not the usual increases that used to greet its shareholders. One chief executive at Zenith, a nineteenth-century Swiss brand that was now part of the luxury goods conglomerate LVMH, told the *Financial Times*, 'There has been a lot of turmoil and no one has any idea what will happen next.'

But other watchmakers took a more relaxed view, as befits an industry that's grown fat on more than 200 years of profit. The Swiss would take a dip, they believed, but the Swiss would then surface triumphantly. The beautiful and impossibly engineered products they made for the world would continue to dazzle with their refinements and complications and unasked-for lunacy, and would forever sell us the time in a way we desire but never need. Tradition and craftsmanship still counted for a lot in the pixellated world; wearing a mechanical watch simply makes us more human, and that is something we may always like to feel. So no need to panic just yet; it wasn't like the Quartz Crisis of the 1970s or anything cataclysmic like that.*

---

* But by September 2015, the situation had worsened again. The value of Swiss watch exports was down 7.9 per cent on the previous year. The biggest declines were

iii) Uh-oh

In September 1975, an advertisement on the front cover of the *Horological Journal* featured a close-up photograph of a chrome-plated day/date battery-powered Timex held between thumb and forefinger in a person's hand, and the line 'Introducing the Quartz watch with the incredible price tag'. There were no gimmicks or feats of endurance in this campaign, no arrows or glass or sledgehammers, although there was a little tag dangling from the side of the watch with a handwritten price: £28.

This was not cheap (£28 was the equivalent of about £250 in 2016), but it was good value for what it promised to do, which was tell the time better than any watch made in Switzerland. Inside the *Horological Journal*, a trade publication founded in 1858, an article called the watch 'the horological bargain of the decade' and 'a milestone in the history of horology'.

'Its accuracy takes it into the middle-upper end of the market place and it is so easy to change parts it is a watch-maker's dream.' The customer fared well too: 'What does a customer require from a watch today? Style, easy to read, accuracy and a fair price? The Timex Model 63 Quartz has all of these in abundance.' What it had above all was the essence of quartz: a tiny piece of crystal that resonated at a high and fixed frequency when powered by a battery. This steady signal was then transmitted to an oscillator, an electronic circuit that regulated the gears that turned the watch hands. The movement itself had been around since the 1920s, but its miniaturisation had only been achieved in prototype by Seiko

---

seen in Hong King and the United States. In the market for watches valued between 200 and 500 Swiss francs, where the Apple Watch did most of its damage, the news was worse still – a year-on-year decline of 14.5 per cent.

and Casio in Japan in the late 1960s. Its price had taken it beyond the general consumer, although the excitement and novelty of quartz in the early 1970s – the very idea of a precision-cut piece of rock not only doing away with the centuries-old movement of winding and power storage but also keeping near-perfect time – had led collectors to Japan and the USA, and they had paid hundreds of dollars for early examples. But now, through mass production and the marketing potential of Timex and its main American rival Bulova (which had developed the Accutron, a watch fitted with a tuning fork in place of the far less accurate standard vibrating balance wheel), the electronic watch represented a change of philosophy. The new quartz Timex of 1975 oscillated at a frequency of 49,152 cycles a second, which was then divided electronically by a microcircuit to drive the hands; each step of the sweeping second hand takes a third of a second. From the outside, the watch looked like any other. But this was a solid-state watch, so called because of its lack of moving parts, and it converted quartz oscillation into electronic pulses driving tiny electronic lights – the digital display lighting up the segments on the face. The tiny alarms that would soon wreck a night at the theatre were also a sign that the Japanese and Americans thought they had seen the future.

The new watches indicated something else as well: the dawn of mass tech-based consumerism. Split-second timing, once the exclusive domain of physicists and technicians, was now available to all, and there was no better symbol of the seismic shift from the mechanical to the electronic world.

How did the Swiss react to this disruption? They oscillated between denial and panic. Between 1970 and 1983, the Swiss share of the watch market fell from 50 per cent to 15, and the industry shed more than half its workforce. The warnings were there as early as 1973: in that year, Timex sold about 30 million watches around the world, a huge increase from 8 million in

1960, and almost half of what Switzerland was capable of. These watches were unjewelled mechanical pieces, a bit clunky and rattly, and they could easily lose or gain a couple of minutes each day. But they only cost about $10, and owners regarded them as disposable. With quartz in the mid-1970s it would overtake the Swiss competition with ease.*

But in the early 1980s, with doom on the horizon, the Swiss fought back with a new philosophy of their own, and something plastic, cheaper and powered by quartz and battery: the Swatch. The Swatch – from its name onwards – injected colour, emotion, youth and fun back into Swiss watches (God knows, the fusty industry needed it), and a series of assured marketing campaigns made every teenager drool. The Pop Swatch made watch collecting feasible for the young. The success of the Swatch made it look as though the Swiss were never in trouble at all. There is a brilliantly seamless (if not entirely accurate) riff about electronic watches in Tom Stoppard's *The Real Thing* (1982), which is a play about loyalty and dedication to a cause. In the first scene, a play within a play, the character Max, an architect slightly worse for drink,

* Timex claims it is 'True Since 1854', but this is being economical with the truth. The Timex Corporation was only established in 1969, the new name for the US Time Corporation, which itself had formed from the ashes of the failing Waterbury Clock Company (est. 1854). The leading force behind the company's post-war success was a shy Norwegian refugee named Joakim Lehmkuhl, who had fled his native country at the time of the Nazi invasion in 1940. When he became president of Waterbury in Connecticut in 1942, the company's experience with time was diverted into making ammunition fuses for the British military. But his biggest asset was what the Swiss had lost – its delight in invention and innovation. The American company Ingersoll had already achieved great success with its $1 watch, even though it was highly unreliable. Lehmkuhl saw no reason why Americans shouldn't benefit from accurate timekeeping that endured, or at least endured until they could afford to spend another $10 on the next one. The watch chimed with the great boom in American consumerism and the desire to purchase patriotically. The watches were sold not through the usual respectable jewellery outlets, but more like soap powder – in F.W. Woolworth and other chain stores, and through mass-market catalogues. It worked.

suspects that his wife has not, as she has claimed, been on a trip to Switzerland. He ponders the correct pronunciation of Basel, and claims,

> You know the Swiss – utterly reliable. And they've done it without going digital, that's what I admire so much. They know it's all a snare and delusion. I can remember digitals when they first came out. You had to give your wrist a vigorous shake, like bringing down a thermometer. And the only place you could buy one was Tokyo. But it looked all over for the fifteen-jewel movement. Men ran through the marketplace shouting 'the cog is dead!' But still the Swiss didn't panic. In fact, they made a few digitals themselves, as a feint to draw the Japanese further into the mire, and got on with numbering the bank accounts.

Stoppard maintained that the days of the digital were numbered, the metaphor 'built into them like a self-destruct mechanism'. But these days Swatch is based solidly on quartz and is the most influential player in the industry. In 2014 its gross sales amounted to more than nine billion Swiss francs, and the Swatch Group is the world's largest watchmaking company, consisting of brands that once would have shuddered at the thought: Longines, Blancpain, Rado, Harry Winston and Breguet – the company which claims to have made the first wristwatch in 1810.*

iv) In Which We Name the Guilty Man

In May 1996, the London-based advertising agency Leagas

---

* Many companies claim to have 'invented' the wristwatch, a development that usually entailed a client taking a pocket watch and strapping it around their arm. Breguet's claim has more foundation: its order books show that a small oval time-piece with a silver dial was made for Caroline Murat, the younger sister of Napoleon Bonaparte, specifically to be attached to a bracelet.

Delaney announced that it had won another huge global account. The company already had contracts for Harrods and Porsche, and now it was to add the high-end watchmakers Patek Philippe to its roster, in a deal valued, according to *Campaign*, at £10 million. The competition had been stiff, including pitches from Bartle Bogle Hegarty and Saatchi, and when the account was awarded, a high-up at Leagas Delaney said, 'This is a pitch which excited the whole agency. We are thrilled to get the business.'

The press release announcing the news stated that Patek Philippe took such immense care over its timepieces that it had sold fewer watches in its 150-year history than Rolex produced in a year. It wasn't clear whether this was a good or a bad thing, or whether Patek's eagerly awaited new advertising campaign would begin to narrow the gap. One of the earliest new advertisements featured a photograph of a man seated at a piano, and on his lap was a child in pyjamas. You couldn't see the face of either man or child, and you couldn't see a wrist either, so there was no watch. The only watch on display lay at the foot of a lot of text in the bottom half of the ad. 'Begin your *own* tradition' the copy began.

> Whatever innovations Patek Philippe introduce, every watch is still crafted by hand. The men's Annual Calendar ref. 5035 is the first self-winding calendar watch in the world to require resetting only once a year. And because of the exceptional workmanship, each one is a unique object. Which is perhaps why some people feel that you never actually own a Patek Philippe. You merely look after it for the next generation.

When the last two lines of the new advert were edited to appear on their own, something new was born: 'You never actually own a Patek Philippe. You merely look after it for the next generation' just stuck, to the extent that it has become one of the most famous in advertising and has appeared unchanged for almost 20 years (and counting). It translates too, although perhaps not quite so elegantly: *'Jamais vous ne posséderez complètement une Patek Philippe. Vous en serez juste le gardien, pour les générations futures.'*

In 2011, when *Creative Review* magazine asked industry experts to name the most enduring or cleverest slogans, the choice was impressive and wide, ranging from 'I Heart NY', 'Refreshes the parts other beers cannot reach' and 'Beanz Meanz Heinz' to 'Careless talk costs lives', 'Keep calm and carry on' and 'Does exactly what it says on the tin'. Gordon Comstock, a columnist at *Creative Review* and a freelance copywriter, chose John Lewis's 'Never knowingly undersold', the *Independent*'s 'It is. Are you?' and Nike's 'Just do it'. But top of his list was 'You never actually own . . .'. Explaining his choice, Comstock wrote that 'The brand runs this line with different photography every year and pays [Leagas Delaney] a million quid. It's probably worth it too . . . It's a confident writer that will leave two adverbs in a headline.'

The confident writer is a man called Tim Delaney, one of the greatest names in British advertising; many would place him in the top ten of the greatest copywriters in the world. Delaney entered the industry as a messenger boy at 15 and has been at the helm of his own company since 1980, running ads of substance for Sony, Philips, Timberland, Glenfiddich, Ordnance Survey maps, Barclays, the *Guardian*, Bollinger, Hyundai, the BBC, the TUC, Adidas and the Labour Party. When he was inducted into The One Club in 2007 (a lifetime-achievement award presented in New York), one of the tributes, from a former colleague of Delaney's named Martin Galton, said, 'In a time when it's unfashion-able to take risks, when we are swimming around in a sea of beige, the world needs Tim Delaney more than ever.' One advertisement his company made for Timberland included a photo of a Native American in full regalia and the copy line: 'We stole their land, their buffalo and their women. Then we went back for their shoes.' Leagas Delaney wrote the line 'There is only one Harrods. There is only one sale.' And, in an advert promoting the Nationwide Building Society in the 1980s: 'If you want to find out how banks became the richest, most powerful institutions in the world, go into the red one day.'*

The 'Generations' campaign, as the Patek Philippe ads became known, featured photographs taken by Herb Ritts, Ellen von Unwerth, Mary Ellen Mark and Peggy Sirota, and showcased such simulated moments as a father and son on a glamorous fishing trip, a father and son on a journey on the Orient Express, and a father showing a son how to tie a tie. There was also a mother laughing with her daughter over life's little luxuries at home. Most of these adverts made me feel queasy, and I sent Delaney an email to tell him so.

I told him I was interested in how one sells a watch to those who don't really need one, and that I admired his Patek campaigns. I also told him that I was upset by those perfect families and their smugness, and that 'I'd like to give the adults a good slap. The deeper problem is, the adverts have made me fairly keen to buy one of those beautiful watches.'

I told him I was interested in talking about the conception of the campaign and its intentions. 'Why are they so effective? And will they just continue until the kids in the photos become adults themselves, and then hand watches down to *their* children? We may reach the end of the world, but those families will still be looking after watches and

---

* My favourite is one for Tripp luggage. A while ago, before all new suitcases had four wheels, the big innovation was luggage that grew bigger. You unzip a compartment and, *voila*, the case is one third as big again. Leagas Delaney's advert featured a fat case and the headline 'The expandable suitcase. Now you can steal the bathrobe as well as the toiletries.'

passing them down – it's mind-blowing, it's like a Charlie Kaufman film.'

Delaney was happy to chat. He explained that the majority of the other famous watch brands had passed from family ownership to the conglomerates, and that it was always his intention to emphasise the fact that Patek was still owned by the same family. 'We had an emotional insight,' he says. The ads are successful 'because of continuity – in the company itself, the family ownership, the design ethos – the watches come from somewhere, they don't just turn up'.

In common with most agencies embarking on work for a new client, Leagas Delaney spent some time looking at previous campaigns to discover what they believed did and didn't work. The campaign featuring famous past owners – Queen Victoria, Einstein – produced some particularly useful research: 'Naturally if you showed that to Americans the first thing they'd say is "Yeah, but what about me?" So that gave rise to "Begin your own tradition", and that in turn gave rise to the line that we have now.'

Delaney conceived the 'Begin your own tradition' idea on a plane. He says he took the 'You never actually own . . .' line and made it into the headline, but says he can't remember who in his agency wrote it originally. 'A number of people claim it,' he says, 'but success has many fathers.'

Viewed as a whole, on the back page of *Esquire*, *GQ* or the *Economist*, the advert tugs at the reader's sense of responsibility and family obligation, not least the creation of dynasty and heritage. It is as aspirational as most other luxury adverts, in this case appealing to someone with new money aspiring to be someone with old money. And of course it relies on the warped concept that to fulfil one's obligation of not owning a Patek watch one must first *buy* a Patek watch. New Patek watches cost from a few thousand to hundreds of thousands, edging towards millions for classic models at auction. Delaney himself wears an Aquanaut, a watch at the modest end of the scale.

I asked him why his campaign had lasted so long. 'I think it's a universal insight, and I think people respond to it,' he says. 'It's not pushy – the thought doesn't run down, it doesn't become less intelligent the more you see it . . . But it doesn't happen through fantastic genius; it happens through a combination of factors and happenstance and it slots into place.'

There have been subtle changes over the years in photography and typography. 'You change with the demands of the culture and the demands of the economy. You're subtly monitoring behaviour of people who can afford watches.' The photos are an attempt 'to show humanity and warmth. Truth . . . It's idealized. Everyone knows it's advertising. You have a strong sense that it's a natural bond between the two people, the father and the son, mother and daughter, so it's palatable, but it's not a photograph of a guy with his real son. It's only a matter of us trying to restrain everything so that it doesn't become saccharine and that it stays palatable within the framework of advertising.'

I asked him whether there were any other watch campaigns he admired, and he thought for less than a second. 'No.'

v) The Most Valuable Watch on the Planet

But here's one he may envy a little. If, as a marketing manager of a famous watch company, you did somehow manage to get the first man on the moon to wear your watch as he set foot on the lunar surface for the very first time, then surely you would have something to brag about and promote for evermore. So imagine the delight at Omega when NASA selected the brand as its official Apollo time-keeper, and the unfettered joy when it was clear that Neil Armstrong – and could there ever be a more perfect name for a watch ambassador? – agreed that he would be wearing an Omega Speedmaster Professional Chronograph as he stepped down from the lunar module onto the Sea of Tranquillity.

Didn't happen. Armstrong went all the way there – *all the way to the damn moon* – with the *intention* of wearing his Omega as he took his one small step onto the moon's surface, but then when the *Eagle* landed he deliberately left his watch behind because the timer in the module was malfunctioning. So step forward Buzz Aldrin. 'Few things are less necessary when walking around on the moon than knowing what time it is in Houston, Texas,' the second man on the moon wrote in his memoir *Return To Earth* in 1973. 'Nonetheless, being a watch guy, I decided to strap the Speedmaster onto my right wrist around the outside of my bulky spacesuit.'

The Omega advertising team sprang into action imme-diately. 'Saying that an Omega is the most trustworthy watch *on Earth* is something of an understatement', one advert ran, and the crowing never abated. 'How can a man in a $27,000 suit settle for a $235 watch?' ran another. An adver-tisement promoting the Speedmaster Mark II had the line, 'And its daddy went to the moon'. Heralding the unlikely American–Soviet/Apollo–Soyuz space mission of 1975, Omega claimed that 'for any other watch the shock would be too much'.

Omega went on all the missions. When, as commander of Apollo 17, Gene Cernan left the last footprint on the moon on 14 December 1972, he had a Speedmaster strapped to *each* arm of his spacesuit; one told Houston time, the other the time in Czechoslovakia, the birthplace of his mother. 'The

Speedmaster is the only thing we took to the Moon that had no modification whatsoever,' the astronaut said, as if reading from a script prepared by the Omega marketing department. 'It was right off the shelf.'*

Today, the so-called 'Moonwatch' is still a hugely attractive USP. The company offers several editions of the Speedmaster, with its ambassador George Clooney happy to wear the updated 2015 model with recessed hour markers and newly designed 'broad arrow' hands as he messes around on his motorbike (Clooney says that his father and uncle also wore Omegas). But you can also get editions called Dark Side of the Moon (zirconium oxide ceramic dial), Grey Side of the Moon (with the metallic-looking dial inspired by moon dust and mint-green luminosity on the bevel) and the ghostly White Side of the Moon that looks like it's been dropped in a tin of Dulux Vinyl Matt but was actually inspired by 'the radiance of the celestial body as seen from Earth'. Uh-huh. Omega is now part of the Swatch Group.**

Which brings us to the most valuable watch on the planet. This would be Buzz's Aldrin's own 42mm Calibre 321 hand-wound Speedmaster Chronograph that he wore with an especially long strap when he went walkabout. How much would such an item be worth? No one knows, and no one

* The Speedmaster was not the first watch in space, of course. As he hurtled in his red-hot Vostok on 12 April 1961, Yuri Gagarin wore a rather less complicated Sturmanskie, a military timepiece produced in Moscow and handed to many Soviet top guns after the war. Today, a stunning new Speedmaster will cost you around £3,500, with more for the special editions. But you can pick up a new Gagarin commemorative version Sturmanskie (quartz rather than mechanical) for £100.
** It is also part of the James Bond empire. Its last outing – a modified Seamaster 300 with the black and grey NATO strap – was in *Spectre* and in glossy boutiques and magazines not long afterwards (the showroom model, costing £4,785, is, predictably enough, limited to 7,007 copies.) When Q (Ben Whishaw) presents Bond (Daniel Craig) with the watch in the obligatory gadgets scene, Bond asks 'Does it *do* anything?' And Q replies, 'It tells the time.' When Bond later finds himself in a tight spot, the watch aids his escape by exploding.

knows where it is, either. His watch went walkabout all on its own: all the Apollo astronauts were asked to hand their watches back after their return to Earth, and they remained the property of NASA in Houston (and some ended up at the Smithsonian in Washington DC). But Buzz's watch went missing not long after he returned it, and it has never been found. So if you want to look under your bed, the reference number on the inside of the back case is ST105.012.

When time was a game: how to have fun at a party in the 1960s.

Chapter Twelve

Time Tactics That Work!

i) The Berry Season

Over the last couple of years I have amassed a number of self-help books on time management, but there is no aggregate book that offers advice on finding enough time to read them all. Most come with exercises and mental-workout programmes, and some recommend going online for bonus lessons and questionnaires. By the time you're finished, you're tired. Among my favourites:

> *18 Minutes: Find Your Focus, Master Distraction and Get the Right Things Done* by Peter Bregman
>
> *15 Secrets Successful People Know About Time Management: The Productivity Habits of 7 Billionaires, 13 Olympic Athletes, 29 Straight-A Students and 239 Entrepreneurs* by Kevin Kruse
>
> *The 26 Hour Day: How to Gain at Least Two Hours a Day with Time Control* by Vince Panella
>
> *It's About Time: Find 5 Extra Hours Each Week* by Harold C. Lloyd
>
> *Time Tactics That Work: 107 Ways to Get More Done* by Gavin Preston
>
> *Five Minutes a Day: Time Management for People Who Love to Put Things Off* by Jean Reynolds PhD
>
> *More Time, Less Stress: How to Create Two Extra Hours Every Day* by Judi James

> *The 12-Week Year: Get More Done in 12 Weeks Than Others Do in 12 Months* by Brian P. Moran and Michael Lennington*

And this is only the beginning, a mere scratching of the surface of the amount of time that can be saved or gained in an hour/day/week/month by following these easy methods/steps/secrets. Why not also try:

> *Two Awesome Hours: Science-based Strategies to Harness Your Best Time and Get Your Most Important Work Done* by Josh Davis
>
> *The Power of a Half Hour* by Tommy Barnett
>
> *The 15-Minute Total Life Makeover: 12 Ways to Dramatically Change Any Area of Your Life in Just 15 Minutes a Day* by Christina M. DeBusk
>
> *75 Secrets Revealed on Time Management Skills: The New Organised You in Just 3 Hours – Volume 1 (10 Mins a Day)* by Joe Martin

Most of these carry similar advice: save mornings for real work; stop multitasking and do one thing well; make time for yourself; get enough sleep; plan a whole day without any meetings. Only occasionally does a novel suggestion leap out. In *15 Secrets Successful People Know About Time Management: The Productivity Habits of 7 Billionaires, 13 Olympic Athletes, 29 Straight-A Students and 239 Entrepreneurs*, for example, the author Kevin Kruse writes that we should all stop making to-do lists. The items on to-do lists never get completed, he argues, they merely get transferred onto other, longer to-do lists. To-do lists prioritise the urgent over the important

---

* Fantastically, should you not have time to read *The 12-Week Year: Get More Done in 12 Weeks Than Others Do in 12 Months* (208 pages), there is also an abridged version available, containing all the gems (34 pages).

(urgent being the water leaking through the ceiling, important being the family photo album that never gets done) and do not distinguish between items that take a short amount of time and a long one, with our natural tendency to knock off the quick ones first. He has research to back this up, and it concludes that 41 per cent of to-do-list items are never completed.* Rather than a to-do list, Kruse suggests a well-maintained and rigorously apportioned calendar.

Kruse also has an answer to the puzzle 'Can three simple questions save you eight hours a week?' The answer of course is yes. He calls these 'Harvard Questions', because they derive from Julian Birkinshaw and Jordan Cohen, two professors claiming in the *Harvard Business Review* that one reason we like to feel busy all the time is because it makes us feel important. But in 2013 the professors found that busyness in itself wasn't actually very productive. When they retrained workers to slow down and think more about their actions, they found that on average their subjects saved six hours of desk work and two hours of meeting time per week. The three questions were: What items on my to-do list can I drop entirely? What items can I delegate to a subordinate? What do I need to be doing but can do in a more efficient way? The key to so many problems of limited time – not just for Kruse, but also for the majority of these authors and researchers – is delegation. You hire someone. If you are Tony Robbins, the motivational life coach and author of such hits as *Awaken the Giant Within*, you hire someone to get your suits from the dry cleaner's so you can concentrate on other things: 'I don't do anything that someone else can do better.' Or if you are Andrea Waltz, the co-author of *Go For No!*, the more you delegate, the more you thrive. Or if you are Lewis

* Impeccable source: an item called 'The Busy Person's Guide to the Done List' on the website idonethis.com

Howes, host of the 'School of Greatness' podcast, 'Focus on what you are great at and hire everyone else to do the rest.' It's the same thing in 30 books: buy time from somebody with time to spare. But what happens if you can't afford to hire somebody else? 'You always can,' says Tony Robbins. 'You'll see.'

Kruse is no novice to time management. He started his own company when he was 22, and it turned out to be a miserable failure (he showered in the local youth hostel). According to his autobiography, it was only when he discovered the power of Wholehearted Leadership and how to Master Your Minutes that he became the man he is today, the founder of several multimillion-dollar companies. Along the way he has amassed plenty of temporal information to transform a day, and thus a week and a life. Kruse's central source of information is the Kruse Group, his time management research bank, and the information that shines brightest is this: 'People who actively look for things to delegate report higher levels of productivity, happiness and energy, and are less likely to feel "overworked and overwhelmed".' In the digital environment, delegation no longer means overloading a beleaguered person on a lower pay scale in an office (i.e. dumping on the less fortunate), but outsourcing with an app or URL; time-saving has become democratic, and a goldmine for start-ups. So Kruse has enlisted a phalanx of workers to help him save time when producing his books (there is Clarissa, a cover designer in Singapore who he's never met; Balaji in India, involved in data mining, ditto; Serena, handling his email enquiries from Thailand; and Camille, a book editor he found on fiverr.com, lives in the US, ditto).

Many of Kruse's epithets may seem banal and oversimplified, but they may also be harder to achieve than they first appear. For example, the 'Time Secrets of 29 Straight-A Students' require exacting self-discipline:

i) Turn off social media.

ii) Don't go out in the evenings, and socialise predominantly with your work peers during study sessions.

iii) Do small tasks that take less than five minutes immediately.

iv) Schedule 'me time'. Be like Caitlin Hale, a medical student in New Jersey: 'I make sure that every night I dedicate at least one hour to myself.'

The 'Time Secrets of 13 Olympic Athletes' are also productive:

i) Don't plan your training schedule on your phone: get a large paper calendar instead as this helps with perspective of what you've achieved so far and what you still need to do.

ii) Don't feel bad about saying no to people.

iii) 'Rest is perhaps the most overlooked and undervalued aspect.'

iv) Be like Briana Scurry, the perfectly named goalkeeper who won gold medals as part of the US women's soccer team in 1996 and 2004, and ask yourself: 'Will this activity help me perform better and therefore help us win gold?' She calls this focus 'white-hot obsessiveness'.

Advice from Kevin Kruse and his cohorts tends to concentrate on saving time in the workplace with a familiar mission: maximise productivity, blitz the opposition, become wealthy, achieve the American Dream (almost all the books are indeed American – hard to see the tribes of Patagonia or Peru being crazy about me time or shaving ten minutes off meetings). These books all tend to have numbers in their titles, and thus measurable targets. But there is also a less driven approach to time management, a softer and more holistic side encompassing a work-life balance. So one may also learn interesting things from:

Overwhelmed: How to Work, Love and Play When No One Has the Time by Brigid Schulte

Time Management for Manic Mums: Get Control of Your Life in 7 Weeks by Allison Mitchell

Managing Time Mindfully: A Mindful Approach to Time Management by Tom Evans

Business Owners: Your Family Misses You: Time Management Strategies That Free up Two Hours a Day and Get You Loved Again by Mike Gardner.

Eat That Frog! 21 Great Ways to Stop Procrastinating and Get More Done in Less Time by Brian Tracy

Eat the Elephant: Overcoming Overwhelm by Karolyn Vreeland Blume

When you are done eating things, you could do a lot worse than start your domestic tune-up with *I Know How She Does It: How Successful Women Make the Most of Their Time* by Laura Vanderkam. 'Time management will always be a popular topic because we all live our lives in hours and we all have the same number of hours,' its author told me. She is also the author of *What the Most Successful People Do Before Breakfast*. 'All the money in the world can't buy you a second more.'

You may, in the parlance of this genre, turn your sneers to cheers: the sentiments in Vanderkam's book impress even as her prose sometimes cloys. We learn that she had an enlightening moment one June afternoon while strawberry picking on a farm in Pennsylvania with two of her children. She noticed the poetic line on an empty fruit box: 'Remember the berry season is short.' The box held about 10lb when level full, and perhaps 15lb when heaped, and she wondered if her life could do the same. 'What you do with your life will be a function of how you spend the 8,760 hours that make a year, the 700,000 or so that make a life.' She resolved to spend more time 'at strawberry farms, as well as rocking toddlers to sleep and pursuing work that alters at least some corner of the universe'.

For Vanderkam, that work has involved sending detailed weekly time grids to 143 working women, providing her with 1,001 (143×7) days with which to study the hourly pursuits of work, home and self. This 'Mosaic Project' was made up of half-hourly tiles throughout the day from 5 a.m. to midnight; participants had to fill in each tile no matter how dull, predictable, repetitive or slightly embarrassing that period had been. If you had spent two hours on Facebook that would be four tiles, and honesty was all. In the middle of March 2014, aged 35, Vanderkam filled out her own time grid, and when she published it I felt like a voyeur. On Tuesday, 18 March, for example, she was up working at 6. This continued for three tiles, and at 7.30 it was breakfast with the kids. She then worked on an unspecified project until 10.30 a.m., when the complexion of the work changed: for two tiles it was now listed as 'Work (brainstorm ideas)'. Emails took over for an hour at 1 p.m., then there was an hour-long interview, and the tiles between 3 and 4 were split between work and a run. So far so boring, but then things got a little more varied: the next work tiles were spent on drafting a piece for *Oprah*, continuing her Mosaic project, and going to the library to write ('novel, 2000 words!'). At 7.30 she ate sushi out, and at 8 she drove home after filling her gas tank. The next tile was reading to her kids and putting them to bed, followed by a tile of TV, a shower tile (*yes!*) and many tiles of bed. Wednesday's highlights included a tile titled 'Work, primp for video call' followed by one that says 'Video call doesn't happen, inefficient!' At 2 p.m. a tile reads '2 p.m. call also doesn't happen'. There is better news later in the day: 'Dinner with family' at 6.30, but then partial disaster: '2 kids to Ikea, J. watch *Frozen*'.

The weekends looked rather different, for that was predominantly family time. On Saturday she gets up an hour later, cleans, spends four tiles at the Scouts' Pinewood Derby, plays outside with the kids and invests five tiles on a date night at a restaurant with her husband. Reading it from afar, one can't help but look for the tile(s) in which she might have had sex, but the only possible hint is Sunday at 10.30 p.m., when the tile billed as 'shower' during the rest of the week becomes 'shower etc.'

Analysing her log once the week was over, Vanderkam was disappointed that her evenings weren't as effective as she would have liked, as she was doing a lot of multi-tasking. If she had to work in the evenings she hoped to have a clearer idea of what she wanted to accomplish, rather than just drifting in and out of her inbox. I asked Vanderkam what she found most surprising about all the time logs she had collected from other people, and she told me she was impressed with the levels of flexibility people have.

> Even women in fairly traditional jobs find ways to move the hours of work around to make the pieces of their lives fit together. I found that about three-quarters of women did something personal during work hours. Of course, the flip side is true too. Three-quarters did something work-related at night, or on week-ends, or in the early mornings. To me, the two are completely related, so it misses the mark to call one good and the other bad.

In the course of her research, Vanderkam exposed some false assumptions. Americans tend to think they are working more hours than their parents did, but the opposite may be true: according to surveys by the Federal Reserve Bank of St Louis, the average working week fell from about 42.4 hours in 1950 to 39.1 hours in 1970. In 2014, the Bureau of Labor Statistics found that the average (non-farm) working week had fallen to 34.5 hours. Averages can be deceptive, of course, not least the suggestion that people are happy working fewer hours; this may mean less pay and thus an inability to enjoy increased leisure time. Working hours are no longer much indication of busyness either.

Vanderkam found what most veterans of survey analysis already know: people tend to lie. 'Looking at the numbers, most people aren't overworked,' Vanderkam says. 'In a decade of writing about time and careers, I've come across studies that show a fascinating tendency of white-collar workers to inflate their work hours.' This applied particularly to those employed in what she calls 'white-collar sweatshops', the traditionally punishing arenas of finance and tech. 'No one wants to be seen as working less than the guy in the next cube.' The observation is backed up by research conducted over decades by the sociologist John Robinson at the University of Maryland and colleagues. Writing in the *Monthly Labor Review* in 2011, and using data from the American Time Use Survey, they found that when they compared estimates of hours worked with detailed time sheets, those who claimed they were working 75-hour weeks were exaggerating by about 25 hours. 'The Executive Time Use Project' at the London School of Economics surveyed more than 1,000 CEOs in 6 countries and reported in 2014 that the average CEO spent 52 hours a week on work activities: a significant figure but not the excessive striving one is familiar with from literature and the movies. Seventy per cent of those in the survey said they worked no more than five days.

'When I get in a sombre mood it makes me angry, because I think there's something insidious going on,' Vanderkam says. 'By exaggerating workweeks, people can make some jobs appear off-limits to those who care about having a life. Making women – and men – think that they must inevitably choose between a particular career and their families will knock a huge chunk of the competition out.'

This may be the true value of these tiles and time logs: beyond merely deepening our desire to exploit every waking minute, they may show users that their lives weren't quite what they thought they were. 'The best outcome for some was changing the stories they were telling themselves,' Vanderkam told me. 'A popular one: working moms don't spend enough time with their kids. One woman looked at her time log and realized she was spending every moment that her school-aged children were awake at home with them. After seeing that, she said that she used to feel guilt, but she didn't feel guilt any more. If she wanted to go to the gym, it was OK.'

ii) The Lean Email Simple System

The study of time management, and the subsequent translation of this knowledge into accessible research and punchy advice in book form, has been going on for a while. The Internet, and a growing awareness of how much time we spend on activities not available to our parents, have hastened the variety and supply of these books, as has the move away from the traditional office and factory-based work towards the freelance and the start-up. But the truly groundbreaking volumes appeared some time before. The most influential appeared in 1989: Stephen R. Covey's *The 7 Habits of Highly Effective People*. Covey, who died in 2012, described himself as a 'lifetime student' of time management, and believed that the essence of the entire field could be simmered down to the phrase 'organize and execute around priorities'. Writing his best-selling book, for instance, became his priority for several months, a level of concentration he attained by following his own principle of putting 'first things first'. He clearly got something right – his publishers claim sales in excess of 25 million copies.*

In the book, Covey classifies three generations of time management advice, each building on the last. The first revolved around the construction of lists, 'an effort to give some semblance of recognition and inclusiveness to the many demands placed on our time and energy'. The second generation he classifies as a period of calendars and appointment books, a desire to look ahead and plan. And the third wave is an attempt to prioritise the demands on one's time, particularly in relation to our values, and to set corresponding goals. But Covey also suggested that the notion of time management was falling from favour; too many lists, and too strict an adherence to targets and goals, hindered human interaction and spontaneity. 'Time management' is really a misnomer, he believed. 'The challenge is not to manage time, but to manage ourselves.' But his conclusions were drawn up 25 years ago; the crowded shelves today suggest that few agreed with him.

And there is, after all, a fourth way. This involves a time management matrix Covey divided into four quadrants:

I. Urgent and Important, i.e. crises and significant deadlines
II. Not Urgent but Important, such as long-term planning and relationship building;
III. Urgent and Not Important, such as responding to distracting emails and non-relevant meetings (i.e. activities that others may judge important but you do not – activities based on the expectations of others)
IV. Not Urgent and Not Important, such as taking a break

---

* There were spin-offs too: the audio book, embedded into the car cassette player of every rep, was the first to sell a million; *Living the Seven Habits*, the follow-up book, suggested personal applications in the real world; and just when you thought there were no more habits, there was *The 8th Habit: From Effectiveness to Greatness*.

from normal pressures to enjoy activities that add
nothing specific to the working day

'Some people are literally beaten up by problems all day
every day,' Covey writes. '[Ninety] per cent of their time is
in Quadrant I and most of the remaining 10 per cent is in
Quadrant IV, with only negligible attention paid to Quadrants
II and III. That's how people who manage their lives by crisis
live.' Others spend a lot of time in Quadrant III, Covey
suggests, 'thinking they're in Quadrant I. They spend most of
their time reacting to things that are urgent, assuming they're
also important.' Where then should one spend one's time?
Clearly not in Quadrants III and IV, for those who live there
'basically lead irresponsible lives'. But it is Quadrant II that
provides the heart of effective personal management. 'It deals
with things that are not urgent, but are important. Not only
what US presidents once called 'the vision thing', but also
writing a personal mission statement, clarifying values, taking
exercise and preparing oneself mentally for the ambitions
ahead. Covey was writing before mindfulness became a
conscious force, but that would have been in Quadrant II too.

The quadrants were intended to apply to a fairly traditional
business environment, but can be adapted to a less formal
and more private digital world. In both, the message is the
same and seemingly obvious: do important things first. Covey
then falls back on mantras of the David Brent variety: effective
people are not problem minded, they're opportunity minded.
They feed opportunities and starve problems.

But before these epithets became mantras – in fact, 82
years before – Arnold Bennett wrote the time management
book to end (it was perhaps thought at the time) all time
management books, and it even had an ironic title: *How to
Live on Twenty-Four Hours a Day*. Bennett is best remembered
for his novels based on life in the Potteries, and perhaps for

the omelette named after him after his stay at the Savoy.* His time management book appeared at the height of his fame in 1910, and was so brief that he claimed it was dwarfed by the length of some of its reviews. Judged by today's standards, his analysis and advice was stern, forthright and patronising; but to his reviewers, and presumably his large readership, his guidance was original and worthwhile.

Not enough time to do all the things you want to do in the evening? Then get up an hour earlier in the morning. Too tired in the morning to get up an hour earlier and worried about not getting enough sleep? 'My impression, growing stronger every year [he wrote in an undated preface to a new edition of the book] is that sleep is partly a matter of habit – and of slackness. I am convinced that most people sleep as long as they do because they are at a loss for any other diversion.' (The doctors he spoke to confirmed this, he wrote.) But how would one start the day without food and servants at the newly proposed, ungodly hour? Why, ask your servant the night before to lay out a tray with a spirit lamp, a teapot and some biscuits. 'The proper, wise balancing of one's whole life may depend upon the feasibility of a cup of tea at an unusual hour.'

Bennett maintained an upbeat tone; life, he believed, was both wondrous and too short, and although time was finite it was also – contradictory as it may seem – our one renewable resource. 'The supply of time is truly a daily miracle,' he proclaimed as if from the pulpit, 'an affair genuinely astonishing when one examines it. You wake up in the morning and lo! Your purse is magically filled with twenty-four hours of the unmanufactured tissue of the universe of your life!' He particularly welcomed the levelling democracy of time – the cloakroom attendant at the Carlton Hotel had as much as the aristocracy she served. Time was not money, as Benjamin

* *Anna of the Five Towns* and *Clayhanger*; haddock and parmesan.

Franklin had proclaimed. Neither wealth nor breeding nor genius was ever rewarded by even an extra hour a day; money could be earned, whereas time was priceless.

Bennett selected some interesting targets, including his own profession. Novels were all very well, but reading them seldom stretched the working day the way a good self-improvement book was able to do. A reader 'deciding to devote ninety minutes three times a week to a complete study of the works of Charles Dickens will be well advised to alter his plans'.

Poetry, on the other hand, 'produces a far greater mental strain' than the novel, and was the highest form of literature: *Paradise Lost*, he attested, was thus by far the best way to spend your leisure time.*

Bennett acknowledged that his advice was perhaps a little too didactic and abrupt, but he pressed on. The key to good time management was to respect a pre-ordered daily programme, but not to be enslaved by it. 'Oh no,' Bennett had heard a beleaguered wife exclaim, 'Arthur always takes the dog out for exercise at eight o'clock and he always begins to read at a quarter to nine. So it's quite out of the question that we should . . . ' The note of finality here, the author suggests, reveals 'the unsuspected and ridiculous tragedy of a career'.

And at all costs one must avoid becoming a prig. 'A prig is a pert fellow who gives himself airs of superior wisdom. A prig is a pompous fool who has gone out for a ceremonial walk, and without knowing it has lost an important part of his attire, namely, his sense of humour.' The lesson, Bennett claimed, is to 'remember that one's own time, and not other

---

* There were a few exceptions: *Aurora Leigh*, a novel by E.B. Browning, was singled out by Bennett as a magnificent story with 'social ideas'; the novel is written in verse.

people's time, is the material with which one has to deal; that the earth rolled on pretty comfortably before one had to balance a budget of the hours, and that it will continue to roll on pretty comfortably whether or not one succeeds in one's new role of chancellor of the exchequer of time.'

Before Bennett there was *Walden* by Henry David Thoreau. Published in 1854 this was, the original survivalist meditation on how to declutter your life and live simply and 'deliberately' in a cabin without going completely fruitcake. Thoreau did go a bit fruitcake, though, and he certainly went pretentious: 'If you have built castles in the air your work need not be lost; that is where they should be. Now put the foundations under them.'

Walden was less a treatise on time management than it was a total soul rethink. Its transcendental showboating was closer to the rhetoric of Seneca and St Augustine than the balanced-life aspirations of Laura Vanderkam or Stephen Covey. But it did have traction. Thoreau held a stargazy and unrealistic vision of the dignity of rural life (he stuck it out in the wild on his ownsome for 26 months), and his tone is both antisocial and elitist. But for those who can't quite bring themselves to cut loose from the Internet, his heady vision of puritan living among the woodland grubs has become a highly effective (if primitive and unattainable) self-help manual. With Thoreau as your guide you don't just learn 18 productivity tips to super-boost your workday, you retune your mind to when the earth was primordial and cold, and everyone knew someone who owned a scythe, and the poor were all secretly happy, and you could sit in a chair by a pond for most of the day and contemplate the navel beneath your hair shirt, and a river ran through it. Or, if you liked the sound of all this but were a bit worried about the deer ticks, you could just get camouflaged and go paintballing.

Of course, we are all time management experts to a degree;

every waking decision requires at least some element of temporal expertise. And even the most self-assured are beset by questions that may be interpreted as crises. Our time is short, so what do we prioritise as worthy of it? Who is to say that strawberry picking is preferable to making a lot of money? Will our children benefit doubly from seeing us for four hours every evening as opposed to two?

And can any of these books really help us in these decisions? Can even the most cogently aligned bullet point and quadrant matrix transform a hard-wired mind? The notion of saving four hours every ten minutes is challenged by *The Slow Fix: Why Quick Fixes Don't Work* by Carl Honoré. The book set its tone with an epigram from *Othello*: 'How poor are they who have not patience! What wound did ever heal but by degrees?'* The quick fix has its place, Honoré argues – the Heimlich manoeuvre, the duct tape and cardboard solution from Houston that gets the astronauts home in Apollo 13 – but the temporal management of one's life is not one of them. He reasons that too much of our world runs on unrealistic ambitions and shabby behaviour: a bikini body within a fortnight, a TED talk that will change the world, the football manager sacked after two months of bad results.** He cites examples of rushed and dismal failings from manufacturing (Toyota's failure to deal with a problem with a

* Honoré has entered these waters before. He is the author of the popular gospel of deceleration *In Praise of Slow* (2004), a persuasive and punchy rationale for the more considered life. It sets out its stall succinctly in the opening paragraph: 'What is the very first thing you do when you wake up in the morning? Draw the curtains? Roll over to snuggle up with your partner or pillow? Spring out of bed and do ten push-ups to get the blood pumping? No, the first thing you do, the first thing everyone does, is check the time.' The clock, he argues (and who can dispute it?), gives us our bearings, and tells us how to respond. Are we early or late? 'Right from that first waking moment, the clock calls the shots.' His book champions another path.

** He says that the average tenure of the professional football manager in England has fallen from 3.5 to 1.5 years in the 20 years since 1992.

proper solution that might have prevented the recall of 10 million cars) and from war and diplomacy (military involvement in Iraq). And then there is medicine and healthcare, and the mistaken belief – held too often by the media and initially the Bill and Melinda Gates foundation – that a magic bullet could cure the big diseases if only we worked faster and smarter and pumped in more cash. Honoré mentions malaria, and the vague but quaint story of a phalanx of IT wizards showing up at the Geneva headquarters of the World Health Organisation with a mission to eradicate malaria and other tropical diseases. When he visited he found the offices somewhat at odds with those of Palo Alto (ceiling fans and grey filing cabinets, no one on a Segway). 'The tech guys arrived with their laptops and said, "Give us the data and the maps and we'll fix this for you."' Honoré quotes one long-term WHO researcher, Pierre Boucher, saying. 'And I just thought, "Will you now?" Tropical diseases are an immensely complex problem . . . Eventually they left and we never heard from them again.'

The proper, applied fix to many problems may provide useful tools far beyond their immediate applications: peace negotiators in the Middle East, perhaps, or teens devoted to multi-level gaming challenges, may have fresh insight into entrenched attitudes. And Honoré has a personal quest too: to find a lasting remedy for his chronic bad back, rather than the instant but transient relief he's put up with for years.

But Honoré is outnumbered. For every Honoré there are 20 quick-fixers with no time for the long haul. And if the quick fix isn't quick enough for the quick-fixers, they may depend on the super-quick fix, the kernels of the nuggets of the gems for people with *really* busy lives. There is, after all, a solution to the problem of not having enough time to read all the time management books: highperformancelifestyle.net. Here, a man called Kosio Angelov, the author of *The Lean*

Email Simple System, has asked 42 productivity management people how they maintain their focus. So Laura Vanderkam and her friends each came up with three bullets to break wasteful daily cycles and help them stay broken. Maura Thomas, for example, the force behind the website Regain Your Time, suggests 1) Be specific and positive: articulate your new single aim (rather than 'spend less time checking email'). 2) Identify your obstacles. 3) Tie new behaviour to a reward such as a coffee treat.

George Smolinski, the '4-Hour Physician', advocates 1) Doing your new habit at the same time and in the same surroundings each day. 2) 'Write it down!' 3) 'Eat an elephant.' (One bite at a time.) And Paula Rizzo, billed on the website as 'List Producer', suggests 1) 'Obviously you must start with a list!' 2) Split up things into small parts. 3) Reward good work with a treat, 'like listening to your favourite song'.

But what happens if your online life is too full to read even these three svelte tips? Then you're in luck. Because all the strategies from 42 specialists have been reduced down like a good French stock.

1. (As selected by 15 experts): Start Small and Break Down Your Workload into Manageable Tasks.
2. (11 votes): Do it Consistently and Don't Break the Chain.
3. (10 votes): Have a Plan and Prepare in Advance.
4. (9 votes): Use an Accountability Buddy – someone who will track your progress and encourage you towards your goals.
5. (8 votes): Reward Yourself.

Good luck everyone!

'What was good to block out the clock? Another clock!'

Chapter Thirteen

Life Is Short, Art Is Long

i) *The Clock* Is a Clock

People tend to be snooty about online features made up entirely of lists, but who wouldn't genuinely enjoy a photo story entitled 'The 21 Most Unusual Horses That Make Even Unicorns Seem Basic'? Or 'These 15 Dogs Would Take It Back If They Could . . . Unfortunately They Must Live In Regret'? It was perhaps inevitable that someone with too much time on their hands would make a list called '8 Films Where People Hang From Giant Clocks'.*

1) *Safety Last!*
2) *Back to the Future*. (A bold tribute to *Safety Last!* as Doc Brown harnesses the power of the Hill Valley clock tower to get Marty McFly back to the present.)
3) *Hugo*. (Another tribute to *Safety Last!* as director Martin Scorsese incorporates a clip of Harold Lloyd, and the whole film, set in a railway station, is inspired by clocks and clockwork precision.)
4) *The Great Mouse Detective*. (Sherlockian animated caper in which the evil Ratigan battles Basil and friends atop Big Ben.)**

---

* The first two are from Dose.com, which calls itself 'Entertainment. Nerd. Style. Hollywood. The World. More.' The '8 Clocks' list is from the list maniacs at BuzzFeed, compiled by a man named Justin Abarca.

** Technically, Big Ben is the nickname of the largest bell in the clock tower rather

5) *Shanghai Knights*. (Another Sherlockian caper featuring Jackie 'all his own stunts' Chan and Owen Wilson. Wilson goes out onto the face of Big Ben, and when he gets there he observes, 'You're about to die – you're on the minute hand of a clock.')

6) *Project A*. (Also featuring Jackie Chan, this time falling from a smaller clock tower after the face springs out from the building, as in *Safety Last!*)

7) *The 39 Steps*. (The 1978 version with Robert Powell as Richard Hannay smashing his way through the glass on Big Ben to ensure the minute hand doesn't reach 11.45, thus preventing a bomb exploding at the Houses of Parliament – not in the original John Buchan story).

8) *Peter Pan*. (Disney version where Peter and the Darlings walk along Big Ben's minute hand en route to Neverland.)

But there is another movie where people hang from clocks, and viewers do too, and that is *The Clock* by Christian Marclay. Here are six reasons to see it:

1) It's a perfectly executed idea. It consists of about 12,000 clips from famous old films showing clocks, watches or the anxiety of timekeeping, and they are pieced together to last 24 hours.

2) It won the main prize at the Venice Biennale in 2011, and its reviews were laudatory. The novelist Zadie Smith judged it 'sublime' in the *New York Review of Books*; the *Times Literary Supplement* found that 'his extraordinary achievement is philosophical, elegant, hypnotic, frequently hilarious'.

3) It will be free to view. Marclay didn't obtain copyright

------

than the four-faced clock itself. And the clock tower is now officially known as Elizabeth Tower.

clearance for the use of his clips, believing they would constitute 'fair use' as an artwork. Accordingly, the institutions that purchased copies to screen the film (six copies in all including the Museum of Modern Art in New York and the National Gallery of Canada) agreed not to charge the public an admission price to see it.

4) You can leave your watch behind. The time shown on every clip – many are just a few seconds long – is synchronised with the outside world. If you are watching it downstairs in the White Cube gallery in Mason's Yard, London, where it was first shown in October 2010, and an alarm clock or grandfather clock on the screen shows 8.40 a.m., then the rush hour is still roaring in Piccadilly up the road. If a clock on a prison wall is showing 1.18 p.m., then you may be watching in your lunch break. *The Clock* is a clock: that is its gimmick and template, and also its unique genius.

5) You can see it at four in the morning. Although most screenings will be during regular museum hours, a stipulation of purchase stated that there would also be a handful of 24-hour screenings. On many occasions there have been queues to get in before daybreak. When Daniel Zalewski put in a night shift for the *New Yorker*, he found the experience akin to reading the novels of Haruki Murakami, 'when characters cross over into another universe'. He advised readers to visit between 10 p.m. and 7 a.m. The film then 'tugs on your body – especially after midnight. The longer you stay up – after Klute, Mr and Mrs Smith and dozens of other characters have gone to bed – the more giddy and delirious you feel, and you become one with the blearily agitated characters onscreen.'

6) It's mesmerising. You may plan to watch for an hour or so, but three hours later you will be struggling to pull yourself away. *The Clock* casts a spell far more powerful

than its feats of research and editing and artistic endurance might suggest. It is a celebration of film and the representation of time within its borders (one is reminded just how willingly we suspend time when watching a movie, and how time is so frequently the unnamed character in the drama). You will emerge from it with a heightened sense of time, reminded, as if you need to be at this late hour, what a dominant role it plays in our lives.

I was late to *The Clock*. I saw it at the Los Angeles County Museum of Art when the film was already five years old, but of course it was timeless. The sign outside the room where it was screening suggested that the work casts time as 'a multifaceted protagonist . . . revealing each passing minute as a vehicle for dramatic possibilities'. It spoke of the clips as 'found footage', which they were, but only in so far as Marclay had employed a team of seven researchers to watch tens of thousands of hours of film to find the suitable material for him to splice together. The sign also said, 'All forms of photography and audio and video recording are prohibited.'

Inside there are white IKEA sofas (Marclay was quite specific about these), and the film is already well under way when I enter at about 11.30. In fact, the film has been underway all the time since this particular screening opened five weeks before, running behind locked doors all night so as not to upset the synchronisation: to turn it off would be like stopping a clock for the hours one doesn't observe it.

There are two other people in the room. The first sequence I see is from *Falling Down*, with Michael Douglas as a man experiencing a day where his whole life appears to be collapsing around him; at about 11.33, in one of the lighter scenes, he is told that McDonald's has stopped serving breakfast at 11.30. Then there's *I Want to Live*, a woman strapped to a chair awaiting execution – the second hand of a clock moves towards her fate as the scene cuts to a telephone that doesn't ring to pardon her. Then there's a clip from an episode of *The Twilight Zone* called 'A Matter of Minutes', in which an American couple have slipped forward two hours into a time loophole in which every minute in history represents a different world that must be continually rebuilt; as one character tells them, 'It's the sound of actual time approaching!' Then it was *Easy Rider*, with Peter Fonda realising his watch was broken, and at 11.42 it was *The Thirty-Nine Steps*. A nice surprise at 11.44 to see another man hanging from a clock in the film *My Learned Friend*, and then perhaps the longest scene of the whole 24 hours – Christopher Walken's wonderful four-minute much-travelled wristwatch monologue from *Pulp Fiction*.

I thought I'd be ready to leave after a couple of hours, but after three I was still feeling the pull that Zadie Smith and many others had experienced. With most video art shown on a loop in a museum one sits on a hard bench and expects a medal of endurance after five minutes, but this had a hold on me as great as anything I had seen at my local cinema. It was a bit like the early days of MTV: even if you didn't like or recognise what was going on at that moment, you knew that the moment after there would probably be something thrilling. And so it was. At 2.36 two scenes from Ingmar Bergman's *Fanny and Alexander* were bisected by one from Woody Allen's *Interiors*, and then it was Harold Lloyd just hanging there.

One may appreciate this huge collage in many ways, from the surface to the subterranean. Every viewer will have his or her own expectations and favourites, and perhaps sigh when that clip appears. But after a short while a more expansive picture emerges: how actors age through their careers (sometimes backwards – look at Jack Nicholson move from wizened wash-up in *About Schmidt* to wild-eyed buck in *One Flew Over the Cuckoo's Nest*; Michael Caine, Maggie Smith and Al Pacino come in for similar cinematic Botox). We also witness the maturing material possibilities of film itself, from the bouncing jagged life force of the silents to the huge swarming vistas of CGI. The trickery, the manipulation of time that permits our escape into make-believe, has been with us for a century; the technology to make this possible has advanced in sync with our capacity to disbelieve it. (And of course the advance of technology has enabled Marclay to put a film lasting 24 hours on a computer file and access it at random, a concept that would have left Harold Lloyd, Fatty Arbuckle and Stan Laurel with sorer heads than any attainable in slapstick. The relative physical properties of celluloid and digital film, particularly as they relate to time, have quite altered the potential artistic landscape.)

I did finally leave for a bit of sun at around 3. But then I felt compelled to go back in, experiencing a new sensation: the film was in charge. Because it would always be running, it had no need for an audience. No one was there to count the box office, and no one would make a loss if no one watched it. It was time without money: a rare thing in both the entertainment industry and the art world.

Marclay himself, in an interview with Jonathan Romney for *Sight & Sound*, explained that beyond the precise alliances of time between those displayed in his found footage and the timing of his film in the real world (which he pieced together hour by hour), he was also interested in more general notions of time, 'so someone waiting has a body language that expresses impatience or longing or boredom. Sometimes it can be more symbolic – memento mori images, like a flower wilting, a petal falling, the sun setting.' One reason the viewer is so compelled by *The Clock* has to do with how the fragmentation and deconstruction of its contents are rendered whole and harmonious. Perhaps only in the cinema will we comfortably surrender our regular expectations of space and time. 'The false continuity that I was trying to create is, to me, more connected to the way time flows,' Marclay says. 'There can be a seamless flow and momentum of a gesture from one film to the next, but it jumps from colour to black and white, and you know it's not true, but you still believe in it.' (It may be no coincidence that Marclay, though born in California, grew up in Switzerland, which trades on the unarguable commodity of time as if there was no tomorrow.)

Romney observed that *The Clock* 'is poised between scholarly focus and fetishistic obsession', which is true, and it does this without losing its sense of playfulness. When he's not making films, Marclay spends much of his time as an artful DJ manipulating recorded sound, and his experience in mixing is here brought to blend and mock the narrative of film: thus Romola Garai, driving a car in *Glorious 39*, which was set in the 1930s but made in 2009, is chased by Burt Reynolds in the 1970s. And Jean-Pierre Léaud in 1970s Paris pursues Alan Wheatley as 'Kolley Kibber' in 1940s *Brighton Rock*.

World cinema beyond Europe and Hollywood is only moderately represented: Marclay's researchers noted how seldom a watch or clock appears in Bollywood, an indication of a society concerned with higher things than punctuality.

There is no directory or index of all the films used in *The Clock*. There is, however, a crowd-sourced Wikia page which takes a decent shot at minute-by-minute compilation.* At the top of the list, which begins at midnight with Big Ben exploding in *V for Vendetta*, contributors are encouraged to 'Feel free to add movie titles and perhaps short scene descrip-

---

* See theclockmarclay.wikia.com. Judging by the full and empty slots, the film has been watched and noted extensively between 10 a.m. and 12.30 p.m., and between 1.30 p.m. and 7.20 p.m. But from 7.20 p.m. to midnight (with the exception of a busy patch from 10.15 to 10.45) there's a barren spell. Did people just not visit during this period? Did they visit and fall asleep? Were they so entranced that no one took notes?

tions if you want. Take care not to confuse A.M. and P.M. Remember, A.M. is morning and P.M. is evening.' And then one of the contributors pointed out that Marclay and his team had done just that, mistakenly slotting a scene from Billy Wilder's *Fortune Cookie* in at 7.17 p.m. rather than 7.17 a.m. The wider point, perhaps, is not that *The Clock* got it wrong, but that anyone noticed.

Five weeks after seeing *The Clock* in LA, I drove to Cambridge, England, to attend the UK premiere of another film that lasted 24 hours. These ambitious films were becoming a genre, a durational art form: to examine the notion of time they had to be about time themselves. *Night and Day* drew much from the idea of *The Clock*, for it was also a collage of old footage, but this time it was drawn not from the fathomless possibilities of every film ever made, but from one source – the archives of the BBC television series *Arena*.

Arena began as a fairly straightforward arts documentary programme in October 1975, but now, 600 or so episodes later, stands not only as one of Britain's most unpredictable and inspiring entertainments, but also (as one would reasonably expect from the longest-running arts documentary series on television) one of its greatest creative resources. It was celebrating its fortieth birthday at the Cambridge Film Festival with an original thought: what if film was tied not to an exact time but a vague one – the idea of breakfast or lunch, or of a rush hour or a Sunday morning. *Night and Day* is a more contemplative endeavour than *The Clock*, a voluminous moodscape rather than a strict tempo, and it makes similarly seamless and compelling viewing. As before, one watches for hours, and time is both central and irrelevant, a magnificent obsession.

The film's subtitle is *The Arena Time Machine*, and it's a battered and well-travelled one. Between noon and 1 p.m., the Rolling Stones arrive in Morocco for a drumming master-class and Luis Buñuel explains how to make the perfect dry Martini. Between 4 p.m. and 5 p.m. Francis Bacon and William Burroughs take tea, while Jude Law performs in a matinee of Pinter's *The Lover*. Between midnight and 1 a.m. Ken Dodd is still on stage and John Lydon remembers punk. Between 2 a.m. and 3 a.m. Nico is in the Chelsea Hotel and Fred Astaire and Frank Sinatra are crooning. Between 6 a.m. and 7 a.m. both Don McCullin and Sebastião Salgado like the light, while Sonny Rollins plays sax on a bridge in New York. Between 11 a.m. and noon, T.S. Eliot considers *The Wasteland* while Peter Blake paints the wrestler Kendo Nagasaki. The talent on offer is immense on both sides of the camera, and one is swept into a rousing tide of optimism for the arts. This is their value. If we spend our time wisely we can both make and appreciate the worthwhile things in this world.

I took a break from the screening to talk to *Arena*'s series editor Anthony Wall, who has been involved with the programme almost from the beginning and is now responsible, with film editor Emma Matthews, for this new grand tour. Wall told me that he saw no reason why *Night and Day* couldn't now run on digital demand continuously and for ever, both online and as an app. Whenever you tuned in, a past subject of the programme would be in step with you. But unlike *The Clock*, *Night and Day* is not a fixed or completed work, and so Wall and Matthews will adapt their choice of material to the seasons (nightfall will be earlier in the winter than in summer) and to the days (when the film is screened at weekends it will have a slower pace and fewer scenes in offices). Wall says:

I've always wanted to find a documentary that never needed to end, and I think I've found it. The extraordinary thing is, you take a sequence that had a predetermined intention, and you cut it up and put it in a different place in time, and it has a whole new meaning. I think as a viewer looking at something over a long time we're attracted to a combination of order and chaos. But the key thing is that you can't stop the film and corrupt the timing, any more than you can stop Big Ben. The film will work on any platform, but my ideal would be to have it on one of those corny picture-frame things where you show your photographs, so you could actually have it as your clock.

The fact that both *Night and Day* and *The Clock* last precisely one day is a significant and engaging trick. It is a natural cycle, of course, the Earth spinning once on its axis. But the duration is only one element: it is the films' internal timings, both precise and emotional, that announce their directors' greatness, and this is not something you can say for some of the other films that demand our attention due to their length. There is Douglas Gordon's *24 Hour Psycho*, for example, an installation in which the Hitchcock film is slowed down to about two frames a second and thus lasts a day (the shower scene lasts about 45 minutes; disturbingly, Janet Leigh lies motionless with her eyes open for more than five minutes). Or *Cinématon*, the life project of director Gérard Courant, who has filmed, over a period of 36 years, almost 3,000 people doing silent things (dancing, staring, eating, laughing, fidgeting), each for a period of 3 minutes 25 seconds, thus ending up with a film that lasts 195 hours or 8 days and

3 hours. It is rarely shown.* For *Arena*'s Anthony Wall, it is the idea of the extended art project that is important, not necessarily the project itself. 'I've yet to meet a single video artist who thinks it's remotely important you should continue watching [their work until the end]. So here's the idea of David Beckham sleeping for 50 minutes – right, I've got that, do I actually have to go and see it? If I do, three seconds will be enough.** When Warhol filmed the Empire State Building [for 8 hours 5 minutes in 1964] he was taking the piss.'

Consideration of time in the movies spools back, as we have seen with the Lumière Brothers and Harold Lloyd, to the dawn of movies themselves. And with the popular success of *Memento* (Christopher Nolan's inspired running of twin

---

* We have long appreciated how technology has dictated the duration and consumption of our entertainment. While cinema has offered us many options to watch (multiple screenings over several weeks), television and radio have been the restrictive mediums. Programme length was dictated by the ease of scheduling in half-hourly slots (few programmes begin at 8.55 p.m., fewer still at 9.17), and by what was once considered to be the length of our attention spans. But then two things happened to wrest time back from the scheduler. The video recorder and Internet streaming seemed, for a while at least, to free us from the tyranny of the screen; we could master our own lives without having to worry about missing the outcome of a cliffhanger. Watching streaming programming today is much like reading a book – the viewer decides on the pace and duration, with binge-watching the equivalent of the 'couldn't put it down' novel. Indeed, in many households, the box set has *replaced* the novel. The result may be that we watch more than ever before, the next episode rolling on automatically almost before we have the chance to turn off ('it's *their* fault!'). The 8- or 10-hour series being released all at once on Netflix or Amazon Video has changed the programmes too, and likely for the better: a series no longer has to grab the viewer in the first episode to ensure they return the following week, and the narrative may enjoy a slower burn (unless it is a series like *24*, in which the intense temporal premise is built into it like an overwound spring). Increasingly a channel will just veg out, especially during holiday periods: 24-hour *Family Guy* and 24-hour *Friends* rolled out like half-hour bulletins on CNN or Sky News.
** A film of Beckham sleeping after a training session at Real Madrid, made by Sam Taylor-Wood, was shown at the National Portrait Gallery in 2004.

narratives in different timeframes), *Boyhood* (Richard Linklater's 12-year fictional study of growing up) and *Victoria* (Sebastian Schipper's nocturnal thriller shot in a single take), the subject continues to fascinate both film-makers and audiences. And then there is *Logistics*. This is a film lasting 37 days. According to the website of Daniel Andersson and Erika Magnusson, the two proud Swedes who had the idea for it, the film is an attempt to answer the Zen-like question 'Where do all the gadgets come from?' The 'gadgets' they had in mind included Kinder Eggs, mobile-phone circuit boards and coffee machines. 'Sometimes the world seems unfathomable,' they reasoned.

The simple answer to their question, perhaps unsurprisingly, is that these gadgets come from China on huge ocean-bound freighters. Cameras were thus attached to trains, boats and trucks, and we watch in horror as one chosen object (a pedometer) is transported very gradually from China to Sweden. The artists had another question: 'Would doing the same freight journey as the products enable us to understand more about the world and the global economy?'

The resulting 37-day attempt to find out is very boring, and you'd have to be a complete idiot to watch it all the way through. Days 1 and 2 are comparatively bearable, partly because they take place on a freight truck and a freight train, and partly because they are day 1 and day 2. Unfortunately for the viewer, days 3–36 are spent at sea, with incredibly slow-moving scenery. A gadget to measure walking pace is on a very slow ship. There are one or two beautiful sunrises, but mostly it's a view from a deck, and the view is of rectangular containers and grey horizons.* It's art, and, as the title suggests, logistics; the artists say it is

---

* Tellingly, when the film was shown at the 2014 Fringe Film and Video Festival in Shenzhen, China, it was in a dramatically shortened version: nine days.

also about 'consumerism and time'. Andy Warhol would
have flipped his wig. Isn't almost all art these days about
consumerism and time?

ii) White People Are Crazy

This is certainly the case in Milton Keynes. Here, at the
beginning of 2015 at the MK Gallery, 25 artists were curated
under the title *How to Construct a Time Machine*.* The show
was put together by Marquard Smith, the head of Doctoral
Studies in the School of Humanities at the Royal College of
Art, and, as one would hope for, offers some of the classic
works on the theme. Visitors are greeted by Ruth Ewan's
revolutionary 10-hour clock hanging above the entrance, and
soon afterwards it's John Cage's *4'33* from 1952, denoted in
the show's catalogue by blank sheet music (the work, his most
famous, a fact that must have rankled the composer at least
a little bit, is 4 minutes and 33 seconds of silence. But of
course it isn't total silence, it is *undirected sound*. The solo
pianist or orchestra assembles, and does nothing for three
movements, but the piece highlights the surrounding environmental sounds – the concert hall, the hum of lights, the
racket inside our heads). When *4'33* was performed at the
Barbican in London in 2010, the audience waited diligently
for the gaps between the three movements before they
coughed; they could have coughed at any time during the
nothing, but they waited until the nothing was over to create
something. Huge applause greeted its conclusion, and the

* The title comes from an essay by Alfred Jarry published in France in 1899:
'Commentary and Instructions for the Practical Construction of The Time
Machine'. It was a cod-scientific examination, couched in the newly emergent
language of modern physics popularised by Lord Kelvin, of how the fantastical time
machine proposed four years before by H.G. Wells might become a reality.

conductor mopped his brow, and the orchestra smiled as they took several bows. It was a silent comedy. Viewing the piece on YouTube, where it has been watched more than 1.6 million times, one encounters the comments:

'Would anyone by chance have the sheet music for this? I've been looking to learn it.'

'The worst point is, the orchestra needed six weeks of rehearsals to get it right.'

'Somebody should have let out a big fart.'

'White people are fucking crazy.'

Then there is *One Year Performance 1980–81 (Time-Clock Piece)* by Tehching Hsieh, a six-minute film in which the Taiwanese artist reflected on his inability to obtain a work permit in the USA. Every hour for a year Hsieh put on a silver-grey factory uniform and punched a time clock but did no work: this activity thus became the artwork, and the film consists of 8,627 still images compressing his endeavours.* Hsieh's stamped time cards showed the passage of time, but he also had another method: he shaved his head at the beginning of the year, and as the time-lapse film progresses, it grows.

In the catalogue to the show, Marquard Smith explains that the subject of art and time is one whose time has come. He refers to a survey by Christine Ross called *The Past is the Present; It's the Future Too: The Temporal Turn in Contemporary Art*, which notes that between 2005 and the book's publication in 2012 there were at least 20 exhibitions on time. In 2014 Marquand kept his own tally, adding shows in Harlem, Amsterdam, Rotterdam, Barcelona and Zagreb and a couple of conferences too. He has no answer as to why this should

---

* For those unfamiliar with the phrase, 'punching the clock' should not be taken literally. The action involves inserting a time card into an electronic stamping machine, thus denoting the time a worker arrives for and leaves work.

be, other than the fact that the subject is exciting, multi-faceted, ever-present and insistent. Displayed together, Marquand has detected a rhythm to his disparate selection of work, noting how they challenge and fold back on each other, and how, by playfully recreating the natural order of past, present and future, they all serve as time machines. And some of them are just plain funny, such as Martin John Callanan's *Departure of All*, an airport departure board listing 25 flights – Amsterdam to Gran Canaria, Melbourne to Dubai, Paris to Riyadh – with all the flights leaving simultaneously at 2.11. And Mark Wallinger's *Time and Relative Dimensions in Space*, a full-scale rethink of a London police box and *Doctor Who*'s Tardis, but in silver, suggesting infinite possibilities for adventure inside, but on the outside only reflections of ourselves.

The cyclical nature of time tends to make artists obsessive, but you'd have to get up very early in the day to be more obsessed with the passing of time than On Kawara. Not long after he moved to New York from his native Japan in 1965, Kawara began his *Today Series*, a collection of paintings consisting only of the day's date. Most were the size of a laptop, exquisitely executed in several layers of Liquitex acrylic, white on a dark background, the letters and numerals arranged in the style favoured by the country in which he was painting that day. Most were painted in New York, so appear as APRIL.27,1979 or MAY.12,1983. The one at Milton Keynes was painted in Iceland, so reads 27.ÁG.1995. On completion, each painting would be put in a box with a local newspaper clipping displaying the date, but if Kawara failed to complete a painting in a day, he would destroy it. Looking at his work had an energising effect on me – one of those things, like a close shave on a bike or recovery from illness, which makes one appreciate how many days one has left. I didn't feel nostalgia; I felt release. Can one place a spiritual value on this kind of singular and possessed art?* Before he died in June 2014, Kawara had painted – and thus completed and perhaps owned – around 3,000 days.

One of my favourites in the Milton Keynes show was, predictably enough, a film called *Safety Last* by Catherine Yass. The film lasts just over two minutes, but consists of just one 12-second clip repeated on a loop (the clip, of course, is Harold Lloyd on that clock, the bit where his weight tips the minute hand from a quarter to three back to half past two). But in Yass's version, the clip disintegrates as it plays, each time becoming grainier and scratchier, until at the end, by its tenth appearance, it is just a storm of static ribbons. Yass re-filmed the original version using colour film, so that the disintegration on the emulsion is both more effective and more beautiful. Or, in the artist's words, 'setting up a space of dream and memory that works against the descriptive linear perspective of the monochrome image'.

I'd known Yass since we were teens. But until I visited Milton Keynes I had no idea she was so interested in Harold Lloyd. She told me she was attracted to *Safety Last!* by its combination of comedy and potential tragedy. She liked the idea of time being pulled backwards, and the disintegration of the image was also a comment on the materiality of film as it became eclipsed by newer technologies.

I asked her why time was such a popular subject for artists

---

* The monetary value is easier. At an auction at Sotheby's New York in 2001, one of his days (FEB.27,1987) sold for $159,750. But some days are worth more than others: in June 2006 at Sotheby's London MAY.21,1985 and JULY.8,1981 each sold for £209,600. In October 2012, also in London, JAN.14, 2011 went for £313,250. And in July 2015, Sotheby's London sold OCT.14,1981 for £509,000. Put the increases down to time, inflation, the growing reputation of the artist, the artist's death in 2014, and craziness.

Kawara's interest in mortality and our temporal span had other outlets too. For a number of years he would send daily telegrams to friends with a simple message: 'I AM STILL ALIVE'.

and creators. Many artists are now looking back at Modernism, she said, and the artistic focus on time certainly stretched as far back as Futurism, Vorticism and Cubism (what was Cubism if not a single plane with several viewpoints considered all at once?). And of course before that there was photography and early film, where time could be frozen and reversed. To a modern artist, the explorative possibilities of time were practically inexhaustible.

A few weeks after *How to Construct a Time Machine* closed, the artist Cornelia Parker made her own contribution to the crowded field. Parker had been approached by HS1, the company that runs St Pancras International Station, in collaboration with the Royal Academy, to make an artwork for a series called *Terrace Wires*. She could do whatever she wanted, so long as it would make travellers arriving and departing on the Eurostar look up at the station's magnificent ironwork roof. Her work would be suspended above the passengers, but what would she put up there? The two previous participants in the project had put up a rainbow wall of Perspex (David Batchelor) and clouds (Lucy + Jorge). Several of Cornelia Parker's witty and challenging works had asked abstract questions about deep time and gravity, not least her famous frozen-in-the-moment blown-up shed (*Cold Dark Matter: An Exploded View*) and an event in Boston called *At the Bottom of This Lake Lies a Piece of the Moon* in which she had thrown a lunar meteorite she had bought on the Internet. 'Instead of us landing on the moon it was the moon landing on us.'

'I think my first thought [when asked to put up work at St Pancras] was no. There is so much going on in the station – how can I compete with that?' But then she had a vision of how it might work. 'I'd just come back from France on the Eurostar, and I was walking down the station, and David Batchelor's piece was up, and it was blotting out the clock. I thought that I could do a piece that blocks out the clock. What was good to block out the clock? Another clock.'

Parker was speaking to about 60 people by the St Pancras champagne bar, near the statue of John Betjeman, and because it was a normal weekday evening the station was busy and loud. We seemed to be the only still thing in the place. The artist explained how she had decided to make a replica of the white clock affixed at one end of the station, but hers would be black, its negative, and it would seem to float. It would be the same size as the original (5.44 metres in diameter, 1.6 tonnes of steel) and hang about 16 metres in front of it, floating directly over passengers' heads. Both clocks would tell the same time, although the time may read slightly differently – give or take half a minute – depending on a passenger's viewing angle. And at another vantage point, the original clock would be entirely eclipsed.* Parker wanted her piece to reflect the rarefied nature of time in a train station – the constant rushing, the anxiety of being late – the idea that time hangs above us like a perilous chandelier, a sword of Damocles. She was also keen to introduce the notion of a slower time reference, a deeper psychological or planetary time. And she wanted to pose a heady astronomical question:

---

* Parker's replica was made by Smith of Derby, whereas the original was made by Dent of London, the same company that made Big Ben. The original clock was not, however, the original at all. This had been sold by British Rail in the 1970s to help fund station renovation (reportedly to an American collector for £250,000) but had been dropped during its removal. The fragments were bought for £25 by a retired train driver named Roland Hoggard, who spent more than a year reconstructing it and securing it to the side of a barn in his garden in Nottinghamshire (the barn had once housed a steam engine). Dent subsequently built a replacement modelled on Hoggard's reconstruction, and improved its accuracy. Its gold-leafed slate hands are now controlled by GPS and checked every minute.

'What would eclipse time, if not time itself?' Parker called her clock, or at least the conceptual idea for the piece, *One More Time*. She said she wondered about having the French time on her clock, an hour ahead of London, but was concerned that this would confuse the passengers, who would assume they were an hour late for their trains. A deliberately wrong clock, especially an authoritative one at an international terminus, was clearly taking the artistic interpretation of time too far. But what if the time on the clock was turned back instead of forward? Perhaps only the future king of England could pull off a trick like that.

Walking back to happiness: Alice Waters and Prince Charles
in an Edible Schoolyard.

Chapter Fourteen

Slowing Down the World

i) A Place Where Time Stands Still

At some point towards the end of the twentieth century, Prince Charles had another one of his bright ideas. Disillusioned with the urban sprawl of the 1980s, the prince announced that callous modern architects had done more damage to the country than the Luftwaffe, and he had decided to do something about it. So he drew up a plan for a community that would combine beautiful dwellings with nearby workplaces and shops, a place where council tenants would mingle with the more prosperous, a place where traditional values would be upheld and kids would play hopscotch in the spotless streets. A powerful man does have that rare and enviable ability to turn back time.

The prince chose a plot of land he owned on the outskirts of Dorchester in Dorset. The patch is part of the Duchy of Cornwall, which consists of 126,000 acres in 22 counties, with the primary function of providing an income for the prince. He called his new town Poundbury, or New Poundbury (there was already an older Poundbury nearby, full of the stuff Charles disliked; the associations with chains Poundland and Poundworld, which sprang up after the new town was christened, are just unfortunate). The place would cover 400 acres and house 5,000 people. If you wanted to stop the world, or at least reduce the speed at which it was changing, this was the place you would put down your deposit.

Poundbury has been open for sneering ever since planning consent was granted in 1989; cynics just arrived on the train from London have a field day. There were no television aerials (ugly), no front gardens (divisive), no front-of-house parking (obstructive), nothing at all unsightly or untidy. There were so many rules that a visitor dropping a sweet wrapper might fear arrest by swooping helicopter.

It is a mistake to think of Poundbury merely as a model village or a new small town. It is also intended as an urban utopia, a vision not just of the Prince of Wales, but of ambitious town planners, fogey architects and all the respectable inhabitants who were slightly fearful of headlines involving pit bull terriers. But it was a hard concept for the media to get its head around. It was not intended as something off the grid like Hebridean or Austrian utopias from the 1930s and 1960s, it was not anti-progress, it was not antisocial or supercilious like the deliberate living of Henry David Thoreau's *Walden*, and there was no cult attached to it (apart from the Cult of Charles). Instead it sought to combine the best of all worlds – the lofty moral compass and manicured decency of herringboned Englishness with the eco-efficiencies and agri-advantages of the Internet age. Rooted in classicism and goodness, the architecture was to be *organic*. Poundbury had nothing against technology, so long as the cables were hidden from view, but there would be none of the dehumanising *froideur* that digitisation normally imbues. Instead, Poundbury would be warm and welcoming, and celebrate all those values considered lost to the mad pace of the industrial world. The attempt was a restoration of decent community under blue skies. Whether such a world ever actually existed in Dorset or elsewhere remains open for discussion.

I first visited in the spring of 2001, after it had been habitable for six years and about 500 people had moved in. It was certainly a novel place, and the novel it most resembled was something by Thomas Hardy. The prince's dream was first drawn up on paper by a town planner from Luxembourg named Léon Krier, who was a connoisseur of the design and planning principles of Albert Speer, chief architect of the Nazis. (He has written a book about Speer, and analysed his cleansing theories of postmodern classicism; rotten modernist buildings, he believed, would produce rotten modern citizens.)

Walking around Poundbury at the beginning of the new millennium was an eerie business, and I wasn't quite sure why. Many of the houses were occupied, but there didn't seem to be many people around. It reminded me of the gated 'communities' I had seen in Florida, except in Poundbury there were no gates and no visible security presence. The architectural principles of this new town reflected the American New Urbanism movement, a high-density enclave designed, as its development director Simon Conibear told me, with the intention of 'rehumanising the domestic environment.' In part, this meant living with less dependence on the car and a renewed trust in public buses, although a survey conducted a few years after it opened found that there were more cars per household in Poundbury than in neighbouring towns. To its credit, Poundbury has little superfluous street furniture, and despite the huge amount of rules imposed on the town at the planning stage, there are few road signs telling you to keep to a speed limit or watch that child, because the roads are themselves rules, with blind corners ensuring that no one can go over 20. And you don't hear much hooting of horns from cars, partly out of politeness, one imagines, and partly because there isn't much to hoot at. Besides, a driver might wake one of the inhabitants, at any time of day.

'This is the street we took the Queen up,' Conibear said. ('It was a bit like a mother inspecting her son's school project,' one resident told me later.) Around every corner there's a financial services bureau or a place offering private healthcare (holistic, palliative, meditative). There is a pub, the Poet Laureate, alongside many specialist shops – blinds, bikes, bridal. The biggest industry in Poundbury is the Dorset Cereals muesli factory on the north-east edge, but this has chosen to remove Poundbury from its address, preferring the less exact but more romantic Dorchester. There were many beautiful buildings but no set style; the stonework and designs (everything from neo-Georgian to Victorian townhouse to a barn conversion) had been lifted from the most picturesque dwellings in Dorset's other villages and grouped together to form, ideally, something that was even more picturesque. Poundbury folk didn't take kindly to my suggestion that their new place of residence looked like a film set from *The Mayor of Casterbridge*; it's not always this quiet, they said, not when the football-mad kids get home from school (not that they're allowed to kick a ball against anyone's front wall). And it wasn't really that quiet anyway, because bulldozers and cement mixers were at work in the distance, building a second phase.

Simon Conibear then took me to the House of Dorchester chocolate factory, and he said, 'If you go around the back, you can get what I call droppings for £1.20 a bag.' I asked him about the Poundbury rules. 'Oh yes,' he said. 'We run it as a sort of draconian conservation area and people like that. They know that the area is not going to be disfigured.' The houses we pass cost from £150,000 to £350,000. The place names – Evershot Walk, Longmore Street, Pummery Square – are named after Duchy estate properties, such as farms. The prince is always consulted. There is one glaring exception: Brownsword Hall, the main focal point, is named after Andrew Brownsword, the man from Hallmark cards who stumped up the money for it.

A few crunchy footsteps from the hall lies the Octagon café, purveyors of fine coffee and panini. The owners Clay and Mary have sunk their life savings into the place and they are proud of the comments in their visitors' book. 'Really nice cakes,' one entry says, 'and comfy settees!'

At one table near the door, Lilian Hart and Rosemary Warren, both retired, were discussing Poundbury's progress. Mrs Warren and her husband were the first people to own a house here, while Mrs Hart and her husband were the second, moving in during January 1995. They adore it, not least the location. 'I can drive to the supermarket and be parked and shopping within four minutes, five at the most,' Mrs Hart said, perhaps slightly more concerned with speed and time economy than the architects of her town had intended. 'I can be at a hospital in two and a half minutes and within 30 seconds I'm in the country. I wanted a new house. At my age I don't want to be doing any maintenance – and it's beautifully insulated.' Both women wished there was an easier route to the airport because, like a lot of Poundbury folk, they usually fly away somewhere warm for the winter. And they'd like a little grocery store and a post office.

'But I have only one severe criticism,' Mrs Hart said. 'We have a playground across from us and it's not big enough. And it's in the wrong place.' She mentioned this to the Duchy people and heard back that there were 'rumours' that it would move. 'Prince Charles does take an interest in our views,' Mrs Warren said. 'When my husband died, he sent me a note.'

Other views met with less enthusiasm. Not much point complaining about the gravel, for instance, as Sue McCarthy-Moore did. 'I have two teenage daughters who are always treading it into the house,' she told me. The gravel is the colour of camels, a cheaper alternative to cobbles and more attractive than tarmac. It is almost everywhere in Poundbury and has the attraction of making everyone audible as they walk around, which helps with the neighbourhood watch.

And then there are other, bigger problems. Jonathan Glancey, the former architecture critic of the *Guardian*, believed 'it doesn't really work on any level. It's overwrought. You have to be gentle and loose with new buildings but there's been far too much effort put into it. The streets feel too wide because, unlike the old villages which inspired it, any new place is built with strict regulations that must allow those huge fire engines through.'

Clearly, it is easier to build model houses than a model community, no matter how many stringent rules and ethical codes its citizens enforce. 'Prince Charles's vision would incorporate men on every corner turning the leg of a chair on a lathe,' Glancey told me. 'But the reality is that people are upstairs in their bedroom furtively downloading who-knows-what from the Internet.'

I returned to Poundbury ten years after my first visit, and another five years after that. In 2016 it is still an intriguing place, and in many ways an admirable one. The vision remains consistent, the place appears to be working socially (it's not the ghost town some had feared), and the popularity of the concept means that the building is still ongoing. There were now about 2,500 inhabitants, about halfway to its target, the junior school is expanding, and the bulldozers and diggers are still on the outskirts, and the outskirts are edging ever closer to Dorchester. People like what they see, and what they don't, and they are still moving in from far-flung English outposts where things, in their estimation, have not worked out so well. You still come to Poundbury because you don't like the speed at which the world is changing, Little England for the UKIP age. The panic button is always close to hand, and the fire engines of the drawing board are now a reality: a huge fire station is now an unmissable feature of the town, reportedly based on a design by the prince himself. Like Poundbury as a whole, it has gained the usual fervent dichotomy of opinion: the locals generally approve, while the purists smirk. Clocking its Georgian grandeur garlanded in drains, the editor of the architecture and design magazine *Icon* called it 'the Parthenon meets Brookside', and suggested that the firefighters 'should be forced to wear Regency breeches and powdered wigs, and rush to their infernos in a red barouche carrying water in wooden pails'. Meanwhile, a reader of the *Daily Mail*, responding to photos in the newspaper, judged it 'much better than the modern tat inflicted on us in city centres!!!'*

Even in his most halcyon cups, Prince Charles must have realised that Poundbury would not be to everyone's taste. Indeed, its idiosyncrasy is part of its appeal. It's certainly not to my taste, but I would always take its vaulted ambition over the generic alternative of the little-boxes estate. The strangest thing of all about it is that, while its future is firmly rooted in the past, there is also something rather forward-thinking about its notion of the good life. In the late 1980s, when Poundbury was first mooted, the West's devotion to greed, speed and the aspirational whirlwind appeared limitless. With the social and environmental cost yet to be factored, and the economy yet to *Belgrano*, many could see no downside to it. But these days the notion (if not the reality) of Poundbury dovetails with the wider pursuit of a different sort of life. Something calmer and less frantic, with room for pensiveness and a re-evaluation of purpose. One sees it in mindfulness, in hit books devoted to colouring, woodchopping and *The Life-Changing Magic of Tidying*, in the elevation of crafting and making, in a longer-term consideration of the environment, in popular

---

* *Icon* marked its 150th issue with a glossary of words that should be banned, many of them integral to the slow living movement: eco, curated, artisanal, craft, experiential, sustainable, Scandinavian and timeless. The latter was defined as 'Adjective: Designed to last but destined to be replaced next year.'

lifestyle magazines named *Kinfolk* and *Oak* and *Hole &
Corner* with their precious emphasis on wooden spoon-
making and design from Scandinavia, and even in the
fanatical devotions of the urban barista. Although disparate
in display, and ripe for parody, these forces are unwittingly
banded together in what has become known as the slow
living movement and the new crafts movement; not so much
a rejection of everything connected with speed, but a way
of living that embraces things more meaningful than instant
gratification and the pursuit of the quick fix. In the book
The Kinfolk Home, for example, which is subtitled *Interiors
for Slow Living*, the editors Nathan Williams and Katie
Searle-Williams explain that 'Slow living is less of a style
and more of a deeply personal mentality . . . Slow living
isn't about determining how little we can live with – it's
about working out what we can't live without.' The goal is
not idleness, but pleasure through care and patience. (One
other notable aspect of slow living is how often the attempt
to describe it begins by describing what it is not.) As with
Poundbury, the movement is an easy thing to parody and
deride. Advocates of the slow life may be regarded as narcis-
sistic, backward-looking, smug and incredibly annoying. Is
the whole thing anything more than sterile romanticism?
The worst insult of all is that its chief practitioners offer
middle-class solutions to first-world problems. But some
parts of the movement are also concerned with matters
beyond the local availability of kale and chia seeds, aware
that at least one element of slow living already equates the
pursuit of simple pleasure with the politics of sustainability,
health security and the entire continuous wealth of nations.
In other words, what began as a desire for nice architecture
and a gentler pace of life is increasingly looking like a viable
way to save both our souls and the planet.

ii) Living Frenchly

Chez Panisse, one of the historic culinary landmarks of California, does not, at first glance, have a great deal in common with Poundbury. The weather outside is kinder, for one thing, and there is a more respectful attitude towards the French. But the founding principles are not so far removed, and they both share a distaste for the homogeneity of modern life. Besides, their respective founders are firm and long-term friends, with Prince Charles a great fan not only of Chez Panisse the restaurant, but also a great many of the political and social objectives to which its owner aspires.

Chez Panisse was established by a woman named Alice Waters in Berkeley in 1971. After chaotic beginnings and multiple crises, the restaurant earned a reputation as the epicentre of American slow food, and Waters became an unlikely champion of all that later became known as 'farm-to-table', with all its attendant core values: seasonal produce, local production, minimal use of pesticides and artificial fertilisers, nothing genetically modified, everything sustainable. The catchword, before it became a dirty word, was artisanal.

Waters was born in New Jersey, but she came of age in mid-1960s Berkeley at the time of free love and free speech; she channels that part of the counterculture that tried to change the world rather than the one that dropped out. She is most frequently described as 'elfin', and usually as indomitable. The writer Adam Gopnik has described her as 'the kind of American woman who a century ago would have been storming through saloons with a hatchet and is now steaming fresh green beans, but with similar motives'.

To Waters, slow food was a mood board: it had little to do with the length a pot stayed on the stove, because a plate of allotment heirloom tomatoes would fit the manifesto just as well. It was all about eating with integrity, and buying with respect for provenance. It was about eating the way we think our parents used to eat, or would have eaten, had they not too been always rushed off their feet.

In 2004, at Alice Waters's request, Prince Charles spoke at a conference organised by the slow food movement in Turin. He too had a definition. 'Slow food is traditional food,' he said at the conference, which was called Terra Madre (Mother Earth).

> It is also local – and local cuisine is one of the most important ways we identify with the place and region where we live. It is the same with the buildings in our towns, cities and villages. Well-designed places and buildings that relate to locality and landscape and that put people before cars enhance a sense of community and rootedness. All these things are connected. We no more want to live in anonymous concrete blocks that are just like anywhere else in the world than we want to eat anonymous junk food which can be bought anywhere. At the end of the day, values such as sustainability, community, health and taste are more important than pure convenience.

The prince believed that the importance of the slow food movement cannot be overstated. 'That is, after all, why I am here . . . to remind people as John Ruskin in the nineteenth century did, back in England, that "industry without art is brutality".'

'Representatives from 151 countries were present at that, and everybody was sceptical about him coming and speaking,' Alice Waters told me, 'but they all stood up at the end.' It was clear from the speech that the slow food movement lies at the heart of the slow living movement. It still may be best described by what it is not: it is not purely about food. It is not even particularly middle class. It has its roots in left-leaning politics and community welfare, and its dawn in north-west Italy speaks of a deeply traditional radicalism fused with a particularly agricultural conservatism.

The 'slow food manifesto' was published in November 1987, although by then its ideology had already been chewed over and digested for many years, principally in the Piedmontese town of Bra. The manifesto was written by the author and poet Folco Portinari, and stated that the world had been infested 'by the virus of fast life', and criticised those who 'can't tell the difference between efficiency and frenzy'. The biggest loss, the manifesto claimed, was the pursuit of pleasure; the joy had gone from the table, which meant that the delight had vanished from life. One galvanising force, as so often with food protests, was the imminent arrival the year before of a McDonald's, in this case near the Spanish Steps in Rome. But it was another unhappy meal in 1982 that inspired a man named Carlo Petrini to wonder whether the price we were paying for mediocre and soulless food served up with the guiding principle of speed of preparation was not, after all, too high.

According to Geoff Andrews, author of *The Slow Food Story: Politics and Pleasure*, Petrini and a group of friends were in Montalcino, Tuscany, when they called in for lunch at the town's Casa del Popolo, the workers' social club. They found the food filthy and cold, and, on returning home to Bra, Petrini wrote an open letter declaring his horror. The food was an insult to the region, and an insult to the region's fine wine. His letter drew both support and ridicule, the latter from those who thought that Petrini, a local councillor with a history of cultural radicalism, should busy himself with more important things than a disappointing lunch. There was much to be radical about: it was the beginning of the era of Italian aspirational hedonism that gave rise to Berlusconi. Petrini argued that there may be nothing as important as food: not so much the chilly pasta he was served in a bowl, more what it represented – a rushed job that disrespected tradition and dishonoured local producers. And thus the central tenet of slow food was formed, a movement that now spans 450 regional chapters in 150 countries and claims more than 100,000 members. In the three decades since it was formed its manifesto has matured from polemic to practicalities. Among its current goals: establishing an 'Ark of Taste' log for each area to record and protect locally grown produce; encouraging local processing and slaughtering; supporting local farms; warning against the health dangers of fast food, such as diabetes and malnutrition; lobbying against food miles and genetic engineering. The movement was defensively protectionist, but its commitment to sustainability made it forward-thinking too. The way many of those in the West will first experience the effects of climate change, for example, will be through a shortage of certain types of food, while the transporting of produce will have made a small contribution to the rate of climate change in the first place.

In his Terra Madre speech in Turin, Prince Charles mentioned Eric Schlosser's pioneering book *Fast Food Nation*. 'The extraordinary centralization and industrialization of our food system has occurred over as little as twenty years,' Charles noted.* 'Fast food may appear to be cheap food, and in the literal sense it often is. But that is because huge social and environmental costs are being excluded from the calculations.' The prince listed a few of the costs: the rise in food-borne illnesses; the advent of new pathogens such as E. coli 0157; antibiotic resistance from the overuse of drugs in animal feed; extensive water pollution from intensive agricultural systems.

* The true timeline stretches further back. McDonald's began in California in the 1940s, and the marketing of its burgers with its Speedee Service System helped to popularise the concept of uniform fast food. But the chain that claims to be the first fast-food outlet, White Castle, traces its history back to 1921: this was the original home of 'the slider', small basic square burgers with onions produced on a factory-style production line and sold for 5 cents. Diners in the original Kansas restaurant were encouraged to 'Buy 'em by the sack', and if you ordered takeaway you could get five burgers for 10 cents.

'These costs are not reflected in the price of fast food, but that doesn't mean that our society isn't paying them.'

Alice Waters became aware of the slow food movement when she first heard Carlo Petrini speak in San Francisco in the late 1980s. 'I heard what he had to say and I guess we just fell into each other's arms. It was very exciting to me.' She became an international vice-president of the movement and began her campaigning journey, but food with an appetite for politics was preceded in Waters's life by something simpler – a love of food alone. Her initial passion for gastronomy had a rich and predictable source, and sauce: the cuisine of France. She first visited in 1965 and it was here that the idea for her own local bistro was born. She liked both the myth and reality of the French table: the mood of maternal warmth, the understanding that wine is a mandatory part of every meal, and the feeling that no one seems particularly eager to return to work after lunch. 'When I came back from that trip I was just in shock to be back in this fast-food culture,' she told me. She resolved to live as Frenchly as possible; she wanted nothing less than to re-enchant the world. She had also fallen for French couture and the *joie de vivre* of the 1930s films of Marcel Pagnol. (These films were virtually a country of their own, where coastal time – the setting is Marseille – is counted in units of love and bonhomie and provincial comical tiffs. One character in these films was named Panisse, and another was Fanny, the name Waters gave her daughter.)

Indeed, to eat at Chez Panisse is partly a food experience but partly also a cinematic one: everywhere you look there are elaborate posters for Pagnol's movies. Waters is seldom at the skillet herself, but her enthusiasms are everywhere. Although the menu was once heavy with traditional French cuisine – the bird-within-a-bird-within-a-bird variety, with everything flambéed and slathered – it lightened up in the

late 1970s after the departure of her star chef Jeremiah Tower.*
These days, the dishes are distinctly Californian, sunny with
Meyer lemons and heartiness, but never overwrought. Rather
than slow food, 'real food' may be the better phrase.

When I visited one evening in September 2015 I ate at
the café upstairs, which is rather cheaper than the main
restaurant downstairs but maintains its standards for seasonal
ingredients cooked simply and superbly. One is not made
aware of the 30-year polemical baggage as one eats the halibut
baked in a fig leaf with fennel, or chicken breast with shell
beans and okra, or the nectarine galette with vanilla ice cream
(actually it is Riverdog Farm chicken and August Fire
nectarine, while downstairs one may also travel to Wolfe
Ranch, James Ranch and Cannard Farm to sample their
tomatoes, quail and lamb; one is eating at a farmers' market
where every ingredient has a story, and the story is usually
superfluous when placed next to the question 'Is it delicious?').
The only jarring element in the whole evening is how fast
the slow food is dispensed, and how non-French and
non-surly everything is. Unlike your checked-cloth table in
a *jardin* in the Dordogne, you will be required to vacate a
couple of hours *après le commencement*.

Waters has long resisted offers to franchise the restaurant
and her name. 'I don't want a restaurant to make money. I
want a restaurant because I want to know the people who
work there and the people who come there. The more you
have, the more you have to take care of.' She has, however,

* Tower was everything Waters was not, although she appreciated the flamboyance
and attention he brought to the kitchen. He went off to New York to set up Stars,
a restaurant where the chefs were all show-offs, each producing circus-style extrava-
ganzas for impressionable customers. Molecular gastronomy found its true
American outlet here, and developed the talents of such chefs as Dominique Crenn.
It was the antithesis of fast food: it was intellectual, labour-intensive and aspired
to art. It was food you couldn't make at home. Chez Panisse meanwhile, returned
to its roots: a beautiful lamb dish, a beautiful hearth-fired chicken dish.

written several cookbooks, and these tend towards the charming. The most touching, although also the most likely to induce queasiness in her detractors, is *Fanny at Chez Panisse*, which Waters and two friends wrote in the voice of her daughter. The book contains recipes and also a little history, and tries to capture the naive ethos of the slow food philosophy. 'I like to be around on Wednesdays because that's the one day the vegetables come in from the Chinos' farm way down in Rancho Santa Fe. The Chino family has the most beautiful farm in the world. There are just rows and rows of every sort of vegetable and they all look like jewels . . .'

Beyond her restaurant and books, her central project is something called 'The Edible Schoolyard', an attempt, according to its literature, to 'transform school lunch from an afterthought to an edible education', and to imbue impressionable minds with the slow food ecosystem. Not surprisingly, Jamie Oliver is a keen supporter, and the project has enchanted the Clintons and the Obamas. 'In my heart I am always one of those people who want to win people over rather than overthrow them,' Waters says. 'Bring them to something beautiful and delicious and their bad behaviour disappears.'

Waters was in her early 70s when we spoke on the eve of Thanksgiving 2015, two weeks after her beloved France had been devastated by the attacks on the culture she had tried to emulate. She was working on her memoir. She said she still felt empowered by the faith of the young people she spoke to, but her own faith seemed to be waning.

> Like everyone else I'm on my cell phone. I do put it away at the table. One of the important things about food is that we use it as a means of communication, but I've been at tables with young people where they're on their phones all the time. The things I was shocked by 40 years ago have now become our dominant culture – our dominant values are fast, cheap and easy,

and the value we place on our food has decreased. What have we improved? Very little. We are just completely imprisoned by this culture.

iii) Faster Food

But we are in a hurry, and we need refuelling; we do not have the time to make a reservation at Chez Panisse or any other Chez. Although infused with wider concerns, slow food still has one very tentacular nemesis. Fast food, the enemy at which it railed against 30 years ago, is still offering instantly gratifying alternatives, and it is still mass-producing predominantly unhealthy food at affordable prices. The biggest problem is that some of it is delicious. The sugar and salt content of the food appeals as much to the receptors in our brain as the brief time it takes to prepare and serve it appeals to our schedules. The dominance of cheap and fast food on our high street – the Pret takeover, the Itsu sushi box, the lunchtime food-truck wok – reflects a move towards slightly healthier (or at least more imaginative) fare on the go, at least in the more affluent parts of the city. The trend is still for fast, although variety and imagination has improved a little too.

But recently a whole new category of fast food has emerged, the sort that makes any food category before it look like an eight-hour pot roast. Typically for our age, the food is only part food; the other part is tech. And as with most things tech, there is one enviable soon-to-be-zillionaire at the heart of it.

At the end of 2012 Rob Rhinehart was a slightly desperate hacker in his early 20s with hopes of a big breakthrough in a new start-up. The idea involved mobile phones, and the business was failing. Rhinehart began to economise with his food intake. He started eating junk, felt terrible on it, and then researched what the body really needed to thrive. He came up with a list of about 30 essential nutrients, and started buying chemicals and vitamins on the Internet in powdered form. He blended these with water, found he looked and felt better after drinking it, and started to blog about it (the first post was called 'How I Stopped Eating Food'). The initial reaction from friends and readers was cynical but curious. Soon some readers of his blog began concocting their own mineral formulas for the perfect nil-by-stove diet.

Rhinehart called his product Soylent, having read the book *Make Room! Make Room!* by Harry Harrison. Written in 1966 and set in 1999, the book envisioned an overpopulated world with scarce resources; its most desirable foodstuff was soylent, a steak made from soya and lentils. (In the subsequent film, *Soylent Green*, inhabitants of New York are sustained by Soylent wafers, which are not made from good things in the ocean, as advertised, but human skin.)

Rhinehart's product began to catch on, and Soylent became a timesaving hit at the crowdfunding company Tilt. Rhinehart and his friends swiftly attracted more than $1 million in investment capital, and Soylent started shipping and attracting international news coverage. When Lizzie Widdicombe of the *New Yorker* went to visit Rhinehart she found him 'healthy-looking, which was encouraging', and surer than ever that he had found the food of the future. He called other food, even things such as carrots, 'recreational food'. You didn't have to cook Soylent, it took 10 seconds or so to drink it, it filled you up and freed you up. What did the yellow-beige fluid taste like? Rhinehart wasn't keen to define it, but Widdicombe reported that it tasted a bit like pancake batter, slightly oaty and grainy. Sucralose masked the taste of the vitamins.

The writer Will Self, on assignment for *Esquire*, went on a Soylent-only diet for five days and found the taste 'slightly sweet, a touch salty, with the consistency of a cheap milkshake and a fairly unpleasant processed aftertaste'. At the end of it, the worst thing he could find to say was that consuming the same thing every day had been extraordinarily boring. Although not much of a foodie, he wondered what it would be like to crunch and masticate again, and hankered for anything that promised variety and spice.

The new food, of course, was never intended as pleasure; it was a *utility*. 'I think the best technology is the one that disappears,' Rhinehart said. 'Water doesn't have a lot of taste or flavour, and it's the world's most popular beverage.' Unlike water, Soylent includes lipids from canola oil, carbohydrates from maltodextrin, and protein from rice. There was also fish oil for omega-3s alongside measures of magnesium, calcium, copper, iodine and Vitamins B2, B5 and B6. On the official Soylent video, which is full of young fit people living desirable-looking lives while drinking the mixture at work or at the gym, Rhinehart says that his training as an engineer taught him that 'everything is made of parts, everything can be broken down'. His video also showed a handsome couple preparing Soylent for their day's activity: three bags blended in a liquidiser with water would provide breakfast, lunch and dinner, cost $9 in total and free up perhaps two hours in your day.

Liquid food has been around for a while, most prominently on space missions and in hospitals. The difference now is that Soylent is not just convenience food but core food: Rhinehart claimed that Soylent makes up about 90 per cent of his total diet. It is a completely new way of thinking about survival and sustenance, if not pleasure, and it is food decoupled from the world we've been used to since Palaeolithic times, bypassing the gastronome or the foodie in favour of the end-user.

Inevitably, Soylent swiftly spawned DIY rivals offering similar ways to streamline your day and gut: these are also available online and called Soylent Red, People Chow 3.0.1, Schmoylent, Queal and Veetal, Ambro, KetoFood, Nano and Joylent. There appears to be a growing market for all of them. Soylent is scaling up every day, and at the beginning of 2016 had attracted about $25 million in funding from investors convinced they had seen the future. One thing they have seen is how the dilemma of feeding a burgeoning global population may rapidly become a problem of the past.

Unsurprisingly, Soylent and its clones are a particular hit in the tech centres of Palo Alto and Mountain View, where to walk away from one's desk on a lunch break for even a few minutes might mean crashing your next big start-up. As the official video says, 'Using Soylent as a resource means that you can take the time you would normally spend preparing, eating and cleaning up after meals, and put that time into other areas of your life. Soylent gives you the freedom to live life the way you want to live.' Thousands of people (yes, the Soylent minority) have now tried Soylent or its online variants as their main source of nutrition, and their binary needs have been catered to in digital ways. Long-term health effects have yet to be correlated.

The effects on one's day, however, are instantly evident. Without food to grow and consume and punctuate our lives we become a different race: we will be less sociable (we are unlikely to sit down at Soylent-time with our friends), less communicable and impressionable (we won't shop for food, we won't be open to new experiences), more homogenous (if and when Soylent goes global, we will all eat the same chemicals), and more open to food poisoning (an epidemic on a science-fiction scale, one corruptible food chain rather than thousands). Fed factory swill, we will become like the animals we used to eat. We may look back even on fast food as good food. Soylent may be the beginning, and it may be the end; freedom never looked so fluid, or so synthetic.

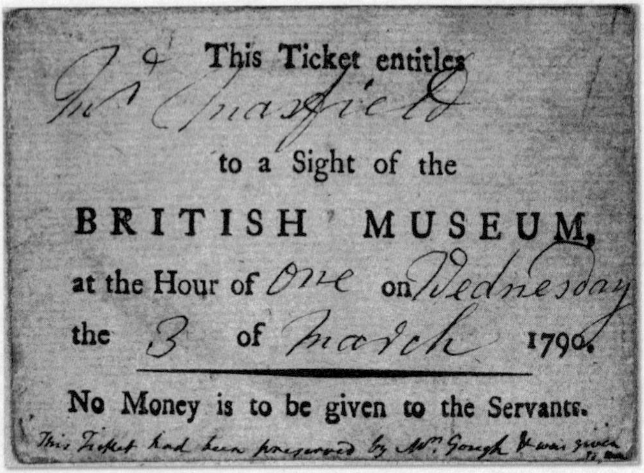

This Ticket entitles

M? Masfield

to a Sight of the

BRITISH MUSEUM,

at the Hour of One on Wednesday

the 3 of March 1790.

No Money is to be given to the Servants.

This Ticket had been preserved by M.º Gough & was given

A new narrative in 1790: a timed ticket to an ordered past.

Chapter Fifteen

The British Museum and the Story of Us

i) The Book of Hours

We conclude this survey somewhere solid: at an institution that marks the passage of time like no other.

Two years after it opened in January 1759, the British Museum published its first catalogue. Its collection was cacophonous – books, prints, jewels, minerals, coins, telescopes, shoes, fossils, Egyptian vases, Roman lamps, Etruscan pots, Jamaican drinking vessels and a mummy – a reflection of the wide interests and hoarding habits of the man who supplied the bulk of its first stock, Sir Hans Sloane.* About 5,000 visitors came to see these objects in the museum's first year, about the same number the museum now attracts in one hour on a rainy Tuesday. Admittance was free, then as now, but in the early days you had to be extremely keen and fit to see your first fossil: you would visit the museum's porter

---

* Sloane was a physician, specialising in dysentery and eyes – one imagines not at the same time – and serving as general physician to Samuel Pepys and three successive monarchs. He also made important advances in the field of smallpox inoculation and the drinking of milk chocolate, something he brought back from his far-reaching travels. He lived to 92, rare in the eighteenth century, and so had ample time to collect. When he died in 1753 he had agreed to sell his collections to the Crown in return for £20,000 to be paid to his family. In London his patch was Chelsea, and he has Sloane Square and other byways of Knightsbridge named after him.

one day to express interest, the porter would check on your address and suitability, you would have to return on another day to receive a signed ticket (if approved), and return on a specified day after that to enjoy the items. An 'under-librarian' would take you around in a group of five, a tour which, according to the museum's own reports, was conducted at a hurried pace to ensure the next quintet didn't lose all interest while waiting.

Among the first objects to be seen after negotiating the huge staircase was a room containing coral and a vulture's head in alcohol. Some of the items reminded visitors of the fairground and freak show: there was a mysterious 'cyclops pig' and a horn from the head of a woman named Mary Davies. Objects such as these seemed to belie the museum's grand objective, which was to be a place 'chiefly designed for the use of learned and studious men, both natives and foreigners, into their researches into several parts of knowledge'.* One room, the precursor of the famous round Reading Room, was set aside, according to the first regulations, for 'the persons so admitted [to undertake research], in which they may sit, and read or write, without interruption', a noble pursuit not yet labelled academia. On its first day this library attracted eight visitors. The patience one needed to gain admittance was nothing compared to the patience one needed to restrain from tying up some of the museum's trustees. John Ward, for example, the professor of rhetoric at Gresham College, London, fretted that most of the objects on display were rather too rarefied for 'ordinary people of all Ranks and Denominations' to appreciate. There was a genuine fear that the eighteenth-century London mob would trash the place.

* 'The Statutes and Rules of the Trustees', 1757.

Many irregularities will be committed that cannot be prevented by a few Librarians, who will soon be insulted by such people if they offer to control or contradict them . . . No persons of superior degree will care to come on those days – a great concourse of ordinary people will never be kept in order. If public days should be allowed, then it will be necessary for the Trustees to have the presence of a Committee of themselves attending, with at least two Justices of the Peace and the constables of the division of Bloomsbury.*

As Ward feared, a museum is a living thing; in a healthy state it will attract all manner of curious people. Even at its opening, the British Museum had long abandoned the Ancient Greek vision of what a museum should be, and from which the name derives: a tribute to and deployment of the Muses, a demonstration of the highest cultural aims and achievements exemplified not through objects but through a salute to the capacity of the human mind; in Alexandria, learned men were paid just to *be* in a hallowed porticoed space, like celebrity 'ambassadors' today. But then came the library and university, and the dissemination of curiosity through other means, and historic and symbolic objects were placed beneath glass. And thus the museum took on a new role, and became a symbol and demonstration of time: time passing, time tracked, time catalogued. In some form at least, a museum is merely a chronology of its specialism, a consistent desire to order and explain events beyond randomness. In Bloomsbury, the temporal ordering of things hung heavier than most.

* As quoted in *That Noble Cabinet* by Edward J. Miller (London, 1974).

In 1759, Buckingham House, now Buckingham Palace, was seriously considered as the British Museum's first home; only its purchase cost to the government – £30,000 compared with £10,250 for a Bloomsbury alternative – ruled it out. So the institution (although it was then more of an experiment) opened at Montague House, a seventeenth-century mansion in Great Russell Street, and there it has stood ever since. We've seen that the displays were only a little more ordered than Portobello Market; one couldn't yet get a cohesive grasp on Britain's place in the world, let alone any idea of the development of the human spirit or adventurous mind.

But a catalogue from 1860, marking the museum's first centenary, suggests an expansion not only of contents but also of vision: there was now a purpose and order to the displays beyond mere accumulation. Some of this purpose manifested itself in the act of unrighteous looting, a demonstration of the rampaging Empire as we scooped up the spoils of war and stole things on our holidays. But broad learning now had a more directed chronology, a directed history rather than a cabinet of curiosities. (The catalogue also suggests the inevitability of the Natural History Museum, to be spun off from the British Museum 30 years later: alongside the Rosetta Stone and the Elgin Marbles the early rooms were home to a wasps' nest, a dodo skull, snail shells, an elk fossil, an iguanodon fossil, a stuffed flamingo, peacocks, unhappy marsupials.) The British Museum was already thinking upon Darwinian lines, with a natural selection edging towards empirical ethnography. *On the Origin of Species* and the work of Alfred Wallace emerged in the late 1850s, and hindsight suggests that the new rooms at the British Museum, while still fusty with a Grecian ideal of beauty and the notion of the higher calling, were already, if often unwittingly, in step with lucid and exhilarating biology. What emerged at the museum in the middle of the nineteenth century was the one thing that modern visitors crave above all else: narrative.*

The ordering of time at the museum was inevitably the work of its curators, and one in particular. Augustus Wollaston Franks was appointed to the Department of Antiquities in 1851, and he swiftly enhanced his reputation as one of the leading antiquarian scholars by establishing new departments in porcelain, glass and other areas. His own experience as a collector, which he regarded as a pleasurable if incurable hereditary affliction, enabled him to obtain important collections of British antiquities before they were split up at auctions. (His dedication to his cause was confirmed when he purchased for the museum the ornate Royal Gold Cup with £5,000 of his own money; acknowledging the coup a few years later, the museum paid him back.)

But Franks's greatest achievement was his friendship with the collector Henry Christy, from whom the museum acquired more than 20,000 objects. Christy made his money in banking and industry, but his passions lay in anthropology, palaeontology and human evolution. Two journeys in particular, to museums in Stockholm and Copenhagen in the early 1850s, revealed something both obvious and striking – a new way that isolated objects could be brought together to tell the story of how cultures varied and grew over time. The British Museum remains grateful to both men, and has dedicated a corner of a room on the ground floor to their legacy. Most other museums are also indebted to them. One of the museum's information panels states that under Franks's guidance, Christy's collection was not only classified and arranged

---

* The story is the key, as much in our generation as when the museum opened. People didn't queue for ever for the Tutankhamun show just to see all the gold; they wanted to be a part of the discovery narrative too. The same with Grayson Perry; here the story was the eccentricity of the artist and the rude unpredictability of his curation.

systematically, but also originally: 'Objects from remote cultures around the world [were placed] alongside those of more familiar civilisations.' Narrow chronology itself was the equivalent of rote learning; true knowledge was to be gained from association.

Time has changed the museum itself. One of its recent biographers, Edward John Miller, who worked there for many years as an archivist and keeper, suggests that too many museums are a product of artistically sterile ages: unable to create masterpieces of their own, they must make do with dusty rooms of antiquities from more virile times. Another biographer, W.H. Boulton, writing *The Romance of the British Museum* in 1931, observed that 'there was a time when a visit . . . would have been regarded as the driest of all dry ways of passing the time on a wet day . . . to the great bulk of the population of London, the whole thing was as dry as the mummies themselves.'

But one thing hasn't changed. The current British Museum is still one of the world's great protectors and promoters of old and heavy objects. In common with so many other museums and art galleries, its displays mark the distinct end of something – an artistic period, a distant civilisation, the deadening thud of institutional approval. Objects in amber are concealed and protected behind heavy glass. But the place is accessible and commercial where once it was constipated and haughty, and it is no longer afraid of the mob. Beyond the porticos and grey columns and heavy grandeur of the Greek Revival facade, and beyond the undevout schoolchildren enjoying their lunch in the Great Hall, the museum has managed to achieve something that goes far beyond the gathering, classification and preservation of treasures: it has maintained the traditions of Franks and Christy by tracking the passing of human time in physical form.

The museum even offers study guides as to how this may best be achieved. There is the conventional display of clocks and watches in Rooms 38 and 39, tracking early turret clocks and domestic mechanical pendulums right through to an Ingersoll Dan Dare novelty watch from the 1950s and a Bulova Accutron vibrating electronic model from the 1970s; the Apple Watch may soon take its place alongside them. Other chambers display time-telling objects from less predictable vantage points. Object one: a carving on a mammoth tusk from about 13,500 years ago. It is one of the tenets of the British Museum that 'at the root of all cultures is a need to organize the immediate and more distant future in order to survive', and one of the earliest demonstrations of this takes the form of the seasonal migrations of animals. Found in a rock shelter at Montastruc, France, the carved tusk shows two swimming reindeer, the leading animal with the markings of a deep autumnal coat. For a hunter this is a good seasonal sign: the reindeer are at their fattest, and their journey through water makes them easier to hunt. The carving, 12.4cm long, would have formed the tip of a wooden spear, and the spear would have killed the reindeer midstream.

Object two: the 3ft 2in intricately carved wooden and nephrite genealogical or 'Whakapapa' stick from New Zealand with 18 notches. Each notch depicted a Maori ancestor of its owner, and as each stick stretched back and back with more and more notches, it established a ceremonial link to the very beginning of time and ultimately a connection with the gods. It was also a tactile symbol of mortality. And then our own colonial timeline obliterated the Maori timeline: these sticks were prized souvenirs of nineteenth-century European naturalists; the very thing that made them desirable was instantly curtailed.

Object three: a tribal and spiritual artwork produced over decades – the museum's carved double-headed wooden dog Kozo. This is a traditional *nkisi* figure, the property of a shaman from the Democratic Republic of Congo. The shaman would listen to a request for healing or the correction of a wrongdoing from a tribe member, and drive a nail or other object into the *nkisi*'s body to unleash its powers. It would take a generation for the sculpture to dispense all its energy and become entirely covered with spikes: part brutal hedgehog, part voodoo grenade.

Object four: the Bedford Book of Hours. One of the most ornate manuscripts to arrive at the museum (now at the British Library), the book is a daily calendar of Christian worship, with illustrated prayers each in their anointed timeslot. Made in Paris between 1410 and 1430, and once owned by a young Henry VI before he took the throne, its 38 biblical images lean heavily upon the travails of the Virgin Mary and the infant Christ (the Annunciation, the Adoration of the Magi, etc. etc.). The eight liturgical hours mark time in their inescapable way, a literary form of clock-work from dawn to dusk: matins, lauds, prime, terce, sext, none, vespers and compline. The lush volume, clasped between velvet, was at one time the property of John, the Duke of Bedford, and to mark his wedding to Anne of Burgundy it was amended to include their vows and heraldic arms. Books of Hours were revered fixtures in wealthy and devout Europe – a preordained guide to the day and a companion for a lifetime.

And objects five and six: a vision of the end of time on two fifteenth-century alabaster panels. The carvings show two signs of the Apocalypse, one in which men emerge from their dwellings senseless and unable to speak, and the other in which all living things die. The Last Judgement and the death of us all would seem a good place to close our tour.

Newer apocalyptic prophecies hold sway in the most brutal of terrorist regimes, and their destruction of antiquities as they rampage through ancient cities speaks to the destruction of time itself. The future evolution of the museum has its own challenges, not least the repositioning of curiosity in the digital age, but to judge by the record number of people through the portico in Bloomsbury each year the basic attraction shows no sign of waning. We yearn for our past on an ordered timeline. The glass cabinet with amber inside: it's the past and the future combined, as romantic and resonant as a fairy tale.

ii) Doomed and Marooned

Once upon a time, the terrible thing that happened at midnight was that your coach turned into a pumpkin. These days we would regard such a thing as humiliating but not so bad. These days the worst that can happen at midnight is that the world comes to an end.

In June 1947, the *Bulletin of Atomic Scientists*, a monthly newsletter, found that it had become a victim of its own success. Its central debate on the responsible control of atomic power had become essential reading for everyone involved in policy making in the post-war years. The bulletin was supported by Albert Einstein, who was then chairman of the Emergency Committee of Atomic Scientists, and its editorial board included those who had worked on the Manhattan Project and other atomic research during the war. As one member put it, 'Never foregoing hope, the scientists who built the bomb sought to secure the world from itself.'

But nuclear annihilation wasn't the only dilemma facing the editorial board: there was also the problem of what to put on the cover. The *Bulletin* had begun as a simple 6-page publication in Chicago in December 1945, and 18 months later it had expanded into a 36-page magazine with contributions from Bertrand Russell and advertisements for devices to measure radioactivity. ('In Science's newest phase . . . it is of paramount importance that the instrumentation be of utmost precision and dependability.') For the first time, the issue of June 1947 was to carry a professionally designed front page (previously there had only been text), and there was some discussion over what the image should be. Someone suggested using a big letter U, the chemical symbol for uranium, but artist Martyl Langsdorf, who was married to the physicist Alexander Langsdorf, came up with something more powerfully persuasive. The contents of each issue would henceforth be printed on a backdrop of a giant clock, so giant that one would only see the top quarter of the face. But this was where the action was: the black hour hand was pointed straight up at midnight, and the white second hand occupied the key region to its left. It was an ominous and abiding image, an image for all time, not least because the first time the clock appeared it read seven minutes to destruction. Indeed it was such a powerful symbol that the message never needed explaining: something awful would happen when the two hands met, and the articles in that issue discussed ways to avoid it. In the first issue in which the clock featured, there were pieces such as 'War Department Thinking on the Atomic Bomb' and 'With the Atomic Bomb Casualty Committee in Hiroshima'. The first editorial began: 'If there is something we cannot afford in dealing with atomic energy, it is muddled thinking, policy based on ignorance, hearsay, prejudice, partisan expediency or wishful thinking.' The rhetoric was as sharp as the graphics.

Who set the clock and how did they decide on the time? The first time the decision was arbitrary and aesthetic. Martyl Langsdorf picked seven minutes to midnight because 'it looked good to my eye' (it was the artist's answer to the marketing departments of watch brands setting faces at 10 to 10 because it showed off the design nicely and seemed to make the watch 'smile'). But subsequently the editor Eugene Rabinowitch took charge. In 1949, after the Soviet Union tested its first atomic bomb, he moved the time to three minutes to midnight.

When Rabinowitch died in 1973 the responsibility for timekeeping transferred to the magazine's Science and Security Board. According to Kennette Benedict, a senior advisor to the *Bulletin*, the board meets to consider the state of the world twice a year, consulting widely with their colleagues across a range of disciplines 'and also seek the views of the Bulletin's Board of Sponsors, which includes 16 Nobel Laureates'. Collectively the great minds have made some important adjustments: in 1953, the minute hand moved to two minutes to midnight in response to the US and Soviet Union both testing thermonuclear weapons within six months of each other. By 1972 we had some breathing time: the SALT and ABM treaties established parity between the nations and agreements on future limitations – the clock was at 12 minutes to. In 1998 the hands stood at nine minutes to midnight, following India and Pakistan staging weapons tests three weeks apart, and it was calculated that Russia and the US together maintained 7,000 warheads ready to fire at each other within 15 minutes.

'The *Bulletin* is a bit like a doctor making a diagnosis,' Benedict says. 'We look at data as physicians look at lab tests and X-rays . . . we consider as many symptoms, measurements and circumstances as we can. Then we come to a judgement that sums up what could happen if leaders and citizens don't take action to treat the conditions.'

As of 2016 the clock has changed time on 21 occasions. Global nuclear destruction is now only one consideration, although still crucial: when North Korea tested atomic weapons in 2015 the *Bulletin* board got itchy fingers, as did everyone else who heard the news. But equally significant are considerations of relations between the superpowers, the threat of terrorism and religious extremism, and the general well-being of the planet in terms of famine, drought and rising sea levels. (In the first issue of 2016, the *Bulletin* carried an article about the sale of nuclear power reactors in the Middle East, and two stories on the relationship between climate change and technology in India and Bangladesh.)

Reacting to the accusation that the Doomsday Clock was a scaremongering device employed for political purposes, Kennette Benedict argued that the minute hand has moved away from midnight almost as often as it has moved towards it, 'and as often during Republican administrations in the United States as during Democratic ones'. The hand was moved furthest away from midnight in 1991, a full 17 minutes, when George Bush signed the Strategic Arms Reduction Treaty with the Soviet Union. It has never been quite clear what anyone is supposed to actually do with the time on the Doomsday Clock. Should we hide when it moves towards midnight and rejoice when it moves back? Is it just a publicity jolly to help serious-minded people take the air once in a while? Will significant policymaking ever be influenced by the clock? At its best, the clock is a reason to debate life-or-death issues that might otherwise be deemed too worthy or too heavy to handle.

Benedict says she is frequently asked 'Where can I visit the Doomsday Clock?', although one hopes not by *Bulletin* writers or its board. She tells people that it is not a real clock, and that no one winds it and the mechanics have not been updated to quartz. But it is easy to see how people may get confused. In January 2016, midway through an hour-long press conference to announce the new time at the National Press Club in Washington DC, a clock was indeed ceremoniously unveiled. And not by no one: by four eminent scientists and two former US secretaries of state. Before the unveiling, Rachel Bronson, the *Bulletin*'s executive director and publisher, announced that the timing on the clock would be revealed in DC and 'simultaneously' at Stanford University in California, a feat that involved the learned men removing a blue cloth drape from the front of a large piece of cardboard on an easel. 'Go ahead, please!' Bronson said as the time for doom approached, and photographers gathered as they might at the launch of a new figure at Madame Tussauds. The men did what they were asked. The sign beneath the cloth showed that the clock hadn't moved. Beneath the graphic hands were the words 'IT IS 3 MINUTES TO MIDNIGHT'. The sound of camera shutters filled the room. The luminaries with cloth in their hands tried not to smile.

Real or not and stopped or not, has there ever been a more useful metaphor for doom? The Doomsday Clock comes with all the inbuilt clichés of disaster – the notion that 'the clock is ticking', the warning alarm bell that threatens to wake us from our slumber – and if it only assumes a striking physical form for the purposes of marketing and news reporting then that is enough. There's something to see where there's really nothing to see. When the *Bulletin*'s press conference announced on 26 January 2016 that the period of time between our present somnambulant state and total oblivion was less than the time it took to properly boil an egg, the clock started trending on Twitter. That's modern doom for you: you have three minutes left to live, and you spend at least some of it tweeting.

Beyond all this, a simple symbol of destruction tells us something about how we regard the clock and fear it. Nothing functions without it: all our communications and navigation systems depend on it, as do all financial transactions and almost all our motivation. The alternative is to sit in a cave and wait for the sun to come up.

Our own personal doomsday scenario is a lot closer than the closest weapons silo. This is the doom of us cowed and diminished by time, of time controlling our lives to such a degree that we feel it is almost impossible to keep up. Or perhaps even worse: we keep up, but other things suffer. We are forever making sacrifices and compromises. There isn't enough time for family, but there isn't enough time for work either, or the things we deem increasingly important, like the dreamy prospect of doing nothing.

And we know this makes no sense, and we don't like what has become of our lives. We crave punctuality, but we loathe deadlines. We count down precisely on New Year's Eve so we may obliterate the hours that follow. We pay for 'priority boarding' so that we may sit on a plane and wait for everyone else to join us, and then when we land we pay to get off early. We used to have time to think, but now instant communication barely gives us time to react. Paradise is a beach and the eternal waves and a good book, but then there's email. Why use Oyster when you can go contactless? Why go contactless when you can Apple Pay? If you don't come in on Christmas Day don't bother coming in on Boxing Day. Order within 1 hour and 27 minutes for next-day delivery. You will meet 15 speed dates in a glamorous setting in a two-hour evening. A search for 'time management' produces 'about' 38,300,000 results in 0.47 seconds. Experience ultrafast speed up to 200Mbps with Vivid 200 fibre broadband. You need 7 hours and 43 minutes to complete this book on your Kindle.

The suffocating notion of iTime has replaced the factory clock, and we have reached the point where it is no longer possible to experience time independently of technology. The phrase to describe the feeling of hopelessness in the face of time is 'frenetic standstill'. I first came across it, and also a version of the parable of the Egyptian fisherman in the introduction, in an influential book by the German sociologist Hartmut Rosa called *Beschleunigung: Die Veränderung de Zeitstrukturen in der Moderne* (2005). The main title translates as *Social Acceleration*, and it is Rosa's contention that we may be in a period of catastrophic stasis caused by a collision of rapid technological expansion and the widespread feeling that we will never achieve the goals we crave. The more we try to 'get ahead', the more impossible becomes the likelihood. The more apps and computer programmes we download to streamline and order our lives, the more we feel like screaming. The Egyptian fisherman had it right, as, astonishingly, did Bono: we are 'running to stand still'.

Optimistically, the more benign form of frenetic standstill is not a new thing. In the terminology of popular media we have been 'living on a hamster wheel' since the 1950s, while we have been 'on a treadmill' since the 1970s. And we can go further back still. In February 1920, in a letter to his colleague Ludwig Hopf, Einstein observed how he was 'being so terribly deluged with inquiries, invitations, and requests that at night I dream I am burning in hell and the mailman is the devil and is continually yelling at me, hurling a fresh bundle of letters at my head because I still haven't answered the old ones'.

And further back still. 'Everything is now "ultra",' Goethe wrote to the composer Carl Friedrich Zelter. 'Young people are . . . swept along in the whirlpool of time; wealth and speed are what the world admires and what everyone strives for. All kinds of communicative facility are what the civilized world is aiming at in outpacing itself.' That was in 1825.

Regrettably, not all of our new acceleration is benign. Rosa concludes his book with a worst-case scenario, an endgame he calls 'the unbridled onward rush into the abyss' – death by time. It will be caused by our inability to balance the conflict of movement and inertia, and 'the abyss will be embodied in either the collapse of the ecosystem or in the ultimate breakdown of the modern social order'. There may also be 'nuclear or climatic catastrophes, with the diffusion at a furious pace of new diseases, or with new forms of political collapse and the eruption of uncontrolled violence, which can be particularly expected where the masses excluded from the process of acceleration and growth take a stand against the acceleration society'. Happy days.

Is it possible to schedule when this collapse of time, this black hole of our own creation, will begin? Will our quest for modernity and advance lead to nihilistic wipeout in months, years or aeons? Unfortunately, this scenario has no definable calendar. Also unfortunately, we may already be spinning within its maelstrom. It is not just cosseted Western lives that suffer: time seems to have reached its terrible conclusion environmentally; practically, ISIS obliterates arte-facts in Iraq and Syria, time's record is destroyed. On a less calamitous precipice, we are already supposed to have reached the end of the novel and the end of history; critically, all social, cultural and political movements are 'post-' if not 'post-post-', and the two ultimate 'post-post' things are, iron-ically, modernism and irony. Acceleration has brought on a plague of cynicism.

Hartmut Rosa's book was translated into English by Jonathan Trejo-Mathys, a social and political philosopher who died from cancer in 2014, well before his time at the age of 35. Unusually for a translator, he wrote a lengthy introduction of his own, examining a recent incident in which time itself, no longer passive or benign, appeared to have adopted human traits of venality and malevolence.

The first was triggered by the financial crisis of 2008. As we know, this occurred through a process of overextension and under-regulation, but recovery was swift, and by 2009 money was being earned and traded again in criminal amounts. This was because there was a new, faster way of earning money than ever before: high-frequency trading.

Never had Benjamin Franklin's notion of 'time is money' been more apt. The outside world came to learn of high-frequency trading at around 2.40 p.m. on 6 May 2010, when a trillion dollars was lost in an instant. After seven minutes of financial freefall, during which the Dow Jones index lost 700 points, a safety mechanism jolted into place on the exchanges to prevent further panic; the 'flash crash' was over almost as soon as it had begun, and within the hour the market had regained most of its losses. But then a similar crash happened four months later. This time, the utility company Progress Energy (107 years old, some 3.1 million customers and 11,000 staff) saw its share value drop 90 per cent in a few seconds. On this occasion, what has been termed 'a wayward keystroke' by a single trader triggered algorithmic mayhem. On both occasions, the losses were caused by the same thing that caused the profits: the almost incalculable speed of glass fibre-optic cables.

The ability of computers to transact billions of dollars' worth of business at very close to the speed of light proved to be a fantastic thing until suddenly it wasn't. The strangest thing of all was that even the most schooled trader at, say, Goldman Sachs couldn't offer a plausible (or at least a public) explanation of what had happened, or how to prevent it happening again, because it all just happened too fast. One explanation, reported in the *New York Times*, suggested the

May 2010 crash had come about through 'a poorly timed trade by a mutual fund in Kansas', but five years later a more unexpected suspect emerged in a leafy London suburb near Heathrow airport. Navinder Singh Sarao, 36, was arrested in Hounslow in April 2015 on charges of 'spoofing' – fraudulently buying and then cancelling commodity orders in such quantities and at such speeds that it had sent the algorithms barmy. Further analysis of the markets over the following few months suggested that this scenario was unlikely, but the fact that the fragility of the economic health of the Western world had been blamed on a man trading, almost mythically, on a high-street computer in his pyjamas in his parents' house was enough cause for concern that we may not be in complete control. (And the fact it had taken five years for the regulators to think they had found their man suggested that we have become quite unable to keep pace with acceleration in the real world. Not so long ago, the worst financial authorities had to contend with was insider trading; how quaint that seems today.) At the time of writing, Navinder Sarao faces 22 counts of market manipulation but has yet to stand trial.

Readers of *Flash Boys*, the gripping account of misdeeds in this high-frequency world by former Wall Street trader Michael Lewis, will be familiar with several new notions of time, not least the tiny increments of advantage or delay that meant the difference between helipad profit and suicidal loss (the biggest scandal seemed to be that telecom carriers Verizon and AT&T were inconsistent in their transmission speeds from Chicago to New York – sometimes data took 17 milliseconds to arrive, whereas the ideal was 12 milliseconds (a millisecond is one-thousandth of a second; it takes about 100 milliseconds to blink). Another strange and worrying change in the new trading environment was the complete lack of a need for human beings to oversee (and thus potentially regulate) any transactions; it used to be people in braces yelling at phones and waving their hands, but now it was millisecond flashes on screens and nothing else.

As Lewis recounts, the really successful traders were the ones who found a way to rig the market beneath the surface of the technology in the 'dark pools', where transactions were hidden from public scrutiny. 'Everyone was telling us it was all about faster. We had to go faster,' one of Lewis's protagonists tells him, before revealing that the real trick was to make some transactions actually go *slower*. High-frequency traders – even the honest ones – tend not to specialise in high morals for the greater good, but here, surely, was one for the whole of society.

Why should we care about what happens in the trading markets? Shouldn't we leave this to the investment pages and the movies? We should care because this is the stuff of great depressions and worse, and in an instant. At the time of writing we are able to transmit information at more than 100 petabits per second over one kilometre of optical fibre. A petabit is 1,000 terabits, while a terabit is 1,000 gigabits; at any rate, it's a speed enabling the download of 50,000 two-hour HD films, enough movies to last more than 11.4 years. In a second. (This is an optimal-condition maximum speed achieved in controlled conditions in Japan, and not yet available from your friendly but disappointing local Internet service provider. But give it time.) The economic upside of this is colossal wealth creation for a few; the downside is a worldwide financial doomsday so catastrophic that it will make all crashes from the 1920s onwards look like losing a coin down a sofa.

And then of course there is the everyday world around us, and the challenge of our climate. The key factor in all the debates about the decline of animal species, and the melting polar regions, and the plastics clogging the oceans, is how much time we have left. How did it get so late so soon?

iii) Those Who Feel Differently

Geologists, cosmologists, ecologists and museum curators
have always had a different way of looking at time, a temporal
layering composed of eras and epochs that may seem reassuringly comforting to anyone concerned with imminent
doomsday: crises and all our modern pressures of time keep
mounting, but the Earth keeps spinning regardless.

The sense of security this provides may prove to be unreliable, so where else should we look for solace? Perhaps to
the Inuit at the North Pole, particularly since the native
Inuktitut language has no word for the concept of time. A
calendar used by a hunter in the Canadian Eastern Arctic in
the 1920s shows where the priorities lay: the days are marked,
and there is a special cross for Sundays following the arrival
of missionaries and Christianity, but the big space in the
middle of the chart is reserved for illustrated tallies of caribou,
polar bear, seal and walrus. Prior to nineteenth-century
European contact, which introduced the dubious merits of
the mechanical watch, time was ruled by the seasons, the
weather, the movements of the sun and moon, and migratory
patterns of edible animals – much like pre-Christian England.
Demarcations came in the shape of flexible Inuit Moons,
which were named after practical considerations such as the
nesting of birds or the break-up of sea ice; in dark winter
months the position of the stars indicated when it was time
to leave the igloo and feed the dogs and prepare fuel for
cooking. When fur traders' clocks were introduced to communities, the Inuit in the Keewatin region initially hung on to
their own interpretations of what the passing hours meant:
ulamautinguaq ('looks like an axe') was 7 o'clock; 12 noon was
ullurummitavik ('time for lunch'), and at 9 o'clock it was
sukatirvik ('time to wind the clock'). So much of this way of
life has now been eroded by Western time and the imposition

of what the Inuit refer to as 'order', although as John MacDonald of the Nunavut Research Institute points out (in a break from supplying this magnificent Inuktitut vocabulary), 'the arrival of spring triggers an irresistible urge to partake of nature's bounty . . . a mass exodus to traditional fishing and hunting grounds ensues . . . Employers' clock-driven schedules fall apart as the new time temporarily gives way to the old.'

Or perhaps we are attracted to the mechanical timekeeping systems of ancient Mexico, which, before the New World encroached, were non-existent: there is no evidence even of a sundial, far less an inclination to measure the day into hours. Alternatively, the ancient Indian system of hours may appeal, complex as it seems: the 24-hour day is familiar enough, but less so its romantic-sounding division into 30 *muhrtas* of 48 minutes or 60 *ghatikas* of 24 minutes. The *ghatika* is then divided into 30 *kala* of 48 seconds or 60 *pala* of 24 seconds. The 60-unit base stretches back to Babylonian origin and persisted until the nineteenth century. The British then ordered almost everything to tick in its shadow, the whole country reverting to Indian Standard Time in 1947, 5½ hours ahead of Coordinated Universal Time (UTC), which was then linked to atomic time controlled by caesium atoms. (Although Calcutta and Bombay held on to their own zones for a few years, and Assam remains unofficially and gleefully on Tea Garden Time, with local growers setting their clocks an hour ahead of the standard to increase productivity.) Venezuela turned the clocks back by 30 minutes for a similar reason in 2007, thus providing what was hoped to be 'a fairer distribution of the sunrise' (or President Hugo Chávez may just have been being political and maniacally perverse, having already changed the country's flag and constitution and moved Christmas to November).

Or perhaps we will plump for the Ethiopian system of

Christmas in January and the 12-hour clock, a logical device where the day begins at dawn rather than midnight. Or maybe the Jamaican soon-come mentality that tends to irritate Westerners on holiday until they fall into step with its gentleness, at which point it is time to fly home. And perhaps, since 15 August 2015, we have even held a sneaking admiration for the horological independence shown by North Korea, where Pyongyang Time was set back 30 minutes as a way of ending the blow inflicted 70 years earlier 'when wicked Japanese imperialists deprived Korea of even its standard time'. Or perhaps not.

Extended temporal possibilities in the modern world have, since 1996, been the promise of the Long Now Foundation, an organisation designed to foster long-term thinking within a framework of 10,000 years. In fact, it was formed in 01996, the extra zero intended to 'solve the deca-millennium bug which will come into effect in about 8,000 years' (so there *is* something to look forward to!)

The Foundation, with its principal spirit-guides Danny Hillis, Stewart Brand and Brian Eno, has poetic and laudable ambitions, and a succinct manifesto based on the notion that 'civilisation is revving itself into a pathologically short attention span'. The aims include: serve the long-view; foster responsibility; reward patience; ally with competition; take no sides; leverage longevity; and 'mind mythic depth'.

But the Foundation is not all talk and wonder. It is also constructing a giant clock (a real clock, a counterpoint to the Doomsday Clock) within a mountain in Western Texas. In 1995, Danny Hillis, a computer engineer, dreamt of a machine that ticked once a year, chimed once a century, and contained a cuckoo that came out to say hello once a millennium. The clock is intended to last 10,000 years, and its pendulum is to be powered by thermal energy (i.e. changes in heat in the surrounding atmosphere). Although the clock under construction in Texas chimes more frequently than originally planned (a visitor must have *some* reward for taking a day's hike just to find it), the principle ethos of its inventor remains intact: 'I think it is time for us to start a long-term project that gets people thinking past the mental barrier of an ever-shortening future.' The clock is part-funded by Jeff Bezos, the founder of Amazon, a nice touch from the man whose company aims to get you essential household items within an hour of ordering.

The Long Now Foundation has also been thinking about how we may archive our current knowledge-base so that we may pass it on not just to the next generation, but to the next stage of life-form. To popularise this long-term perspective, one may also take out a Long Bet, a wager formed not over an election or sporting season, but over, say, a half-century. Kevin Kelly, the bookmaker in this scenario, has taken on challengers to many predictions, including the proposition that 'By 2060 the total population of humans on earth will be less than it is today' and 'There will be only three significant currencies used in the world by 2063, and more than 95 per cent of countries in the world will use one of them.' Don't lose that betting slip.

One may take out a membership in the Long Now way of thinking, and by the middle of 02016 more than 7500 had paid to join. Like all good clubs, there are tiered privileges. A Steel Member pays $96 annually for tickets to live events and access to live streaming seminars, as well as several other enticements and 10 per cent off in the Long Now shop. A Tungsten Member ($960 a year) gets all of the above, and also a Long Now book and a special Brian Eno CD. The goodies are not really the thing, of course: you are investing in the long-term future, or at least in the belief that there may be one.

Neuroscientists tell us that we live our conscious states about half a second behind real time – the delay between our brain receiving signals, sending them out, and getting the message that something has been done. The time between deciding to snap our fingers and seeing or hearing this action is always longer than we think, because our brain edits out the delay and constructs its own fluid story. We are always behind even in the now, and we can never catch up.

What to do? Is there a more philosophical approach to time than the Doomsday Clock and the bureaucratic headache of the time zone? Not that he's a great sage or anything, but Woody Allen frequently has a levelling take on these things. The answer to life's short and gloomy span may just be to watch more Marx Brothers movies, as he does in *Hannah and Her Sisters*: he's feeling suicidal, tries to shoot himself but bungles it, and in the daze that follows wanders into a movie theatre where they're showing *Duck Soup*. The Marx Brothers are playing the helmets of guards like a glockenspiel, and slowly the world seems to make sense to him again: why not just enjoy life when you can? One of Allen's other semi-autobiographical characters, Alvy Singer in *Annie Hall*, long ago pronounced that life is 'full of loneliness and misery and suffering and unhappiness, and it's all over much too quickly'.

Allen restated his philosophy in an interview a few years later, but now there was another solution: 'I do feel that it is a grim, painful, nightmarish, meaningless experience, and that the only way you can be happy is if you tell yourself some lies and deceive yourself – and I'm not the first person to say this, or the most articulate person on it, it was said by Nietzsche, it was said by Freud: one must have one's delusions to live.' The opposite course is too unthinkable, or at least unlivable – the notion that everything we care for so much in our lives will soon be swept away. We struggle our whole lives to make enough money, to give enough love, to get the things we think are important, to *do* the things we think are important, to right some wrongs, to help others, to advance our understanding of the universe, to advance technology and the ease of living – and if we consider ourselves artists we try to create beauty and truth – and we try to do this all in the narrow time span available to us, and then every 100 years we're all swept away and another bunch of people try to do the same. Time – and not even geologists' *deep time*, just the time that comes after the time we have now – just keeps on rolling right along. The old Negro spirituals had it right from the start.*

The most prominent vision of freedom in our lives is invariably wrapped up with visions of time standing still: a freedom from the tyranny of the clock. Advertisers have found no more powerful single image of bliss than a deserted sandy coastline. In literature this symbol has been defined by the German philosopher Walter Benjamin in terms of the Parisian *flâneur* wandering the city at glittering dusk, taking a turtle for a walk, going at the turtle's pace.**

---

* Deep time is a geologist's equivalent of the Patek Philippe advert: you never actually live on the earth, you merely look after it for the next species or ice age. The phrase distinguishes our time (the time in Switzerland, the time on our iPads) from a slightly longer time, specifically the age of Earth, some 4.45 billion years. It's a sobering distinction: think about our insignificance on the planet for too long and you'd never get out of bed.

** We first met Walter Benjamin in a footnote in Chapter 2. The vision of the turtle appears in his *Arcades Project*, written from 1927–40, in which the author observes what he believes will be authentic Paris from the streets. The notion of the *flâneur* dates as far back as Baudelaire a century before. The link between tortoises and time goes all the way back to Aesop (I'm using turtles and tortoises interchangeably here, American style), but its most pertinent connection may be as a punchline to the anecdote at the start of an obscure book called *A Brief History of Time*. Here, Stephen Hawking considers the absurdity of cosmology and the consistency of the world. The world, attests 'a little old lady' attending a lecture by a famous scientist ('some say it was Bertrand Russell'), is flat, and supported on the back of a giant tortoise. 'But what supports the tortoise?' the scientist asks. And the answer comes back, 'But it's turtles all the way down!'

The cosmologist Carl Sagan said it eloquently in 1994, in the early pages of his book *Pale Blue Dot*. When, in February 1990, the spacecraft Voyager 1 was about to exit the solar system, it took a photograph of Earth from about 3.7 billion miles away at Sagan's request ('Pale Blue Dot' is also the name of the photograph). Our planet did not, as was to be expected, seem terribly significant in the picture. But its true insignificance in the beautiful firework of light rays was unutterably humbling: a particle so small it was easy to dismiss as a piece of dust on the lens. 'Look again at that dot,' Sagan implored.

> That's here. That's home. That's us. On it everyone you love, everyone you know, everyone you ever heard of, every human being who ever was, lived out their lives. The aggregate of our joy and suffering, thousands of confident religions, ideologies, and economic doctrines, every hunter and forager, every hero and coward, every creator and destroyer of civilization, every king and peasant, every young couple in love, every mother and father, hopeful child, inventor and explorer, every teacher of morals, every corrupt politician, every 'superstar', every 'supreme leader', every saint and sinner in the history of our species lived there – on a mote of dust suspended in a sunbeam . . .
>
> Our posturings, our imagined self-importance, the delusion that we have some privileged position in the Universe, are challenged by this point of pale light . . . There is perhaps no better demonstration of the folly of human conceits than this distant image of our tiny world.

Every superstar indeed. And what was Sagan's message after all this shrinkage of the world and the exposure of our folly? Just to be a little kinder to each other.

The physicist Richard Feynman had yet another take: we are at the very beginning of time for the human race. If we don't destroy ourselves, the purpose of the time we have here is to grant time to those who come after us. We leave messages and evidence and progress where we can. We are 'atoms with curiosity', and that alone gives us purpose as the tiniest speck of matter in the spinning universe. We can only laugh and delight at the futility of it all.

Our own brief dash – that hyphen between the dates on our gravestones – is all we have against this cosmic insignificance. Which is why this book has been concerned with practical matters, key moments when some of our most fleeting thoughts on time came into focus for a short while. Here's another one. In 2011, Randy Newman – best known for his songs for the *Toy Story* movies but loved also for his sad and witty parables of grown-up American life – performed a small show in front of an invited audience in the London showroom of Steinway and Sons. 'The song I'm going to play for you today is called "Losing You",' Newman began.

> Most of my songs, I don't know where they come from. Unless it's an assignment, someone's paying me to do a movie or something. But in this case my brother was a doctor, an oncologist, dealt with cancer. Early in his career he had a 23-year-old kid who was a football player, who had brain cancer, and he died very quickly. He was a star athlete – gone. And the parents of the kid talked to my brother, and they said, 'We lost family 40 years ago in the extermination camps in Poland. And we got over that, eventually we got over it. But we don't have time now to get over this.' And it's a big idea, in a way.

It *is* a big idea, and one that resonates. We are concerned with the precise minutiae of time, the train times, the ticking watch, but when we step back to consider the wider perspective it can be almost too much for us. We don't have to be Einstein to know that all time is relative: it may be enough to have lost loved ones too early, or be struggling against the ravages of serious illness. Life is too short, and full of misery, and we spend most of our time figuring out how to survive or extend it, for it's all we have for sure.

But there is another message here. We have never met the young football player or his family, and we may not admire Randy Newman or his song, but we all understand the layered complexities of the passage of time. Newman roots the complexity in a story – both in his introduction and the song – because telling stories is the best way of marking the passage of time that we know. Stories are also the best way of making *sense* of time, and we have been using them to navigate our way long before time was a studied discipline, and certainly before clocks. Allen's and Freud's wilful 'delusions' are also just stories, studied diversions from the reality of mortality. This is the reason we are attracted not only to the artefacts in the British Museum but also to slow food and Cartier-Bresson's photographs, and why the Beatles' *Please Please Me* and Beethoven's Ninth still enthral: in all their humanity lies the story of us.

Throughout this book we've seen how people have written the modern story of time in their own way. Railway pioneers threw the world into motion until those who made timetables settled it again. Watchmakers complicated things while time gurus simplified them. Christian Marclay moved the minute hand as Harold Lloyd hung on. Ruth Ewan revolutionised the calendar while Buzz Aldrin wore a watch on the moon. Roger Bannister ran to glory and Nick Ut ran to war.

Our obsessions with time have taken us to the edge but not over it. The old stories offer a vision of the future, and our pale blue dot keeps spinning towards a fate we can influence more than we think.

Epilogue:

Humility Watch

I am about to buy a new watch. New to me, at any rate: the watch was made in 1957, three years before I was born, and a short while later (according to the engraving on the back of the case) was given to a railwayman in appreciation of 45 years' service on the London Midland Region. It has 15 jewels, thin blue steel hands and gold numerals. It keeps good time for a wind-up machine manufactured in England almost 60 years ago, but the man selling it to me in a shop overlooking the Thames near Blackfriars Bridge won't let me leave with it, as he believes its inaccuracy is intolerable. At its best the watch will lose or gain about 15 seconds a day. But at the moment it is losing 72 seconds a day.

The measurement was gauged on a time machine called the Multifunction Timegrapher, a small box that amplified its movement and produced a digital readout. 'All of watch-making is about the distribution of tiny amounts of force and the introduction and control of tiny amounts of friction,' the salesman says, as if he is describing life itself. 'On your watch, the balance on one side is probably slightly mushroomed – it's been hit and things have happened to it that have made it slightly flattened. Whereas on the other side it's more like it was when it left the factory – nicely domed, with a very small point of contact.'

After his diagnosis is complete, he says I should come back for the watch in a few days, once he's recalibrated it. When I return a week later he says, 'It looks pretty honest.

It's a very confident statement. See how you get on with it.'

I got on it with it well and wore it with pleasure. When I had my bike accident it tumbled over the handlebars with me and emerged unscathed. It was made by Smiths of Cheltenham, a company with roots in horology from the 1860s. Smiths' proudest day came in May 1953 with the first ascent of Everest by Sir Edmund Hillary ('I carried your watch to the summit,' the company's adverts proclaimed. 'It worked perfectly.') Ever since the ascent, a gold-cased Smiths timepiece was the gift *par excellence* for career long-service, and in 1957 a retiree named O.C. Walker had been presented with the 15-jewel De Luxe I'm wearing now. He had served his time, and the railways wanted him to be certain about the time he had left.

My salesman was a 40-year-old Londoner named Crispin Jones. Jones was thin, wiry and gentle in his manner, and prematurely balding; he looked like a cherubic version of Jude Law. Selling vintage watches was only a sideline for him. His main line was selling items that encouraged the purchaser to think of time in a new way.

Jones trained as a sculptor and then studied computer design, and after a while he began combining the two. A few years ago he made an office desk that answered questions. The questions were things like 'Will my love be returned?' 'What do my friends think of me?' 'Will I find my lost item?' The questions were contained on cards, 30 in all, and to obtain the answers the user had to place them over a metal slot on the desk. 'It was an attempt to use the computer in a similar way that ancient civilisations used oracles,' Jones said. 'The catch was, the metal slot became hotter and hotter as the answer came up.' A barcode was concealed in the pattern on the card, so when you dropped it onto the slot you triggered an electronic reader that slowly produced an answer on a dot matrix. The answer to 'Will my love be returned?' would produce the answer 'Yes . . . if . . . you . . . stay . . . true . . . to . . . your . . .' By the time the answer got to 'true' the card slot would be getting quite hot, but if you withdrew your hand the system would reset and you wouldn't see the whole answer. The last – very hot – word was 'ideals'.

Jones was interested in the way modern technology was changing our lives: what it gives and what it takes away. In 2002 he did some experimental work with mobile phones, at a time when the etiquette was uncertain. 'There were no silent carriages and everyone was still talking annoyingly loudly in public.' Jones built a phone that delivered a variable level of electric shock to a user talking too loudly, and a phone that knocked rather than rang. If the call was for a simple catch-up, the knock could be made soft and unassuming; but if the call was urgent, the knock would be loud and insistent.

And then he started thinking about watches. 'The watch is interesting,' he mused, 'because we don't think of it as technology the way we do about phones or computers. And it's an incredible survivor: most technologies that are 10 years old look incredibly outdated, so that if I use a phone from 10 years ago it's almost a provocation, and it makes me look massively eccentric. But you're wearing your wristwatch from the 1950s and it doesn't seem extraordinary.' He observes that many of us tend to have the same sort of phones these days, but watches remain one of the few outward signs of our personality. 'And with watches you can weave in a lot of interesting stories and remap the concepts of how we think about time.'

At the Royal College of Art, Jones had been influenced by former student Anthony Dunne, whose book *Hertzian Tales* argued for a more considered critique of electronic products, not least a re-examination of everyday objects on aesthetic grounds. In 2004 Jones wrote a manifesto posing two questions: 'How could a watch undermine its wearer?' and 'What if the watch could express some of the negative aspects of the wearer's personality?' But his most provocative question was 'How can the watch represent time in a different way?'

With assistance from design colleagues Anton Schubert, Ross Cooper and Graham Pullin, Jones set out to provide practical answers. They made working prototypes of several watches, only one of which bothered to tell the accurate time. They were all a little clunky, a mix of rosewood, steel and an electronic LED display, with rechargeable batteries that lasted five days. The watches were rectangular rather than round, and they looked like a possible prototype of the Apple Watch.

Jones gave them deliberately pretentious Latin names. First up was The Summissus, subtitled 'The Humility Watch'. This was 'an object designed to remind people that death should be prepared for at any time'. The watch had a mirror face and alternated between flashing the time and the message 'Remember you will die'.

The Avidus was 'The Stress Watch'. This reflected the feeling we have of time speeding by when we are stressed, and time slowing down when we are relaxed. The wearer would press the two metal contacts on the face, and a pulse would activate the display. The more stressed the user, the faster the time would run; the more relaxed the user, the slower, and a meditative state would cause the time to run backwards.

The Prudens was 'The Discretion Watch'. This is a watch that can be read without looking at it – in a meeting say, or when on a date, so as not to appear bored or rude. The watch was worn as two opposing faces on the front and back of the wrist, and when the wearer rotated their arm in the air, a pulse would be transmitted to the wrist corresponding to the correct hours and minutes.

Then there was Fallax, 'The Honest Watch', which projects the wearer's integrity. Many watches aim to reflect the owner's wealth and status, but Fallax has a purer intention: by wearing two finger straps, the watch becomes a lie detector and the word 'LIES' flashes up on the face to alert those close to you that you may not be trusted.

The Adsiduus was 'The Personality Watch', flashing up a random series of messages both positive and negative: 'You are amazing' or 'You have no real friends' or 'Your future will be worse'.

And finally there was the Docilus, 'The Internal Watch', transmitting a small and unpleasant electric shock at unpredictable intervals, leading to the greater internalisation of time and a decreased dependency on both the watch and strict timekeeping.

Taken en masse, the watches represented a Proustian daydream that threatened to become a nightmare. Of all the timekeepers I had met, Jones was the wittiest, and the one who thought the longest about the implications of time's advance. There was no doubt in his mind that time was dominating our lives, but was it doing so in meaningful and constructive ways? And if not, could it be bent back to do so? In 2005 Jones decided to ready some of his prototypes for production.

The workshop of Mr Jones Watches is in Camberwell, south-east London, about four miles from his shop by the Thames. It is a reassuringly ramshackle and industrious place, a well-lit single room with a racing bike hanging on a wall alongside a post-war poster encouraging efficiency. Almost all the horizontal surfaces are covered in watch parts, watch tools, watch-part manufacturing machines, watch regulating machines, watch packaging and watches – a strewn decade of experiment and invention. Metal cabinets beneath the desks contain more of the same. The room is part laboratory, part museum, part explosion.

The first watch Jones made was a new version of The Summissus. He renamed it The Accurate, and placed the word 'remember' on the hour hand and 'you will die' on the minute hand. The watch still had a reflective face – the wearer confronted by their own mortality – but this time it was round, which made it look less like an art project. Its purpose, as with almost all of Jones's other designs, was now refocused to be a little less negative and a bit more encouraging: time could be charming as well as perplexing and uncontrollable.

The next watch Jones designed was The Mantra, a 'positive/negative suggestion watch' like The Adsiduus. The watch had a narrow window, and as each half hour passed the disc revealed a message. A positive statement was followed by a negative one: 'Be the Best'; 'Always Be Alone'; 'You're Blessed'; 'Stay Dull'. 'Over time,' Jones wrote in his catalogue, 'the Mantra makes the meek more confident and the arrogant more humble.' The watch was inspired by the theories of French psychoanalyst Émile Coué, whose 'optimistic auto-suggestion' promoted the healing power of positive thought. (Coué's prime example was championed by Frank Spencer in *Some Mothers Do 'Ave 'Em*: 'Every day, in every way, I'm getting better and better.')

The initial reaction to the early designs was encouraging, and Jones was pleased with the level of intrigue he created, not least after his work was featured on the influential watch blog The Watchismo Times. For further inspiration, Jones then enlisted the help of a few people outside the watch world. The cyclist Graeme Obree, famous for his hour-long endurance stints on his bike, helped with a watch called The Hour. The plan was to note the passing of each one with a significant word, and to spend the time considering its worth. The words included 'value', 'enjoy', 'seize', 'reflect' and 'engage'. There was also Dawn West Dusk East, a watch designed with the artist Brian Catling that attempts to slow down time by showing one dot revolving every 12 hours; the time would be about 4.15 or about 4.30 but you couldn't be sure, and would it matter?

Another collaborator was Professor Jonathan Gershuny, the co-director of the Centre for Time Use Research at the University of Oxford. The Average Day consisted of a regular set of watch hands and two rings of information on the dial. There were no numbers, but instead the wearer was informed what the average European would be doing at any particular time. On the a.m. dial, 7.30–8 is 'Wash', 8.15–9 is 'Travel', 10–11 is 'Work', 11–12 'Meeting', while the p.m. dial becomes 12.15–1 'Eat', 5.15–6.30 'Social Life', 8.15–11 'TV'. The challenge to the wearer is to break free from the routine.

The business found its customers. The watches, produced in editions of 100, cost between £115 and £600, with most around £200. Profits went back into new designs and new lathes and printing equipment, so that by the spring of 2015 Jones was making and assembling all the parts apart from the basic quartz or mechanical movements (which came either from the Far East or Switzerland). And in this way Mr Jones Watches contributed to the resurrection of the British watch industry, and made his customers think about time in an original way. The obsession remains, but the obsession is slightly different.

My favourite Jones design was called The Cyclops, which he says was 'basically ripped off' from a watch called the Chromachron. The Chromachron had been designed by Tian Harlan in Switzerland, and told the time by revealing a different colour segment each hour. The Cyclops did the same in a more subtle way, with a black hoop slowly passing over a disc with small dots of colour at the perimeter of its dial. There was no minute hand, so the user would experience a vaguer sense of time passing, something its maker called 'a relaxed kind of accuracy'.

This was an extraordinary thing to contemplate, a time-keeper without a minute hand. We have spent more than two industrialised centuries battling time – running for the train, striving for the tape, holding on against a streamlined world – and now there was a chance to let it all slide. It would be like leaving the city to plough the fields. Who among us would be equal to the task?

Acknowledgements and Further Reading

A broad narrative history such as this requires a lot of backup, both printed and personal, and I'm grateful to everyone who offered help and suggestions along the way. The idea for the book came from Anya Serota, and was guided through to completion (and enriched greatly along the way) by my editor Jenny Lord. The entire dedicated team who worked on the book at Canongate is worthy of praise, so thank you Jamie Byng, Jenny Todd, Anna Frame, Jenny Fry, Alan Trotter, Vicki Rutherford, Laura Cole and Allegra Le Fanu. Seán Costello conducted a fastidious copy edit, and Pete Adlington designed the alluring jacket. As always, my agent Rosemary Scoular was an invaluable support.

The subject of time is so vast that I was always pleased to receive thoughts on direction. Jay Griffiths, who has written enticingly about the subject herself, first came up with the parameters of obsession. Not everyone I interviewed for this book appears in the final version, so I would also like to thank Terry Quinn, Lucy Pilpin, Lucy Fleischman, David Spears and Cat Gibbard. My friend Andrew Bud read the manuscript for errors only he could spot, and once again he's saved my blushes. And for suggestions of books, angles and contacts thanks to Naomi Frears, John Frears-Hogg, Mark Osterfield, Sam Thorne, Fanny Singer, Daniel Pick, Brad Auerbach, Jeremy Anning and Kim Ellsworth.

Small sections of the watch and photo chapters have previously appeared in a different form in Esquire, and in Johnny Davis I am blessed with a particularly accommodating editor there. An earlier version of the Poundbury story previously appeared in BA High Life, so thank you Paul Clements. Many thanks to Kipper Williams for the inspired Mayfly cartoon that opens the first chapter.

Many of the books that follow were sourced from the London Library, one of our great research institutions, and as ever I am grateful to its staff. Rather than a complete bibliography, the list is intended as an inspiration for further exploration.

Andrews, Geoff, *The Slow Food Story: Politics and Pleasure* (Pluto Press: London, 2008)

Bannister, Roger, *The First Four Minutes* (G.P. Putnam's Sons: New York, 1955)

—— *Twin Tracks* (The Robson Press: London, 2014)

Bartky, Ian R., *Selling the True Time: Nineteenth-Century Timekeeping in America* (Stanford University Press: Stanford, 2000)

Beethoven, Ludwig van, *Letters, Journals and Conversations*, edited, translated and introduced by Michael Hamburger (Thames and Hudson: London, 1951)

Brookman, Philip (ed.), *Helios: Eadweard Muybridge in a Time of Change* (Corcoran Gallery of Art Exhibition Catalogue: Washington DC, 2010)

Brownlow, Kevin, *The Parade's Gone By* (University of California Press: Berkeley, 1992)

Burgess, Richard James, *The History of Music Production* (Oxford University Press: Oxford, 2014)

Conrad, Joseph, *The Secret Agent* (J.M. Dent & Sons Ltd: London, 1907)

Crary, Jonathan, *24/7: Terminal Capitalism and the Ends of Sleep* (Verso Books: London, 2013)

Dardis, Tom, *Harold Lloyd: The Man on the Clock* (Penguin: New York, 1983)

Dohrn-van Rossum, Gerhard, *History of the Hour: Clocks and Modern Temporal Orders* (University of Chicago Press: London, 1996)

Eagleman, David, *The Brain: The Story of You* (Canongate: Edinburgh and London, 2015)

Falk, Dan, *In Search of Time: Journeys Along a Curious Dimension* (National Maritime Museum: London, 2009)

Freeman, Eugene and Sellars, Wilfrid (eds), *Basic Issues in the Philosophy of Time* (Open Court: Illinois, 1971)

Garfield, Simon, *The Last Journey of William Huskisson* (Faber and Faber: London, 2002)

Gleick, James, *Time Travel* (Fourth Estate: London, 2016)

Glennie, Paul and Thrift, Nigel, *Shaping the Day: A History of Timekeeping in England and Wales 1300–1800* (Oxford University Press: Oxford, 2009)

Griffiths, Jay, *Pip Pip: A Sideways Look at Time* (Flamingo: London, 1999)

Groom, Amelia (ed.), *Time: Documents of Contemporary Art* (Whitechapel Gallery: London, 2013)

Grubbs, David, *Records Ruin the Landscape: John Cage, the Sixties, and Sound Recording* (Duke University Press: Durham, NC, and London, 2014)

Hammond, Claudia, *Time Warped: Unlocking the Mysteries of Time Perception* (Canongate: Edinburgh and London, 2013)

Hassig, Ross, *Time, History, and Belief in Aztec and Colonial Mexico* (University of Texas Press: Austin, 2001)

Hoffman, Eva, *Time* (Profile Books: London, 2011)

Honoré, Carl, *In Praise of Slow: How a Worldwide Movement is Challenging the Cult of Speed* (Orion: London, 2004)

—— *The Slow Fix: Lasting Solutions in a Fast-Moving World* (William Collins: London, 2014)

Howse, Derek, *Greenwich Time and the Discovery of the Longitude* (Oxford University Press: Oxford, 1980)

Jones, Tony, *Splitting the Second: The Story of Atomic Time* (Institute of Physics Publishing: Bristol and Philadelphia, 2000)

Kanigel, Robert, *The One Best Way: Frederick Winslow Taylor and the Enigma of Efficiency* (Little, Brown: London, 1997)

Kelly, Thomas Forrest, *First Nights: Five Musical Premieres* (Yale University Press: New Haven, Conn., 2000)

Kern, Stephen, *The Culture of Time and Space 1880–1918* (Weidenfeld and Nicolson: London, 1983)

Klein, Stefan, *Time: A User's Guide* (Penguin: London, 2008)

Koger, Gregory, *Filibustering: A Political History of Obstruction in the House and Senate* (University of Chicago Press: Chicago, 2010)

Landes, David S., *Revolution in Time: Clocks and the Making of the Modern World* (Belknap Press of Harvard University Press: Cambridge, Mass., 1983)

Levine, Robert, *A Geography of Time: On Tempo, Culture and the Pace of Life: The Temporal Misadventures of a Social Psychologist* (Basic Books: London, 1997)

Lewisohn, Mark, *The Beatles – All These Years: Volume One: Tune In* (Little, Brown: London, 2013)

Macey, Samuel L., *The Dynamics of Progress: Time, Method and Measure* (University of Georgia Press: Athens and London, 1989)

McEwen, Christian, *World Enough & Time: On Creativity and Slowing Down* (Bauhan Publishing: Peterborough, New Hampshire, 2011)

Mumford, Lewis, *Art and Technics* (Oxford University Press: Oxford, 1952)

O'Malley, Michael, *Keeping Watch: A History of American Time* (Viking Penguin: New York, 1990)

Perovic, Sanja, *The Calendar in Revolutionary France: Perceptions of Time in Literature, Culture, Politics* (Cambridge University Press: Cambridge, 2012)

Phillips, Bob, *3:59.4: The Quest for the Four-Minute Mile* (The Parrs Wood Press: Manchester, 2004)

Pirsig, Robert M., *Zen and the Art of Motorcycle Maintenance* (The Bodley Head: London, 1974)

Quinn, Terry, *From Artefacts to Atoms: The BIPM and the Search for Ultimate Measurement Standards* (Oxford University Press USA: New York, 2011)

Rooney, David, *Ruth Belville: The Greenwich Time Lady* (National Maritime Museum: London, 2008)

Rosa, Hartmut, *Social Acceleration: A New Theory of Modernity* (Columbia University Press: New York, 2013)

Sachs, Curt, *Rhythm and Tempo: A Study in Music History* (Columbia University Press: New York, 1953)

Shaw, Matthew, *Time and the French Revolution: The Republican Calendar, 1989–Year XIV* (Boydell Press: Woodbridge, 2011)

Sobel, Dava, *Longitude: The True Story of a Lone Genius Who Solved the Greatest Scientific Problem of His Time* (Penguin: London, 1995)

Solnit, Rebecca, *Motion Studies: Eadweard Muybridge and the Technological Wild West* (Bloomsbury: London, 2003)

Vance, Jeffrey and Lloyd, Suzanne, *Harold Lloyd: Master Comedian* (Harry N. Abrams Inc.: New York, 2002)

Whitrow, G.J., *What Is Time?* (Thames and Hudson: London, 1972)

Young, Michael Dunlop, *The Metronomic Society: Natural Rhythms and Human Timetables* (Thames and Hudson: London, 1988)

Zimbardo, Philip and Boyd, John, *The Time Paradox: Using the New Psychology of Time to Your Advantage* (Rider Books: London, 2010)

Picture Credits

While every effort has been made to contact copyright-holders of illustrations, the author and publishers would be grateful for information about any illustrations where they have been unable to trace them, and would be glad to make amendments to further editions.

INDEX

References to images are in italics; references to footnotes are indicated by n.

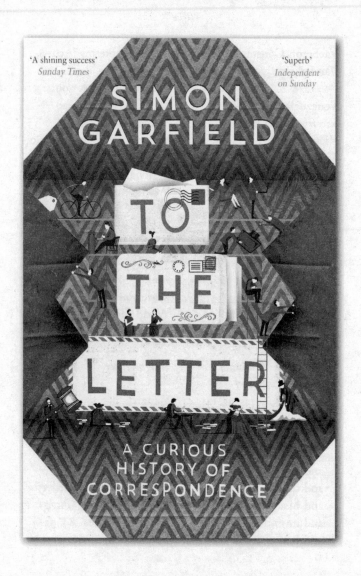

'A shining success'
Sunday Times

'Superb'
Independent on Sunday

SIMON
GARFIELD

TO

THE

LETTER

A CURIOUS
HISTORY OF
CORRESPONDENCE

'A wonderfully elegant history' *Observer*

CANON GATE

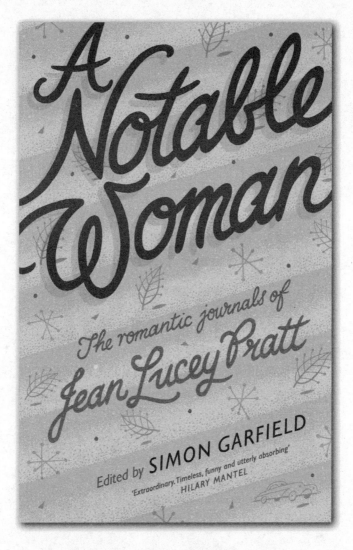

A Notable Woman

The romantic journals of
Jean Lucey Pratt

Edited by SIMON GARFIELD

'Extraordinary. Timeless, funny and utterly absorbing'
HILARY MANTEL

'Funny, tender and gripping'
Rachel Cooke, *New Statesman*

CANON GATE

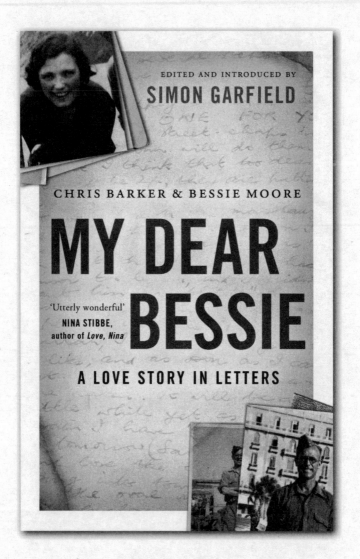

EDITED AND INTRODUCED BY
SIMON GARFIELD

CHRIS BARKER & BESSIE MOORE

MY DEAR
BESSIE

'Utterly wonderful'
NINA STIBBE,
author of *Love, Nina*

A LOVE STORY IN LETTERS

'An immensely affecting set of letters'
Financial Times

CANON||GATE